741.5
Sny

Snyder, Scott.

W9-AFM-294

34711202871812

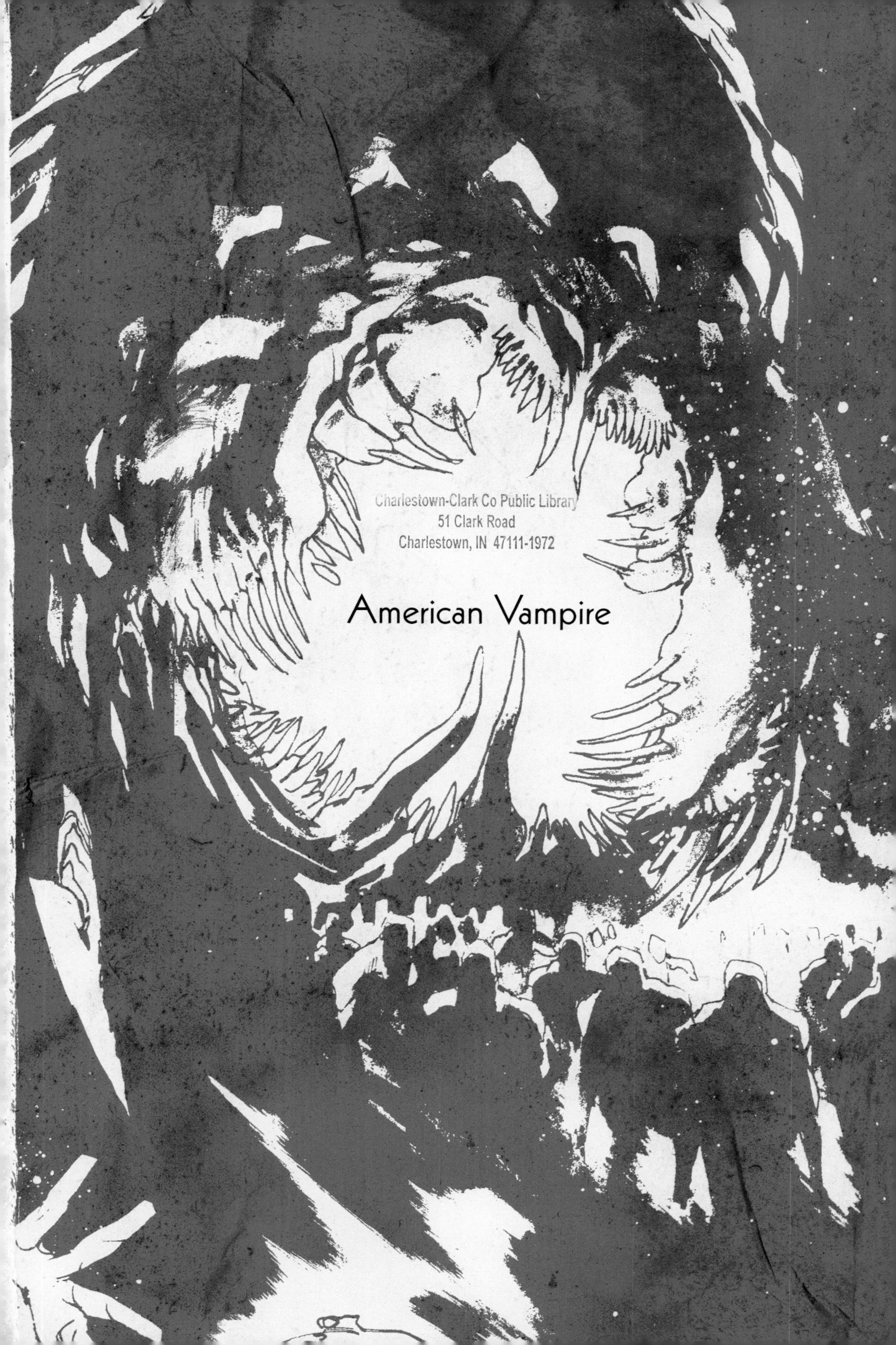

American Vampire

AMERICAN

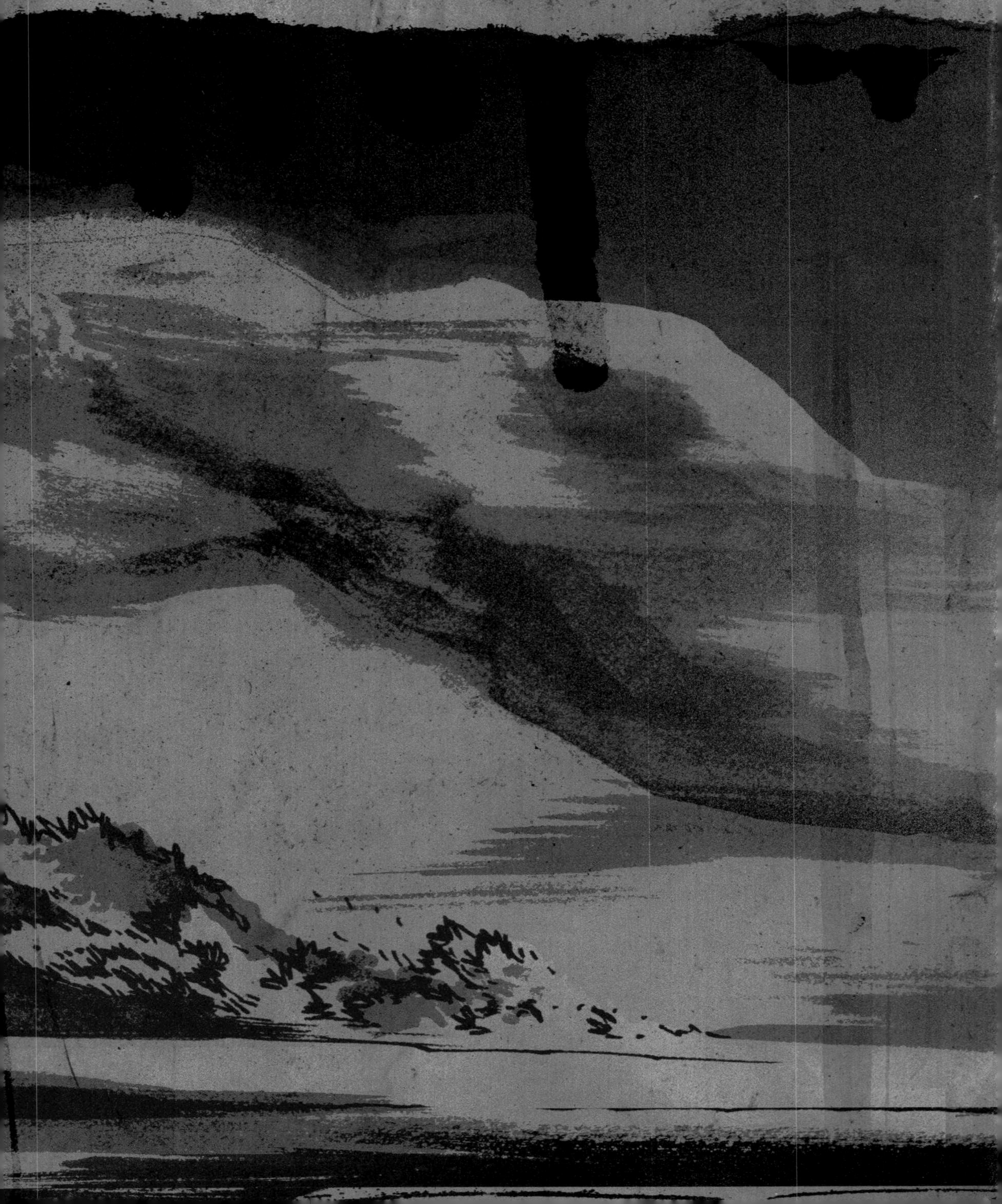

VAMPIRE

VOLUME SEVEN

Scott Snyder Writer

Rafael Albuquerque

Matías Bergara Artists

Dave McCaig Colorist

Steve Wands Letterer

Rafael Albuquerque
Collection Cover Art

American Vampire created by
Scott Snyder and
Rafael Albuquerque

Mark Doyle Editor – Original Series
Sara Miller Assistant Editor – Original Series
Peter Hamboussi Editor
Robbin Brosterman Design Director – Books
Louis Prandi Publication Design

Shelly Bond Executive Editor - Vertigo
Hank Kanalz Senior VP – Vertigo & Integrated Publishing

Diane Nelson President
Dan DiDio and Jim Lee Co-Publishers
Geoff Johns Chief Creative Officer
Amit Desai Senior VP – Marketing & Franchise Management
Amy Genkins Senior VP – Business & Legal Affairs
Nairi Gardiner Senior VP – Finance
Jeff Boison VP – Publishing Planning
Mark Chiarello VP – Art Direction & Design
John Cunningham VP – Marketing
Terri Cunningham VP – Editorial Administration
Larry Ganem VP – Talent Relations & Services
Alison Gill Senior VP – Manufacturing & Operations
Jay Kogan VP – Business & Legal Affairs, Publishing
Jack Mahan VP – Business Affairs, Talent
Nick Napolitano VP – Manufacturing Administration
Sue Pohja VP – Book Sales
Fred Ruiz VP – Manufacturing Operations
Courtney Simmons Senior VP – Publicity
Bob Wayne Senior VP – Sales

AMERICAN VAMPIRE VOLUME 7

Published by DC Comics. Compilation Copyright © 2015 Scott Snyder
and DC Comics. All Rights Reserved.

Originally published in single magazine form in AMERICAN VAMPIRE:
SECOND CYCLE 1-5 © 2014 Scott Snyder and DC Comics. All Rights
Reserved. All characters, their distinctive likenesses and related elements
featured in this publication are trademarks of DC Comics. Vertigo is a
trademark of DC Comics. The stories, characters and incidents featured in
this publication are entirely fictional. DC Comics does not read or accept
unsolicited ideas, stories or artwork.

DC Comics, 1700 Broadway, New York, NY 10019
A Warner Bros. Entertainment Company.
Printed in the USA. First Printing.
ISBN: 978-1-4012-4882-6

Library of Congress Cataloging-in-Publication Data

Snyder, Scott, author.
  American Vampire volume seven / Scott Snyder, author ; Rafael
Albuquerque, artist.
    pages cm
  ISBN 978-1-4012-4882-6 (hardback)
  1. Vampires—Comic books, strips, etc. 2. Graphic novels. I.
Albuquerque, Rafael, 1981- illustrator. II. Title.

PN6727.S555A49 2014
741.5'973—dc23

                    2014034203

SUSTAINABLE
FORESTRY
INITIATIVE

Certified Chain of Custody
20% Certified Forest Content,
80% Certified Sourcing
www.sfiprogram.org
SFI-01042
APPLIES TO TEXT STOCK ONLY

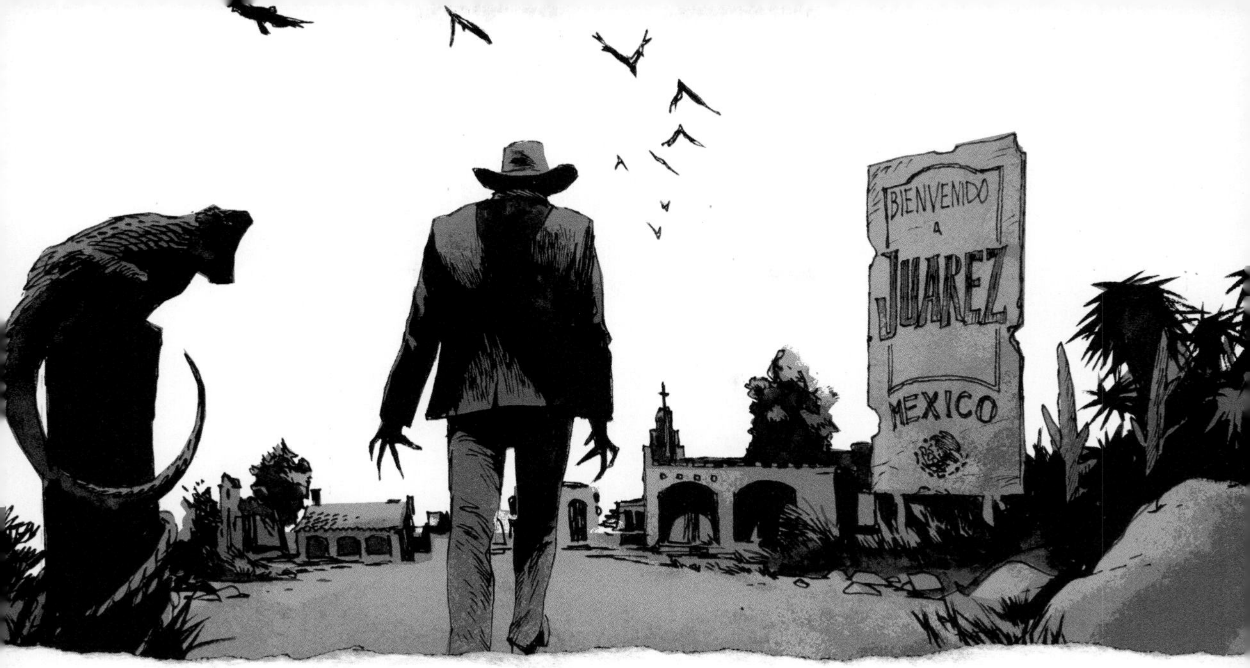
BIENVENIDO
A
JUAREZ
MEXICO

AMERICAN VAMPIRE

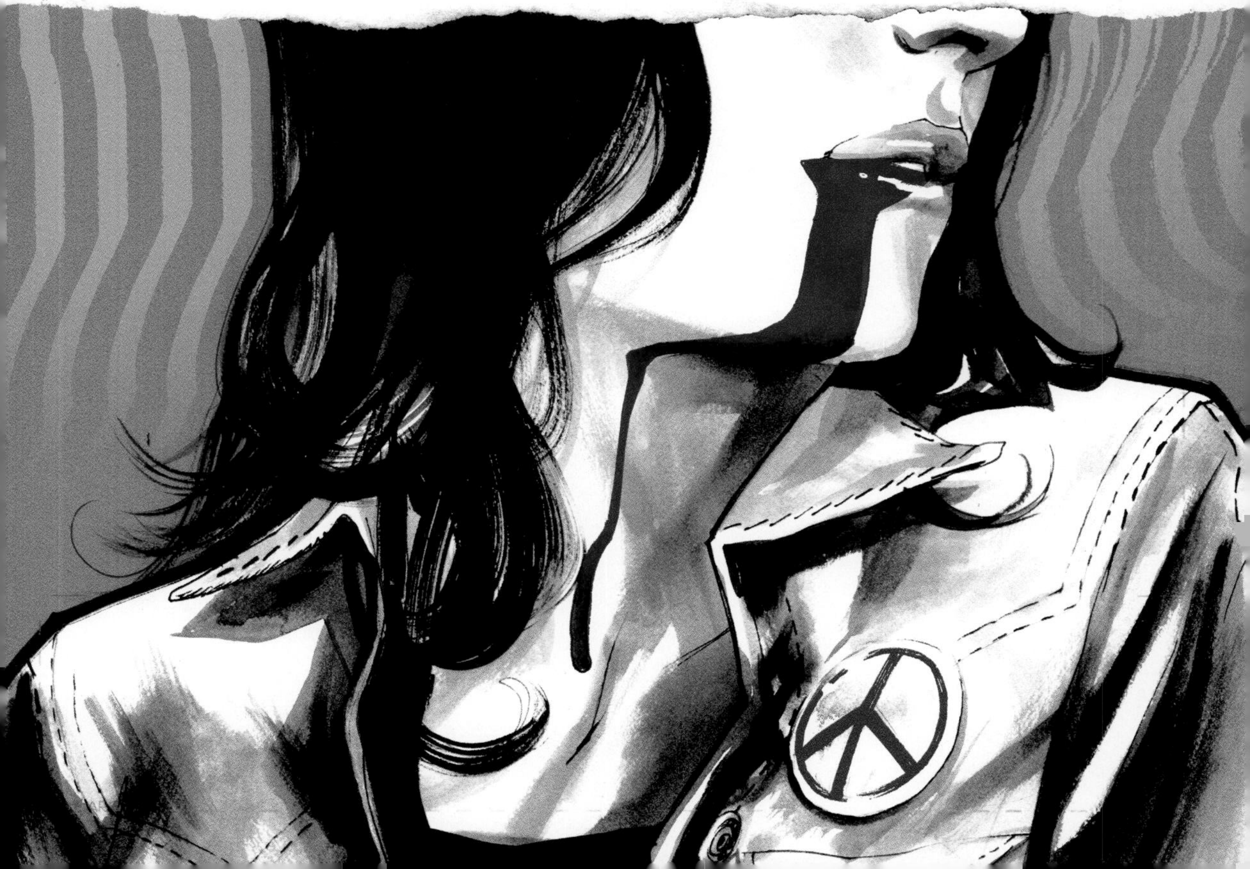

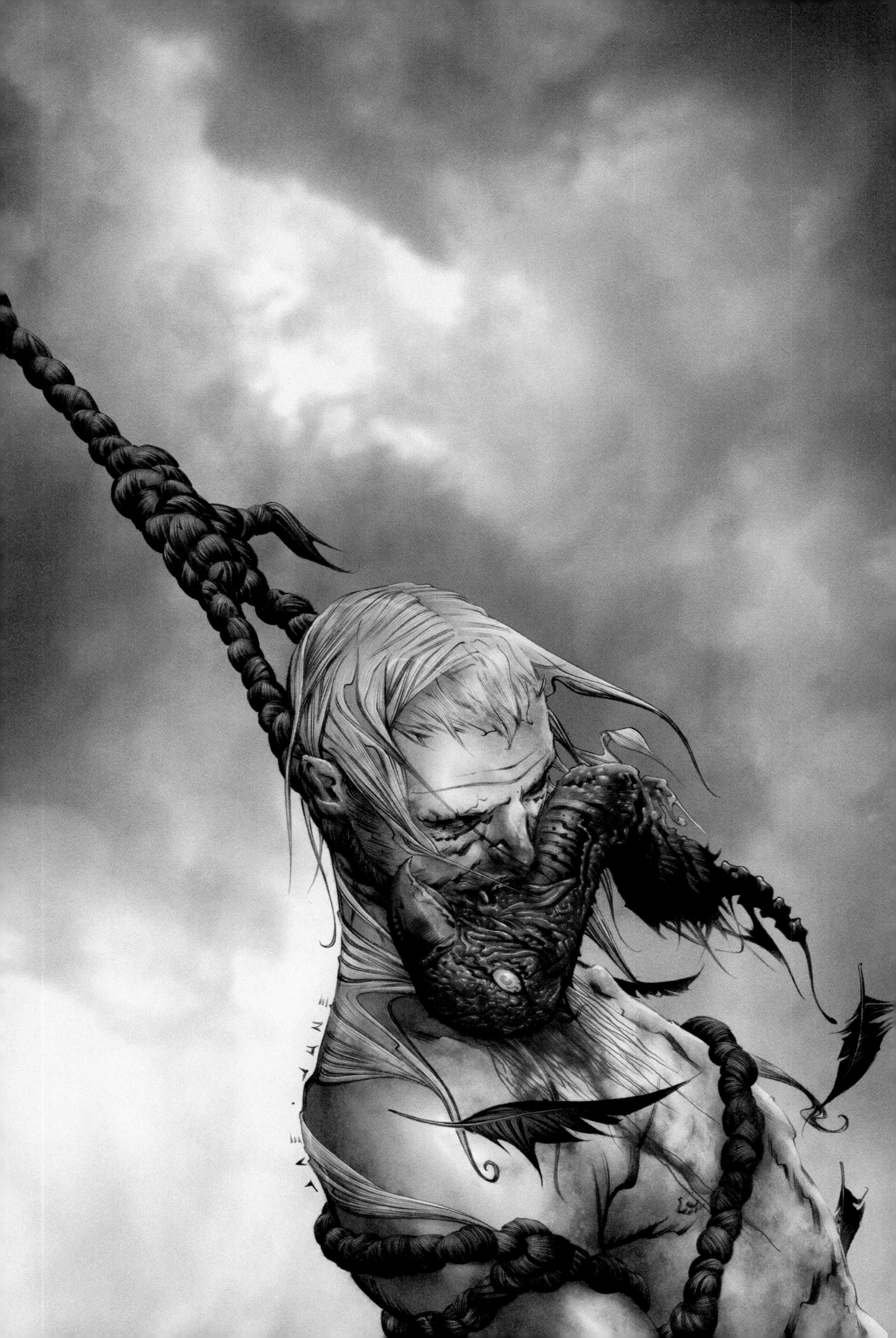

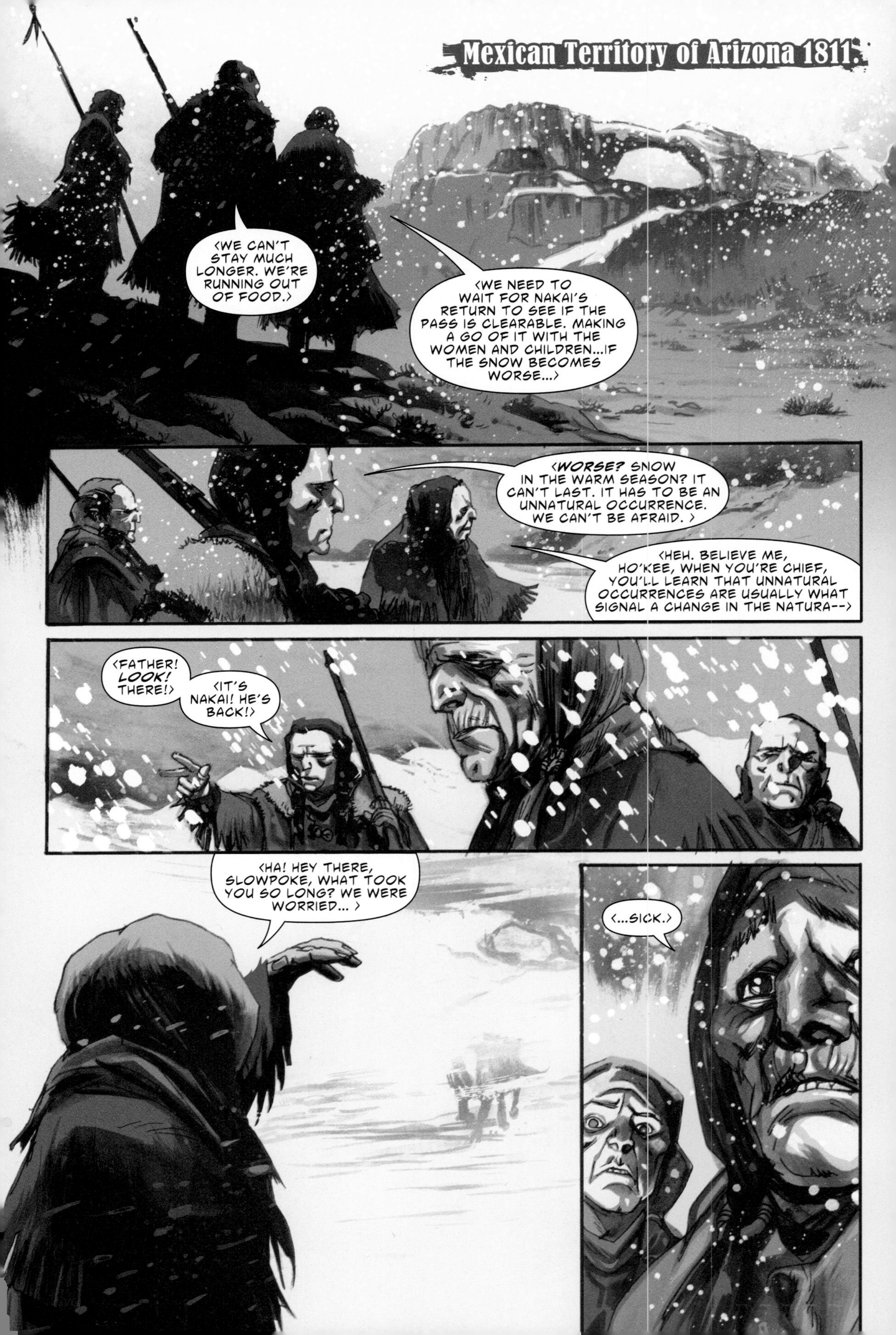

Mexican Territory of Arizona 1811.
<WE CAN'T STAY MUCH LONGER. WE'RE RUNNING OUT OF FOOD.>
<WE NEED TO WAIT FOR NAKAI'S RETURN TO SEE IF THE PASS IS CLEARABLE. MAKING A GO OF IT WITH THE WOMEN AND CHILDREN...IF THE SNOW BECOMES WORSE...>
<WORSE? SNOW IN THE WARM SEASON? IT CAN'T LAST. IT HAS TO BE AN UNNATURAL OCCURRENCE. WE CAN'T BE AFRAID. >
<HEH. BELIEVE ME, HO'KEE, WHEN YOU'RE CHIEF, YOU'LL LEARN THAT UNNATURAL OCCURRENCES ARE USUALLY WHAT SIGNAL A CHANGE IN THE NATURA-->
<FATHER! LOOK! THERE!>
<IT'S NAKAI! HE'S BACK!>
<HA! HEY THERE, SLOWPOKE, WHAT TOOK YOU SO LONG? WE WERE WORRIED... >
<...SICK.>

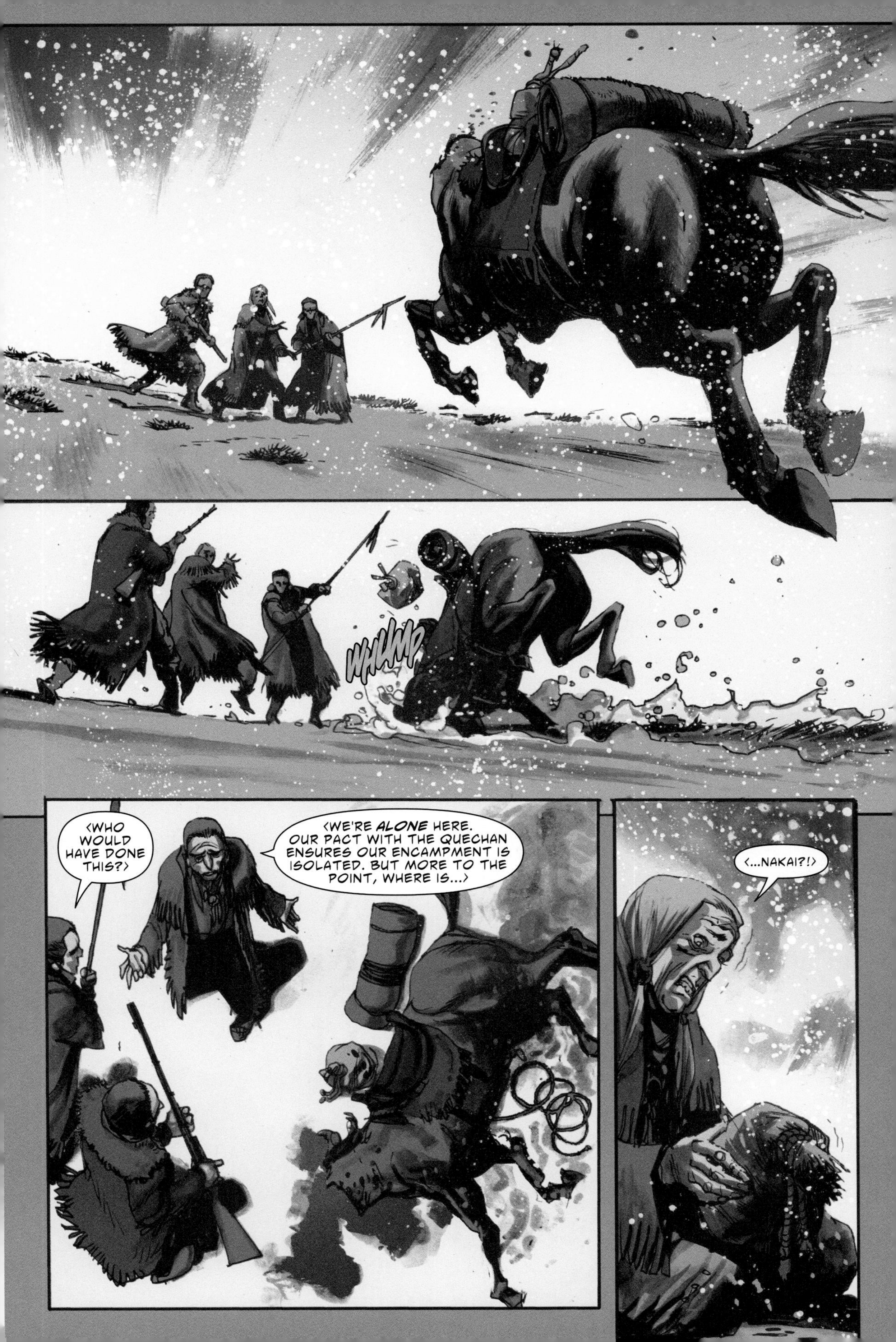
WHUMP
<WHO WOULD HAVE DONE THIS?>
<WE'RE ALONE HERE. OUR PACT WITH THE QUECHAN ENSURES OUR ENCAMPMENT IS ISOLATED. BUT MORE TO THE POINT, WHERE IS...>
<...NAKAI?!>

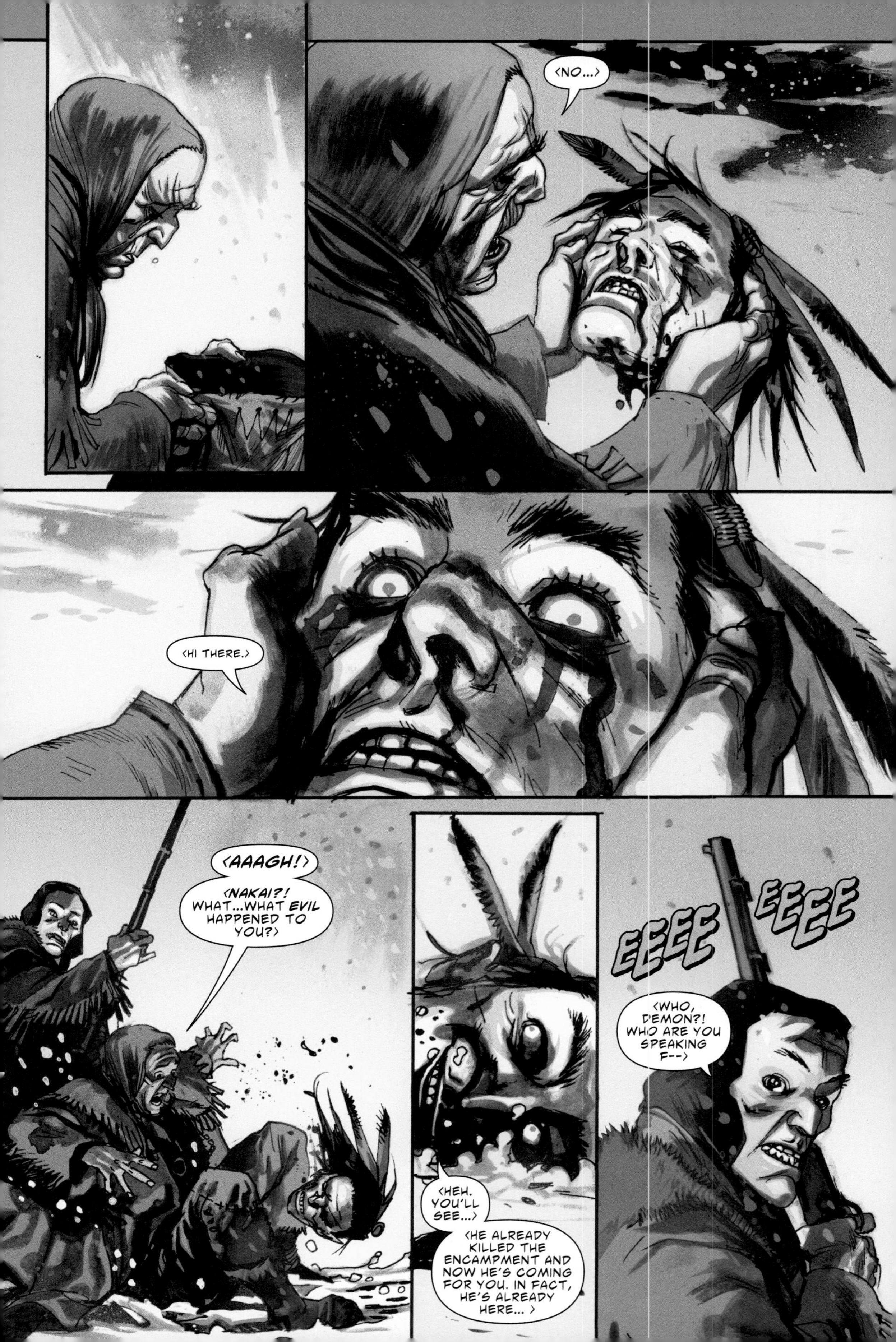

‹NO...›
‹HI THERE.›
‹AAAGH!›
‹NAKAI?! WHAT...WHAT EVIL HAPPENED TO YOU?›
EEEE EEEE
‹HEH. YOU'LL SEE...›
‹HE ALREADY KILLED THE ENCAMPMENT AND NOW HE'S COMING FOR YOU. IN FACT, HE'S ALREADY HERE... ›
‹WHO, DEMON?! WHO ARE YOU SPEAKING F--›

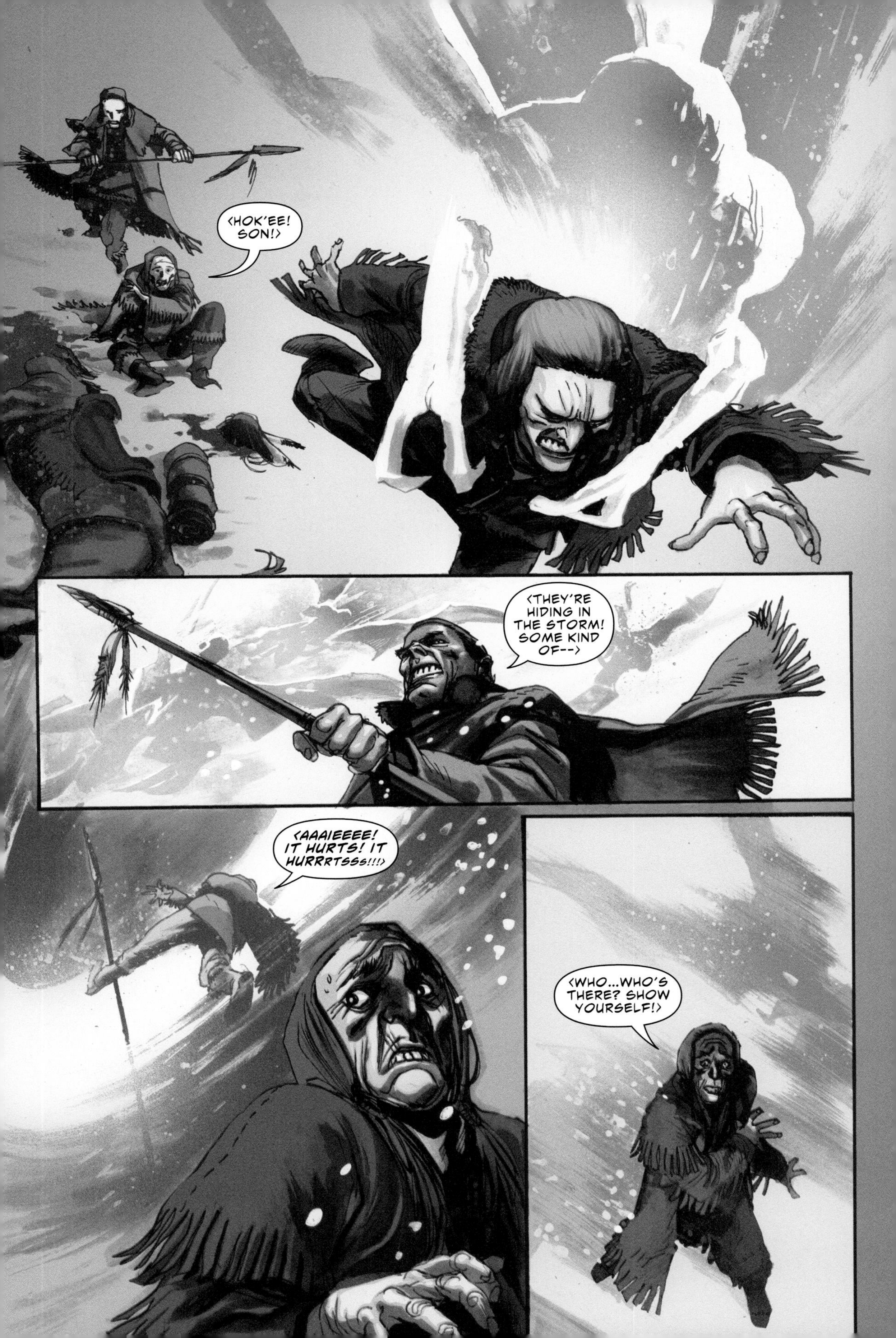

<HOK'EE! SON!>
<THEY'RE HIDING IN THE STORM! SOME KIND OF-->
<AAAIEEEE! IT HURTS! IT HURRRTSSS!!!>
<WHO...WHO'S THERE? SHOW YOURSELF!>

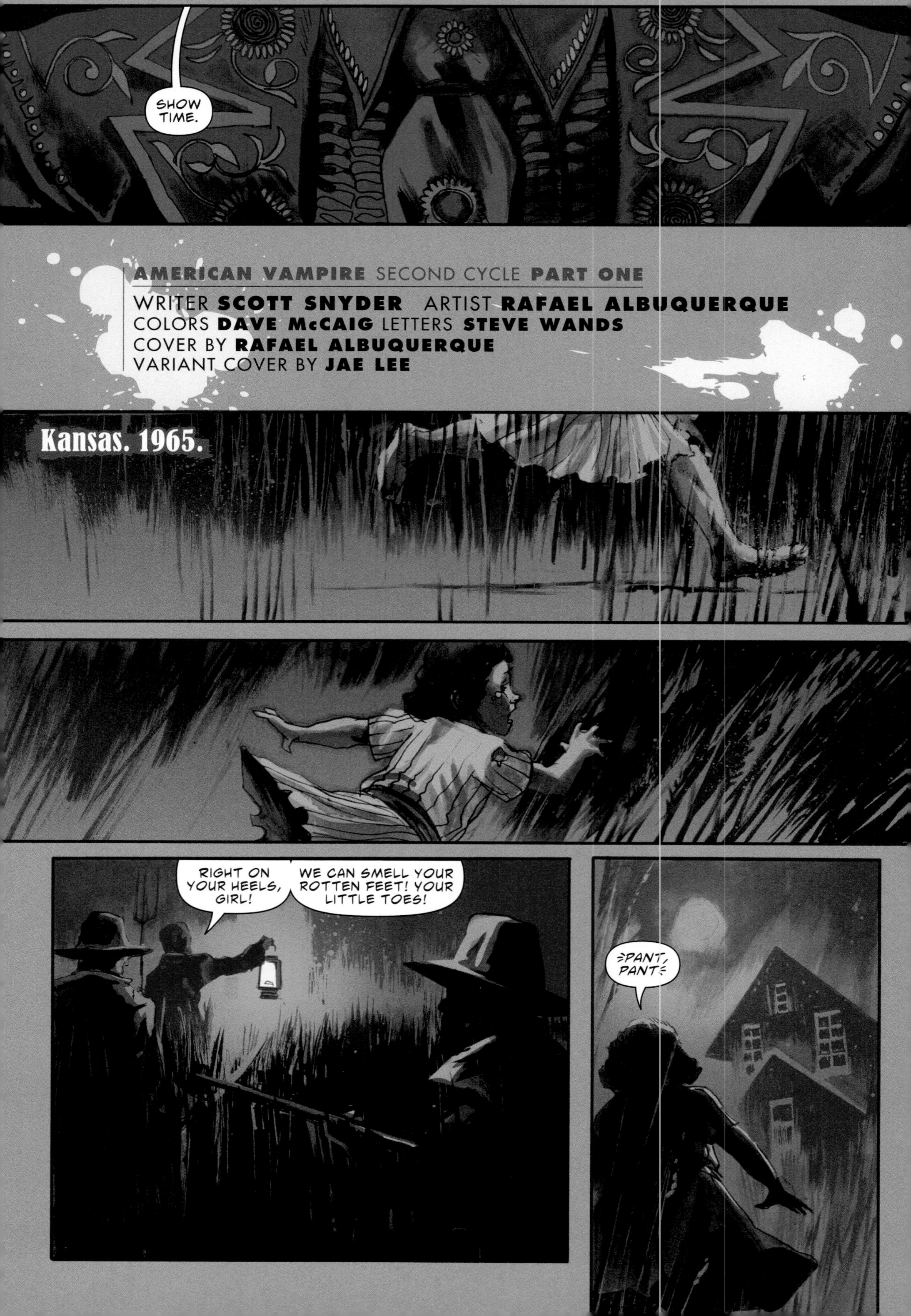
SHOW TIME.
AMERICAN VAMPIRE SECOND CYCLE PART ONE
WRITER SCOTT SNYDER ARTIST RAFAEL ALBUQUERQUE
COLORS DAVE McCAIG LETTERS STEVE WANDS
COVER BY RAFAEL ALBUQUERQUE
VARIANT COVER BY JAE LEE
Kansas. 1965.
RIGHT ON YOUR HEELS, GIRL!
WE CAN SMELL YOUR ROTTEN FEET! YOUR LITTLE TOES!
PANT, PANT

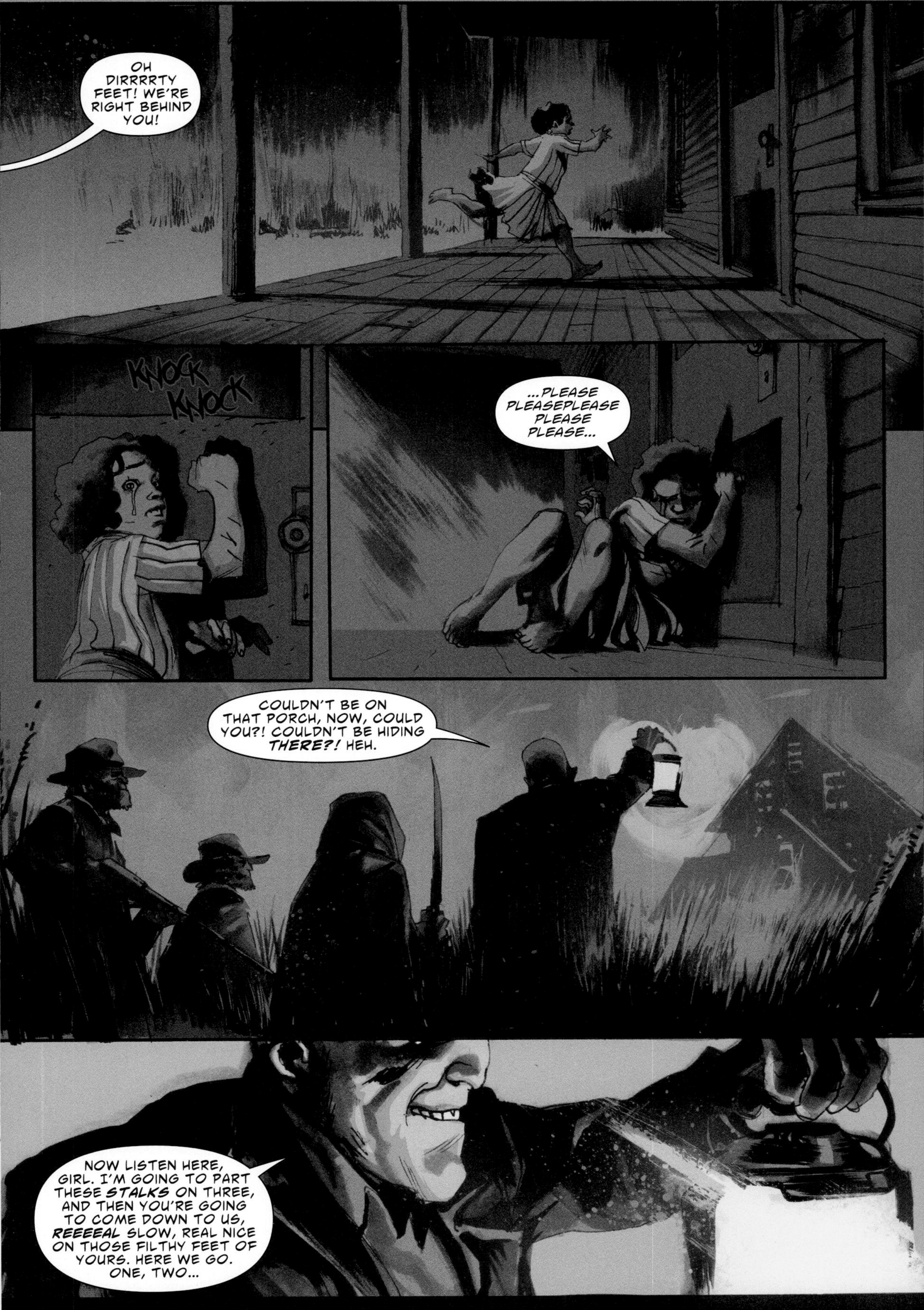
OH DIRRRRTY FEET! WE'RE RIGHT BEHIND YOU!
KNOCK KNOCK
...PLEASE PLEASEPLEASE PLEASE PLEASE...
COULDN'T BE ON THAT PORCH, NOW, COULD YOU?! COULDN'T BE HIDING THERE?! HEH.
NOW LISTEN HERE, GIRL. I'M GOING TO PART THESE STALKS ON THREE, AND THEN YOU'RE GOING TO COME DOWN TO US, REEEEAL SLOW, REAL NICE ON THOSE FILTHY FEET OF YOURS. HERE WE GO. ONE, TWO...

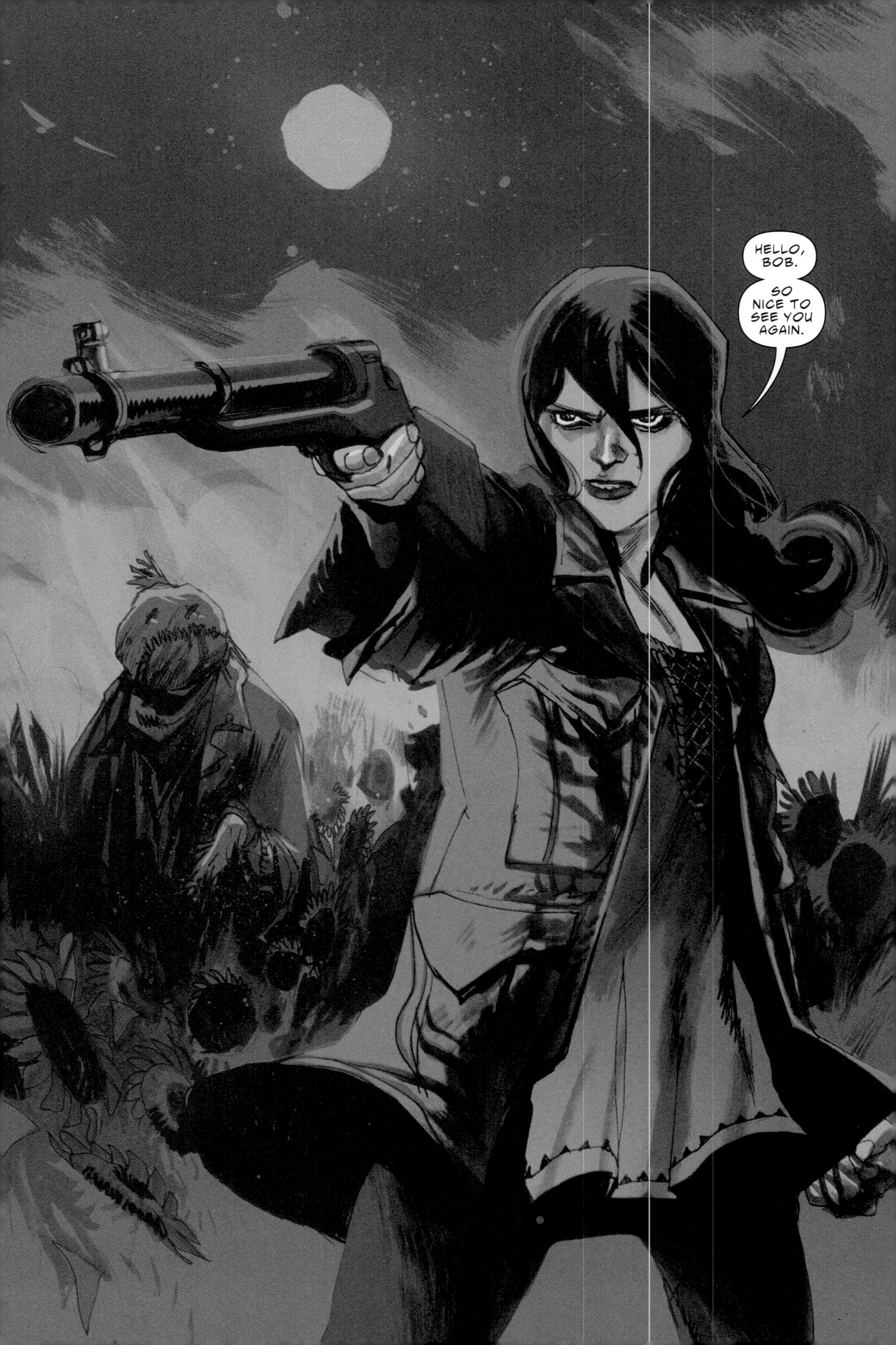
HELLO, BOB.
SO NICE TO SEE YOU AGAIN.

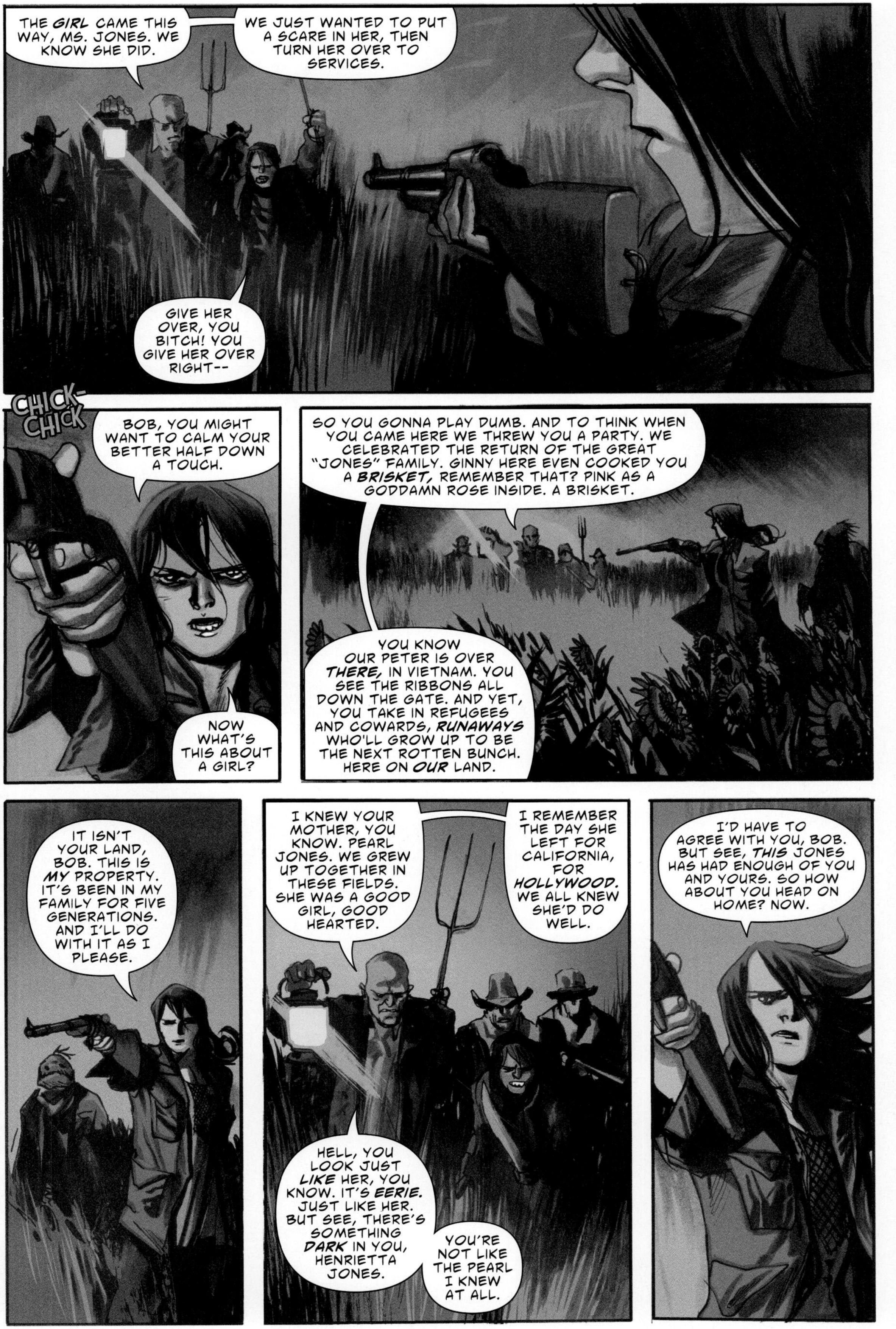
THE GIRL CAME THIS WAY, MS. JONES. WE KNOW SHE DID.
WE JUST WANTED TO PUT A SCARE IN HER, THEN TURN HER OVER TO SERVICES.
GIVE HER OVER, YOU BITCH! YOU GIVE HER OVER RIGHT--
CHICK-CHICK
BOB, YOU MIGHT WANT TO CALM YOUR BETTER HALF DOWN A TOUCH.
NOW WHAT'S THIS ABOUT A GIRL?
SO YOU GONNA PLAY DUMB. AND TO THINK WHEN YOU CAME HERE WE THREW YOU A PARTY. WE CELEBRATED THE RETURN OF THE GREAT "JONES" FAMILY. GINNY HERE EVEN COOKED YOU A BRISKET, REMEMBER THAT? PINK AS A GODDAMN ROSE INSIDE. A BRISKET.
YOU KNOW OUR PETER IS OVER THERE, IN VIETNAM. YOU SEE THE RIBBONS ALL DOWN THE GATE. AND YET, YOU TAKE IN REFUGEES AND COWARDS, RUNAWAYS WHO'LL GROW UP TO BE THE NEXT ROTTEN BUNCH. HERE ON OUR LAND.
IT ISN'T YOUR LAND, BOB. THIS IS MY PROPERTY. IT'S BEEN IN MY FAMILY FOR FIVE GENERATIONS. AND I'LL DO WITH IT AS I PLEASE.
I KNEW YOUR MOTHER, YOU KNOW. PEARL JONES. WE GREW UP TOGETHER IN THESE FIELDS. SHE WAS A GOOD GIRL, GOOD HEARTED.
I REMEMBER THE DAY SHE LEFT FOR CALIFORNIA, FOR HOLLYWOOD. WE ALL KNEW SHE'D DO WELL.
HELL, YOU LOOK JUST LIKE HER, YOU KNOW. IT'S EERIE. JUST LIKE HER. BUT SEE, THERE'S SOMETHING DARK IN YOU, HENRIETTA JONES.
YOU'RE NOT LIKE THE PEARL I KNEW AT ALL.
I'D HAVE TO AGREE WITH YOU, BOB. BUT SEE, THIS JONES HAS HAD ENOUGH OF YOU AND YOURS. SO HOW ABOUT YOU HEAD ON HOME? NOW.

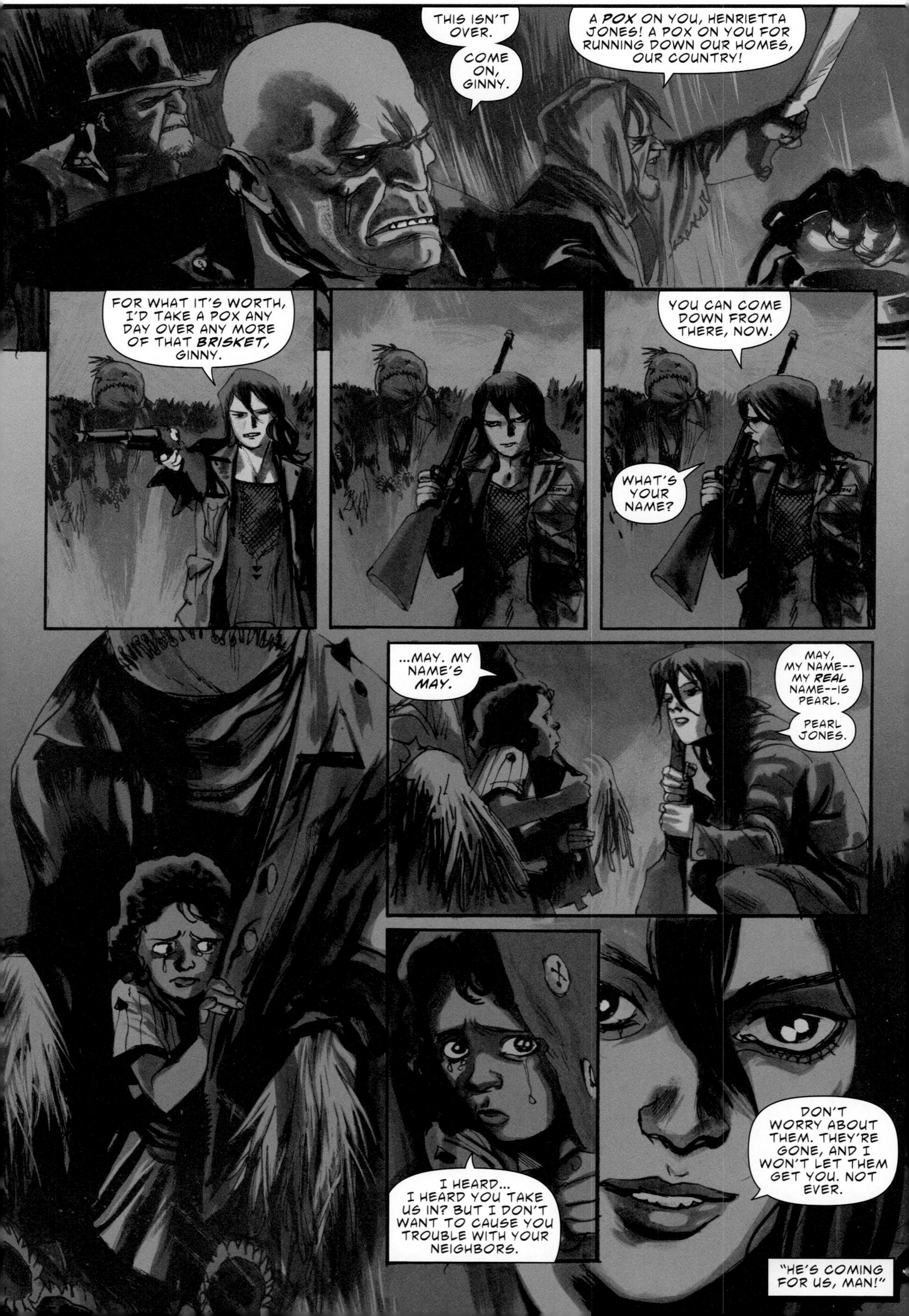
THIS ISN'T OVER.
COME ON, GINNY.
A POX ON YOU, HENRIETTA JONES! A POX ON YOU FOR RUNNING DOWN OUR HOMES, OUR COUNTRY!
FOR WHAT IT'S WORTH, I'D TAKE A POX ANY DAY OVER ANY MORE OF THAT BRISKET, GINNY.
YOU CAN COME DOWN FROM THERE, NOW.
WHAT'S YOUR NAME?
...MAY. MY NAME'S MAY.
MAY, MY NAME-- MY REAL NAME--IS PEARL.
PEARL JONES.
I HEARD... I HEARD YOU TAKE US IN? BUT I DON'T WANT TO CAUSE YOU TROUBLE WITH YOUR NEIGHBORS.
DON'T WORRY ABOUT THEM. THEY'RE GONE, AND I WON'T LET THEM GET YOU. NOT EVER.
"HE'S COMING FOR US, MAN!"

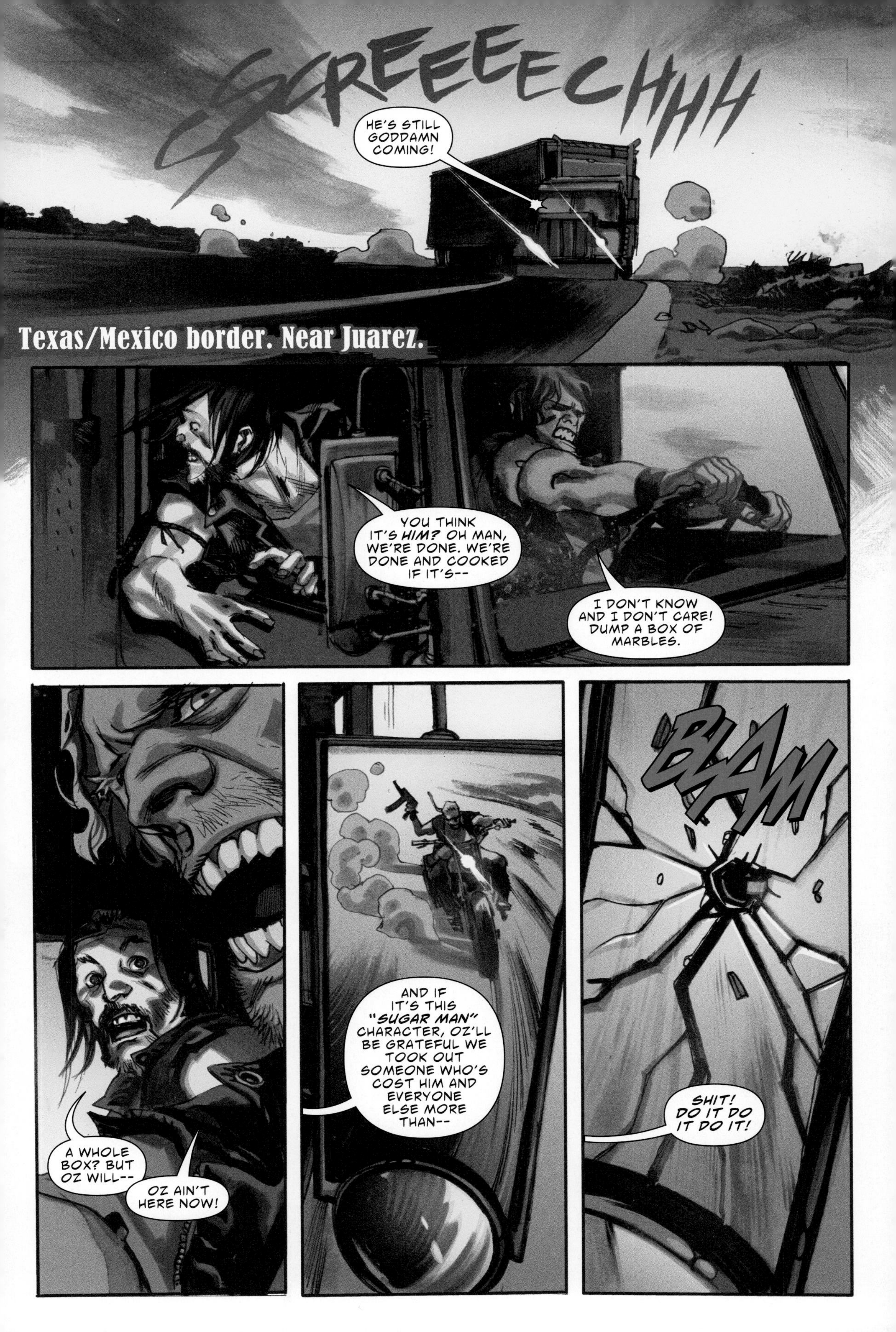
SCREEEECHHH
HE'S STILL GODDAMN COMING!
Texas/Mexico border. Near Juarez.
YOU THINK IT'S HIM? OH MAN, WE'RE DONE. WE'RE DONE AND COOKED IF IT'S--
I DON'T KNOW AND I DON'T CARE! DUMP A BOX OF MARBLES.
A WHOLE BOX? BUT OZ WILL--
OZ AIN'T HERE NOW!
AND IF IT'S THIS "SUGAR MAN" CHARACTER, OZ'LL BE GRATEFUL WE TOOK OUT SOMEONE WHO'S COST HIM AND EVERYONE ELSE MORE THAN--
BLAM
SHIT! DO IT DO IT DO IT!

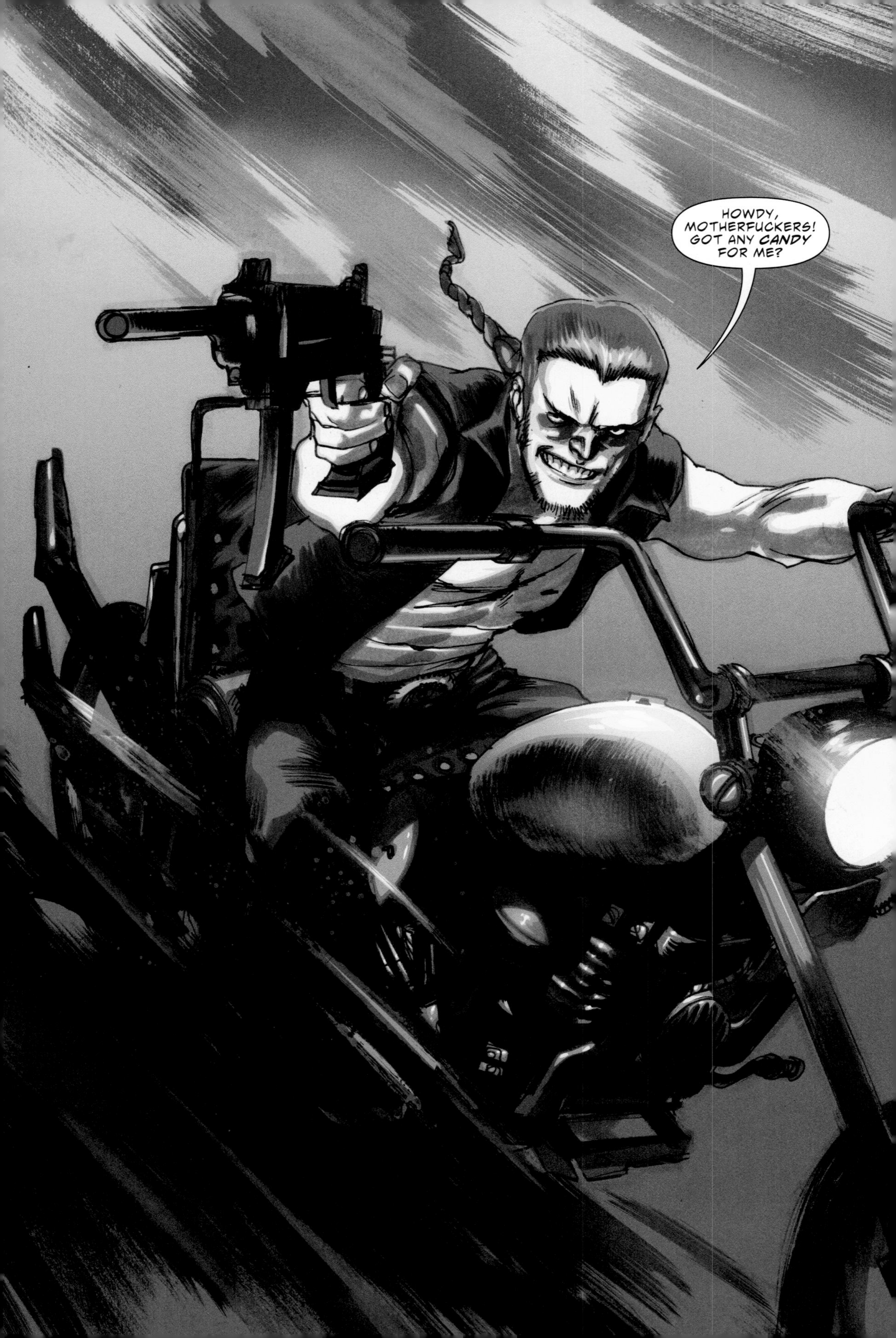
HOWDY, MOTHERFUCKERS! GOT ANY *CANDY* FOR ME?

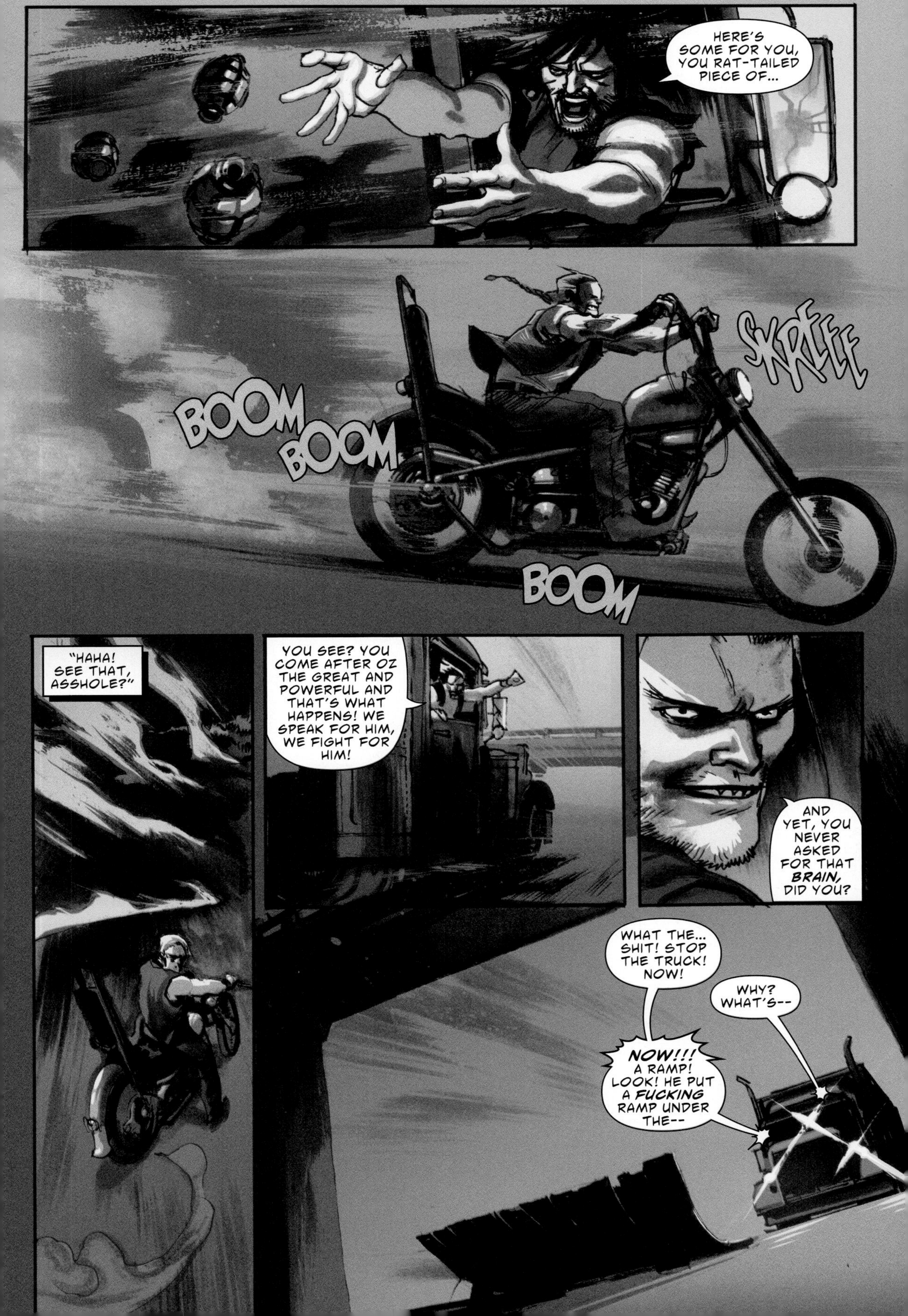
HERE'S SOME FOR YOU, YOU RAT-TAILED PIECE OF...
SKREEE
BOOM
BOOM
BOOM
"HAHA! SEE THAT, ASSHOLE?"
YOU SEE? YOU COME AFTER OZ THE GREAT AND POWERFUL AND THAT'S WHAT HAPPENS! WE SPEAK FOR HIM, WE FIGHT FOR HIM!
AND YET, YOU NEVER ASKED FOR THAT *BRAIN,* DID YOU?
WHAT THE... SHIT! STOP THE TRUCK! NOW!
WHY? WHAT'S--
NOW!!! A RAMP! LOOK! HE PUT A *FUCKING* RAMP UNDER THE--

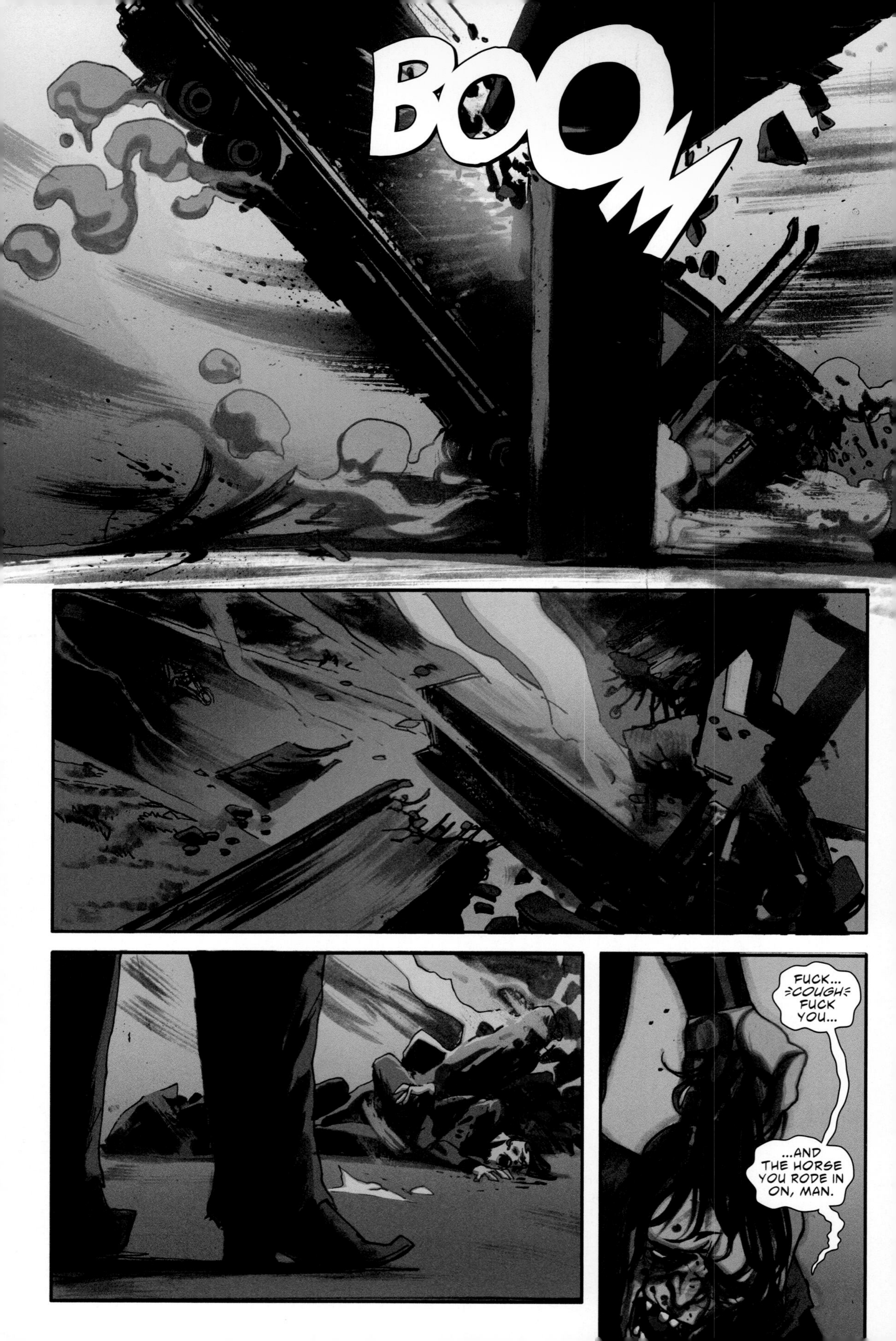
BOOM
FUCK... =COUGH= FUCK YOU...
...AND THE HORSE YOU RODE IN ON, MAN.

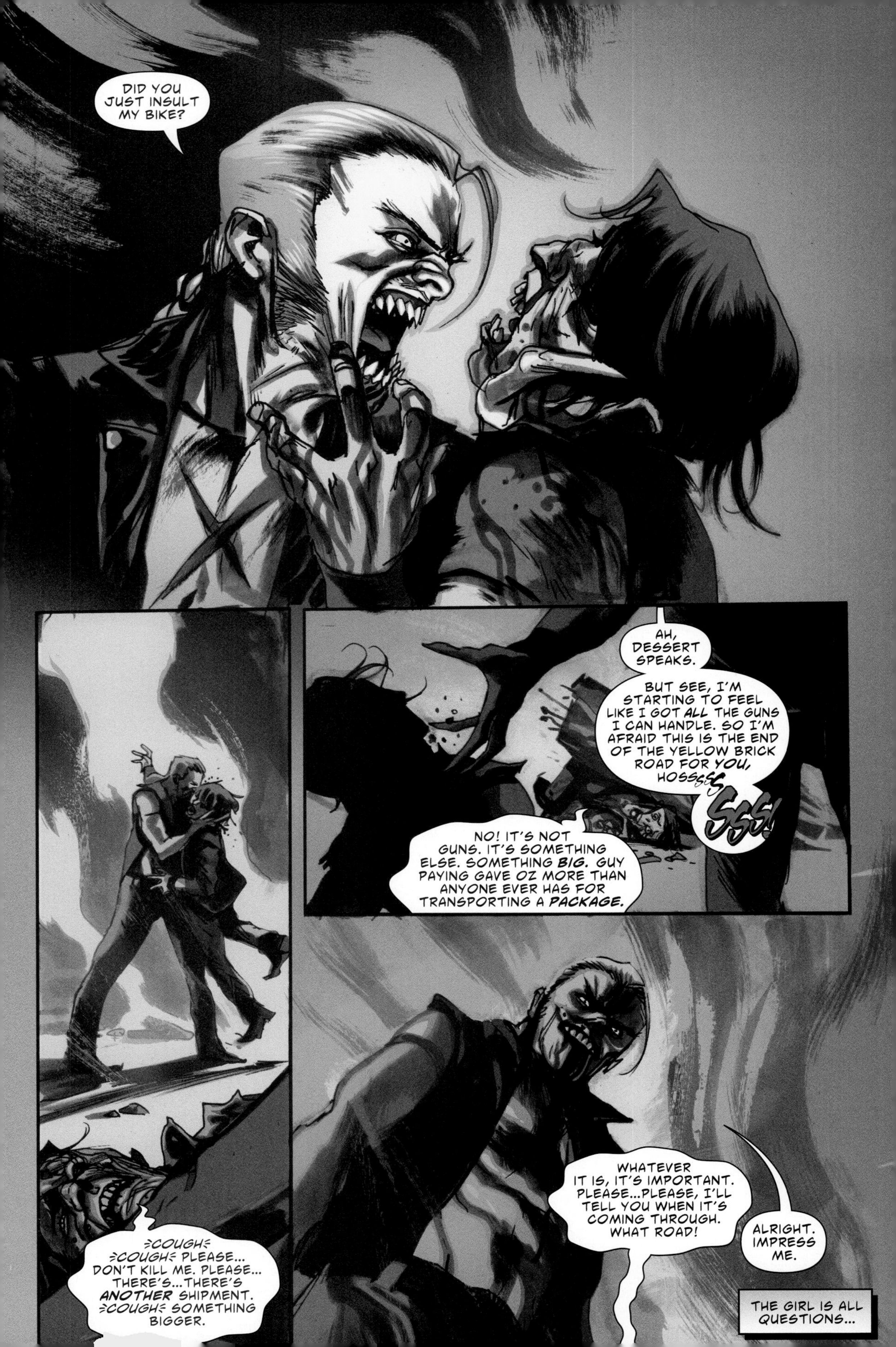
DID YOU JUST INSULT MY BIKE?
AH, DESSERT SPEAKS.
BUT SEE, I'M STARTING TO FEEL LIKE I GOT ALL THE GUNS I CAN HANDLE. SO I'M AFRAID THIS IS THE END OF THE YELLOW BRICK ROAD FOR YOU, HOSSSSS
SSS!
NO! IT'S NOT GUNS. IT'S SOMETHING ELSE. SOMETHING BIG. GUY PAYING GAVE OZ MORE THAN ANYONE EVER HAS FOR TRANSPORTING A PACKAGE.
=COUGH= =COUGH= PLEASE... DON'T KILL ME. PLEASE... THERE'S...THERE'S ANOTHER SHIPMENT. =COUGH= SOMETHING BIGGER.
WHATEVER IT IS, IT'S IMPORTANT. PLEASE...PLEASE, I'LL TELL YOU WHEN IT'S COMING THROUGH. WHAT ROAD!
ALRIGHT. IMPRESS ME.
THE GIRL IS ALL QUESTIONS...

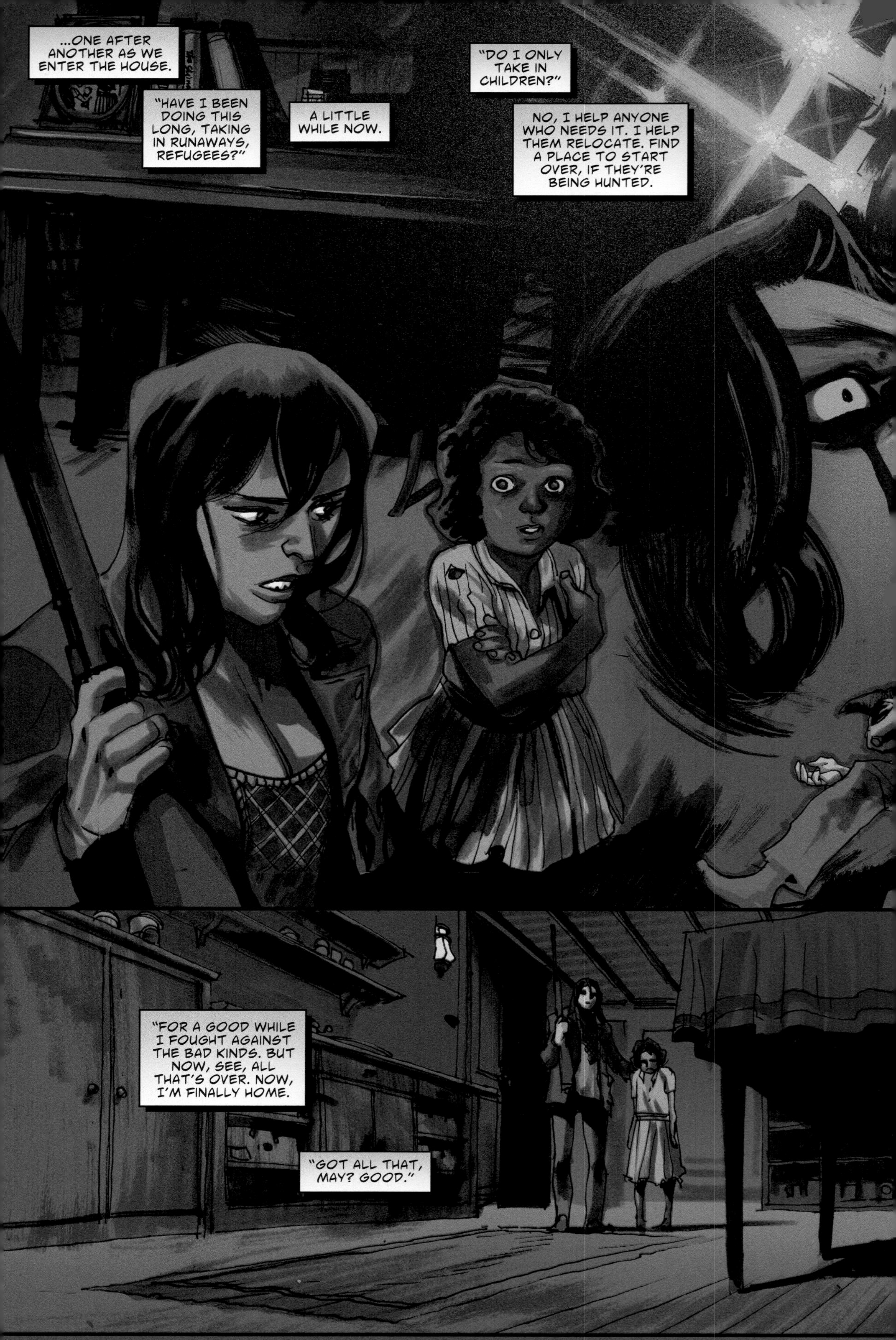
...ONE AFTER ANOTHER AS WE ENTER THE HOUSE.
"HAVE I BEEN DOING THIS LONG, TAKING IN RUNAWAYS, REFUGEES?"
A LITTLE WHILE NOW.
"DO I ONLY TAKE IN CHILDREN?"
NO, I HELP ANYONE WHO NEEDS IT. I HELP THEM RELOCATE. FIND A PLACE TO START OVER, IF THEY'RE BEING HUNTED.
"FOR A GOOD WHILE I FOUGHT AGAINST THE BAD KINDS. BUT NOW, SEE, ALL THAT'S OVER. NOW, I'M FINALLY HOME.
"GOT ALL THAT, MAY? GOOD."

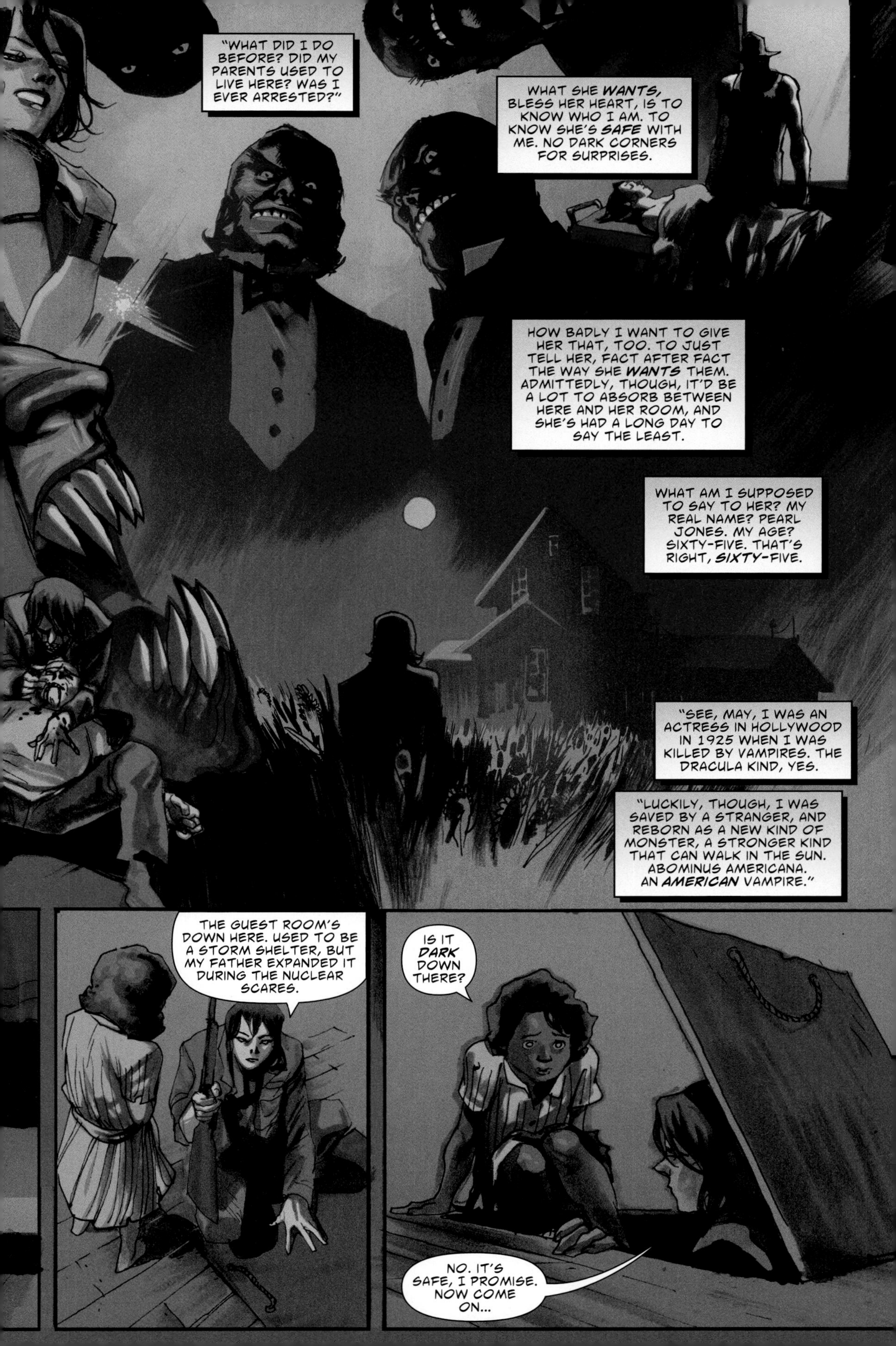
"WHAT DID I DO BEFORE? DID MY PARENTS USED TO LIVE HERE? WAS I EVER ARRESTED?"
WHAT SHE WANTS, BLESS HER HEART, IS TO KNOW WHO I AM. TO KNOW SHE'S SAFE WITH ME. NO DARK CORNERS FOR SURPRISES.
HOW BADLY I WANT TO GIVE HER THAT, TOO. TO JUST TELL HER, FACT AFTER FACT THE WAY SHE WANTS THEM. ADMITTEDLY, THOUGH, IT'D BE A LOT TO ABSORB BETWEEN HERE AND HER ROOM, AND SHE'S HAD A LONG DAY TO SAY THE LEAST.
WHAT AM I SUPPOSED TO SAY TO HER? MY REAL NAME? PEARL JONES. MY AGE? SIXTY-FIVE. THAT'S RIGHT, SIXTY-FIVE.
"SEE, MAY, I WAS AN ACTRESS IN HOLLYWOOD IN 1925 WHEN I WAS KILLED BY VAMPIRES. THE DRACULA KIND, YES.
"LUCKILY, THOUGH, I WAS SAVED BY A STRANGER, AND REBORN AS A NEW KIND OF MONSTER, A STRONGER KIND THAT CAN WALK IN THE SUN. ABOMINUS AMERICANA. AN AMERICAN VAMPIRE."
THE GUEST ROOM'S DOWN HERE. USED TO BE A STORM SHELTER, BUT MY FATHER EXPANDED IT DURING THE NUCLEAR SCARES.
IS IT DARK DOWN THERE?
NO. IT'S SAFE, I PROMISE. NOW COME ON...

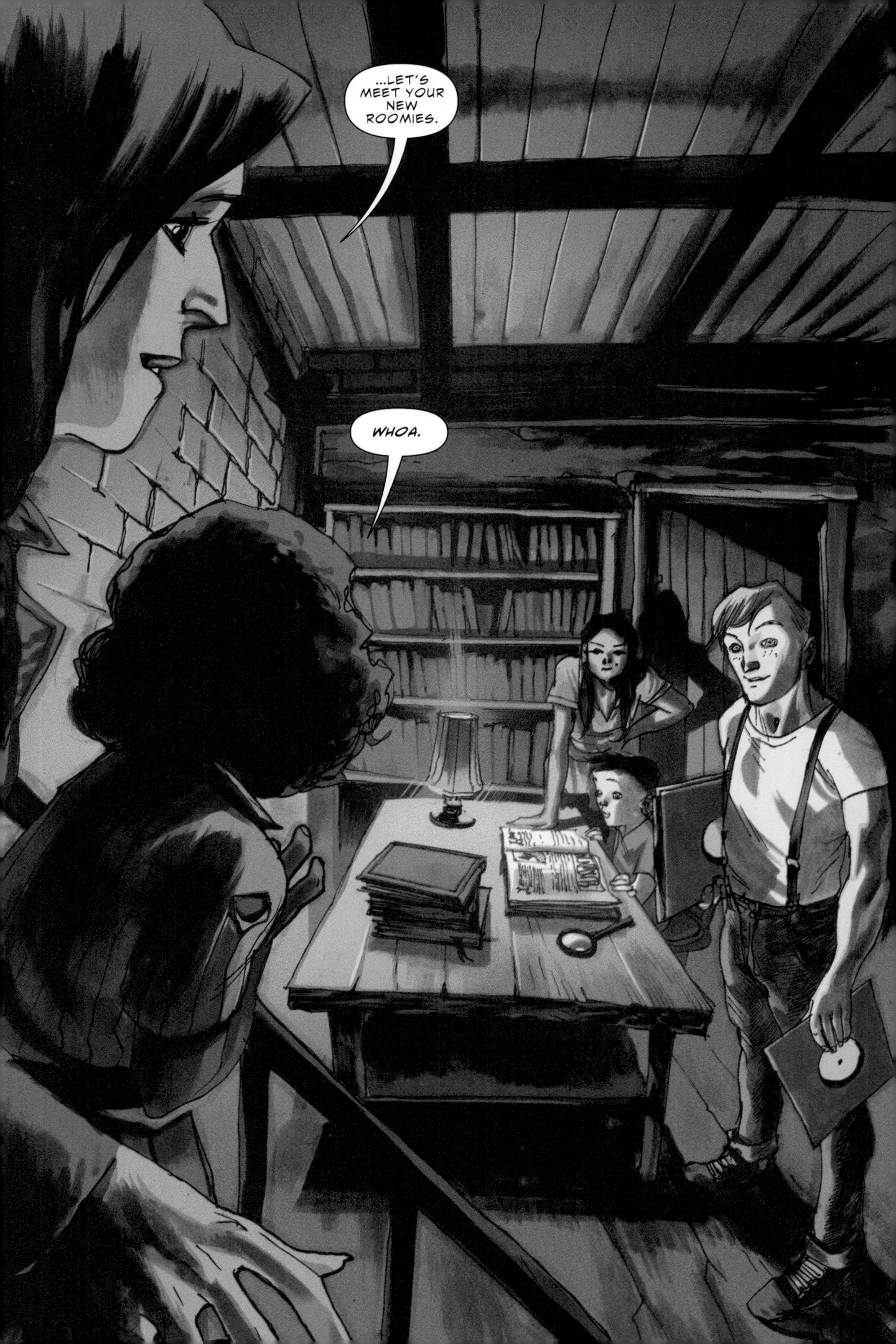
...LET'S MEET YOUR NEW ROOMIES.
WHOA.

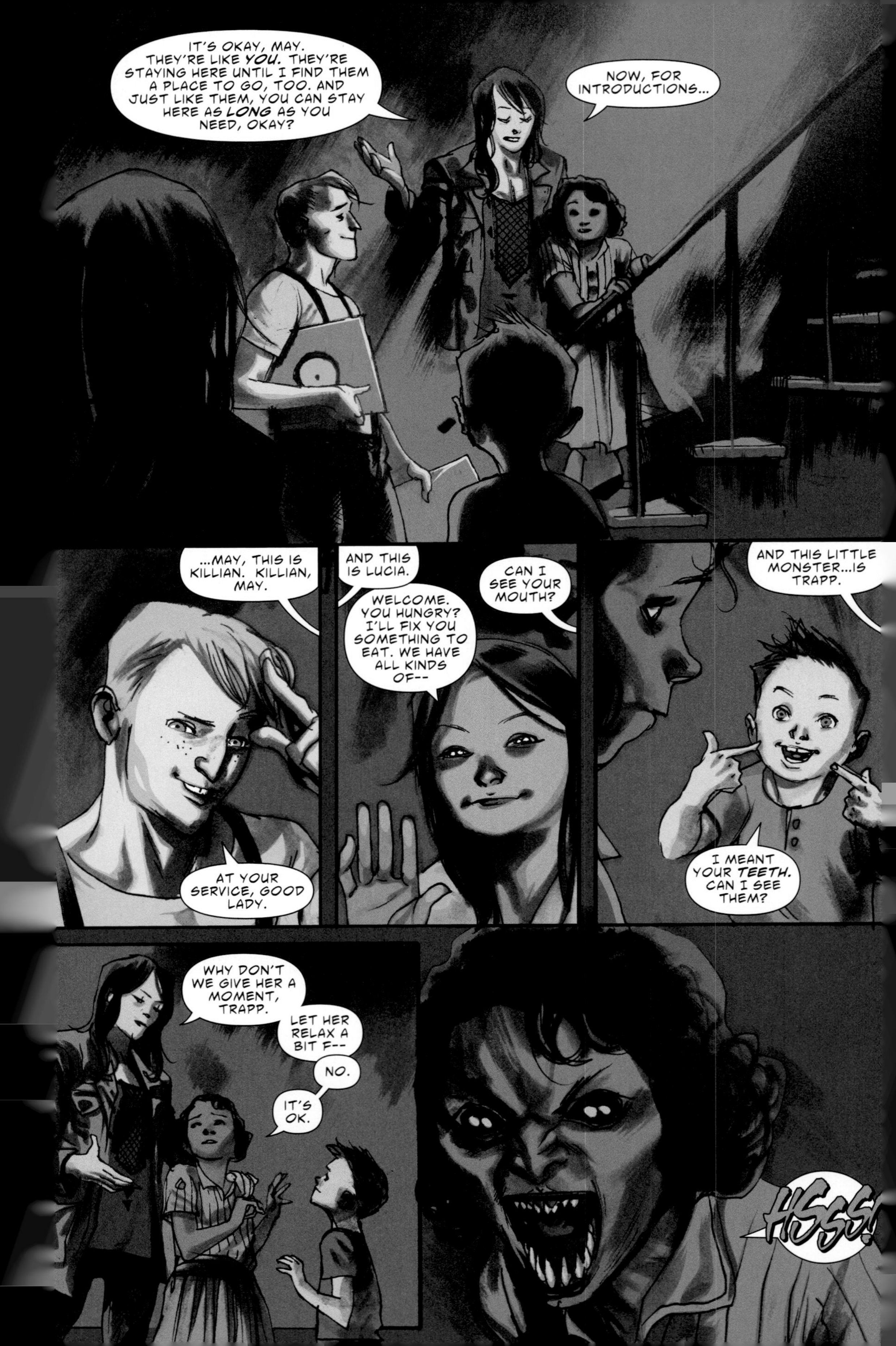
IT'S OKAY, MAY. THEY'RE LIKE *YOU.* THEY'RE STAYING HERE UNTIL I FIND THEM A PLACE TO GO, TOO. AND JUST LIKE THEM, YOU CAN STAY HERE AS *LONG* AS YOU NEED, OKAY?
NOW, FOR INTRODUCTIONS...
...MAY, THIS IS KILLIAN. KILLIAN, MAY.
AT YOUR SERVICE, GOOD LADY.
AND THIS IS LUCIA.
WELCOME. YOU HUNGRY? I'LL FIX YOU SOMETHING TO EAT. WE HAVE ALL KINDS OF--
CAN I SEE YOUR MOUTH?
AND THIS LITTLE MONSTER...IS TRAPP.
I MEANT YOUR *TEETH.* CAN I SEE THEM?
WHY DON'T WE GIVE HER A MOMENT, TRAPP.
LET HER RELAX A BIT F--
NO.
IT'S OK.
HSSS!

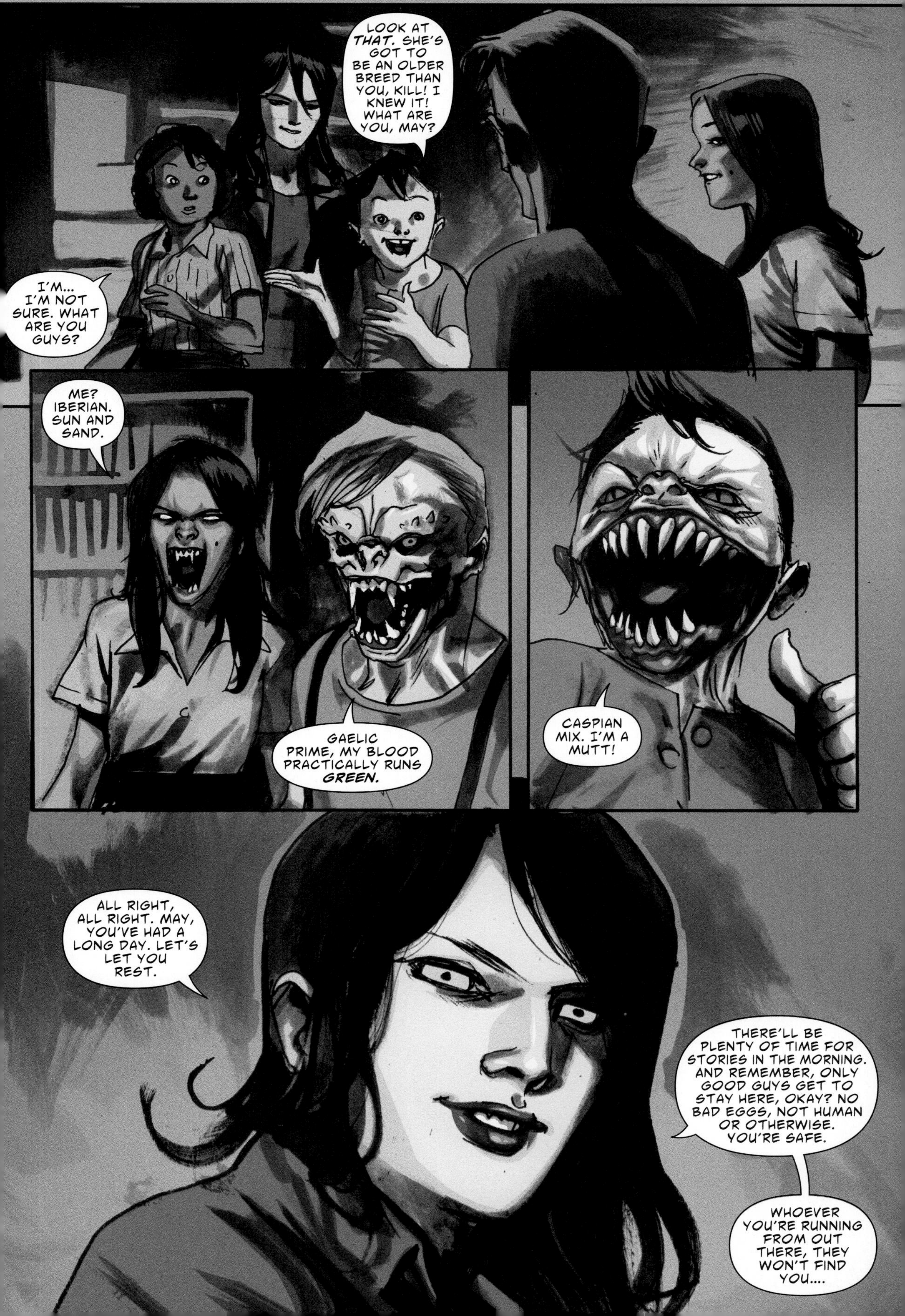
LOOK AT THAT. SHE'S GOT TO BE AN OLDER BREED THAN YOU, KILL! I KNEW IT! WHAT ARE YOU, MAY?
I'M... I'M NOT SURE. WHAT ARE YOU GUYS?
ME? IBERIAN. SUN AND SAND.
GAELIC PRIME, MY BLOOD PRACTICALLY RUNS GREEN.
CASPIAN MIX. I'M A MUTT!
ALL RIGHT, ALL RIGHT. MAY, YOU'VE HAD A LONG DAY. LET'S LET YOU REST.
THERE'LL BE PLENTY OF TIME FOR STORIES IN THE MORNING. AND REMEMBER, ONLY GOOD GUYS GET TO STAY HERE, OKAY? NO BAD EGGS, NOT HUMAN OR OTHERWISE. YOU'RE SAFE.
WHOEVER YOU'RE RUNNING FROM OUT THERE, THEY WON'T FIND YOU....

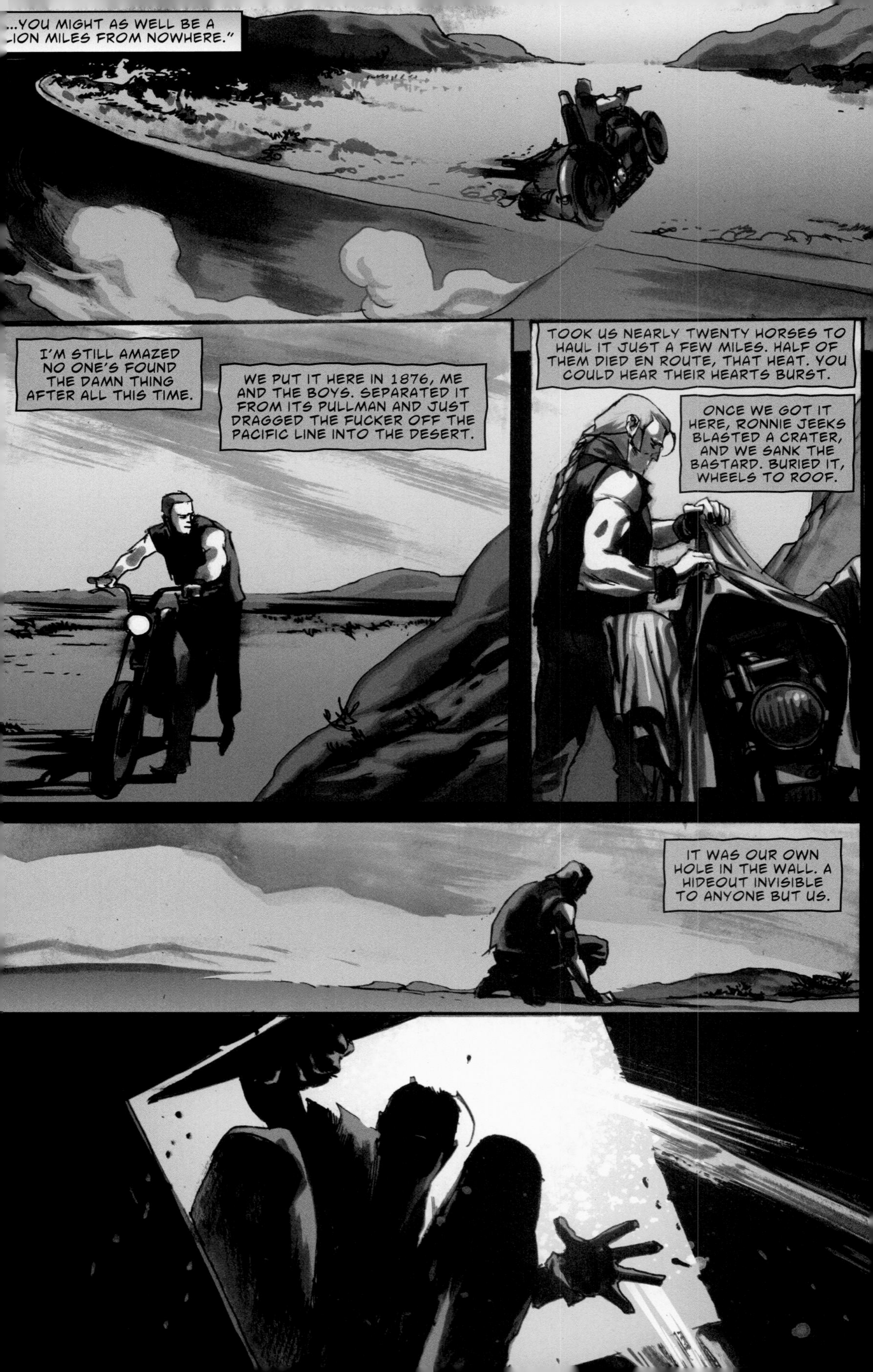

...YOU MIGHT AS WELL BE A LION MILES FROM NOWHERE."
I'M STILL AMAZED NO ONE'S FOUND THE DAMN THING AFTER ALL THIS TIME.
WE PUT IT HERE IN 1876, ME AND THE BOYS. SEPARATED IT FROM ITS PULLMAN AND JUST DRAGGED THE FUCKER OFF THE PACIFIC LINE INTO THE DESERT.
TOOK US NEARLY TWENTY HORSES TO HAUL IT JUST A FEW MILES. HALF OF THEM DIED EN ROUTE, THAT HEAT. YOU COULD HEAR THEIR HEARTS BURST.
ONCE WE GOT IT HERE, RONNIE JEEKS BLASTED A CRATER, AND WE SANK THE BASTARD. BURIED IT, WHEELS TO ROOF.
IT WAS OUR OWN HOLE IN THE WALL. A HIDEOUT INVISIBLE TO ANYONE BUT US.

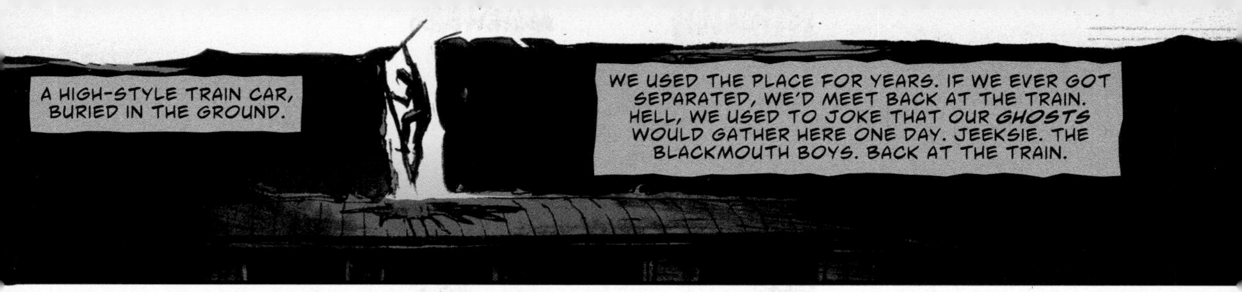

A HIGH-STYLE TRAIN CAR, BURIED IN THE GROUND.
WE USED THE PLACE FOR YEARS. IF WE EVER GOT SEPARATED, WE'D MEET BACK AT THE TRAIN. HELL, WE USED TO JOKE THAT OUR *GHOSTS* WOULD GATHER HERE ONE DAY. JEEKSIE. THE BLACKMOUTH BOYS. BACK AT THE TRAIN.

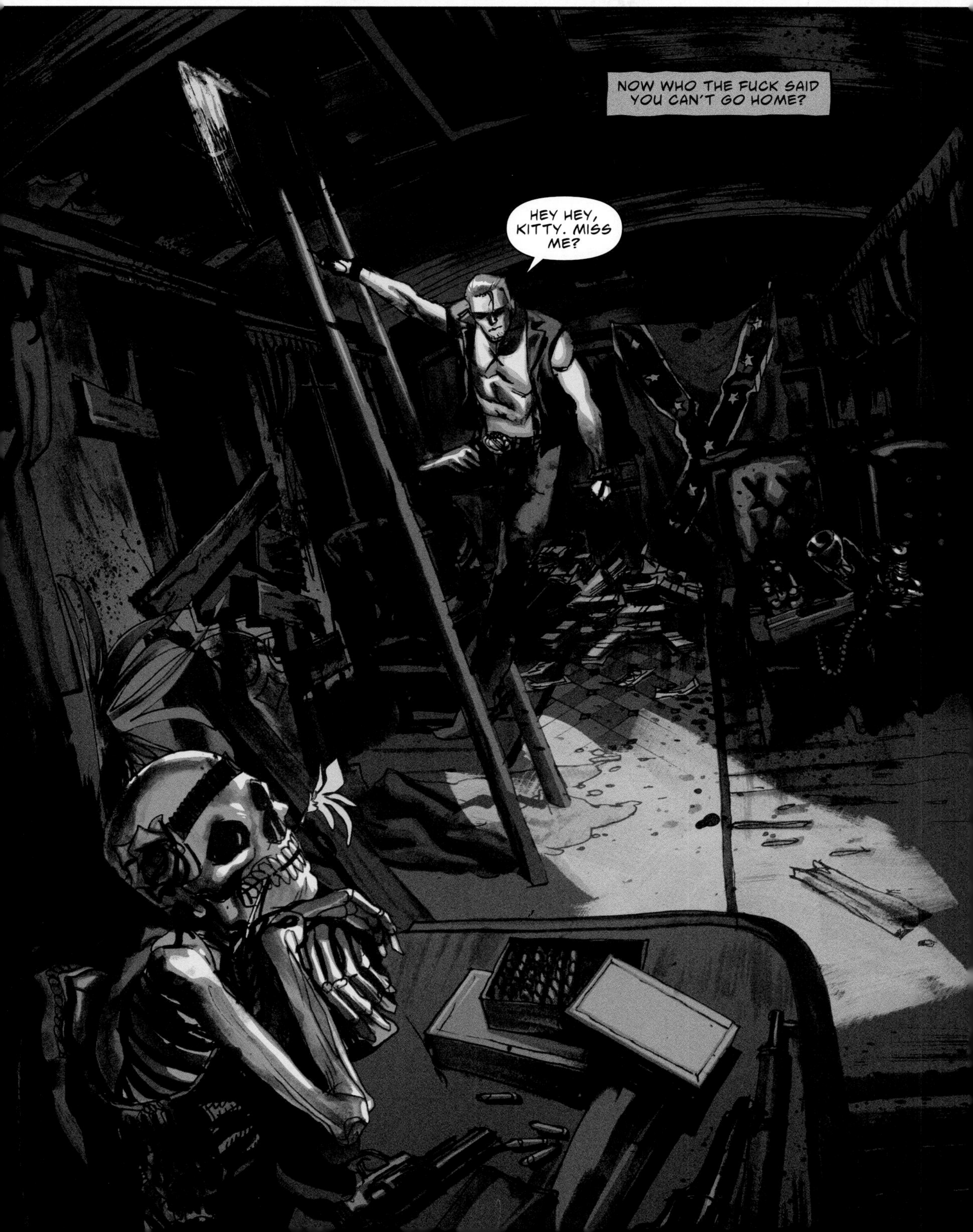

NOW WHO THE FUCK SAID YOU CAN'T GO HOME?
HEY HEY, KITTY. MISS ME?

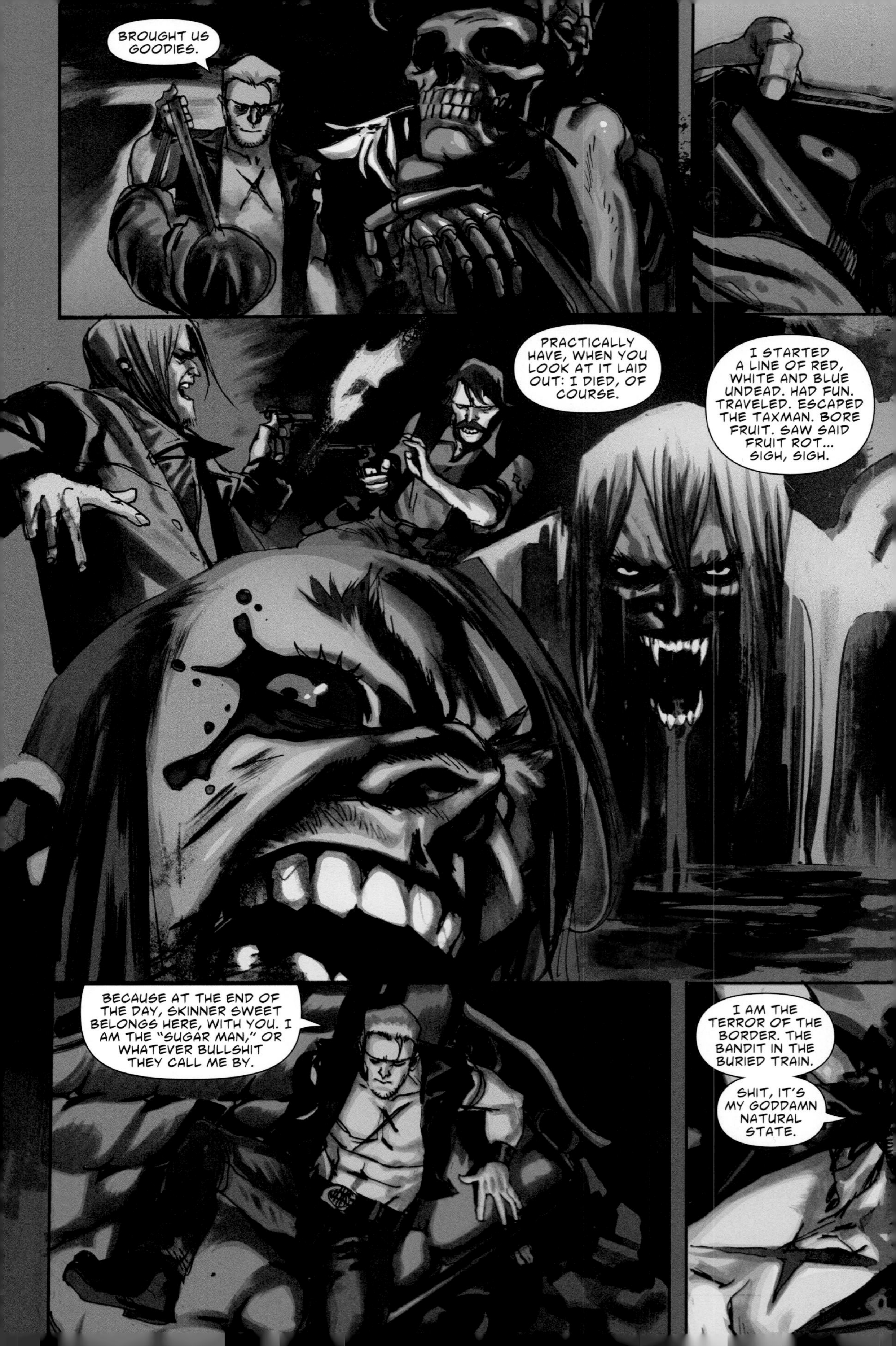
BROUGHT US GOODIES.
PRACTICALLY HAVE, WHEN YOU LOOK AT IT LAID OUT: I DIED, OF COURSE.
I STARTED A LINE OF RED, WHITE AND BLUE UNDEAD. HAD FUN. TRAVELED. ESCAPED THE TAXMAN. BORE FRUIT. SAW SAID FRUIT ROT... SIGH, SIGH.
BECAUSE AT THE END OF THE DAY, SKINNER SWEET BELONGS HERE, WITH YOU. I AM THE "SUGAR MAN," OR WHATEVER BULLSHIT THEY CALL ME BY.
I AM THE TERROR OF THE BORDER. THE BANDIT IN THE BURIED TRAIN.
SHIT, IT'S MY GODDAMN NATURAL STATE.

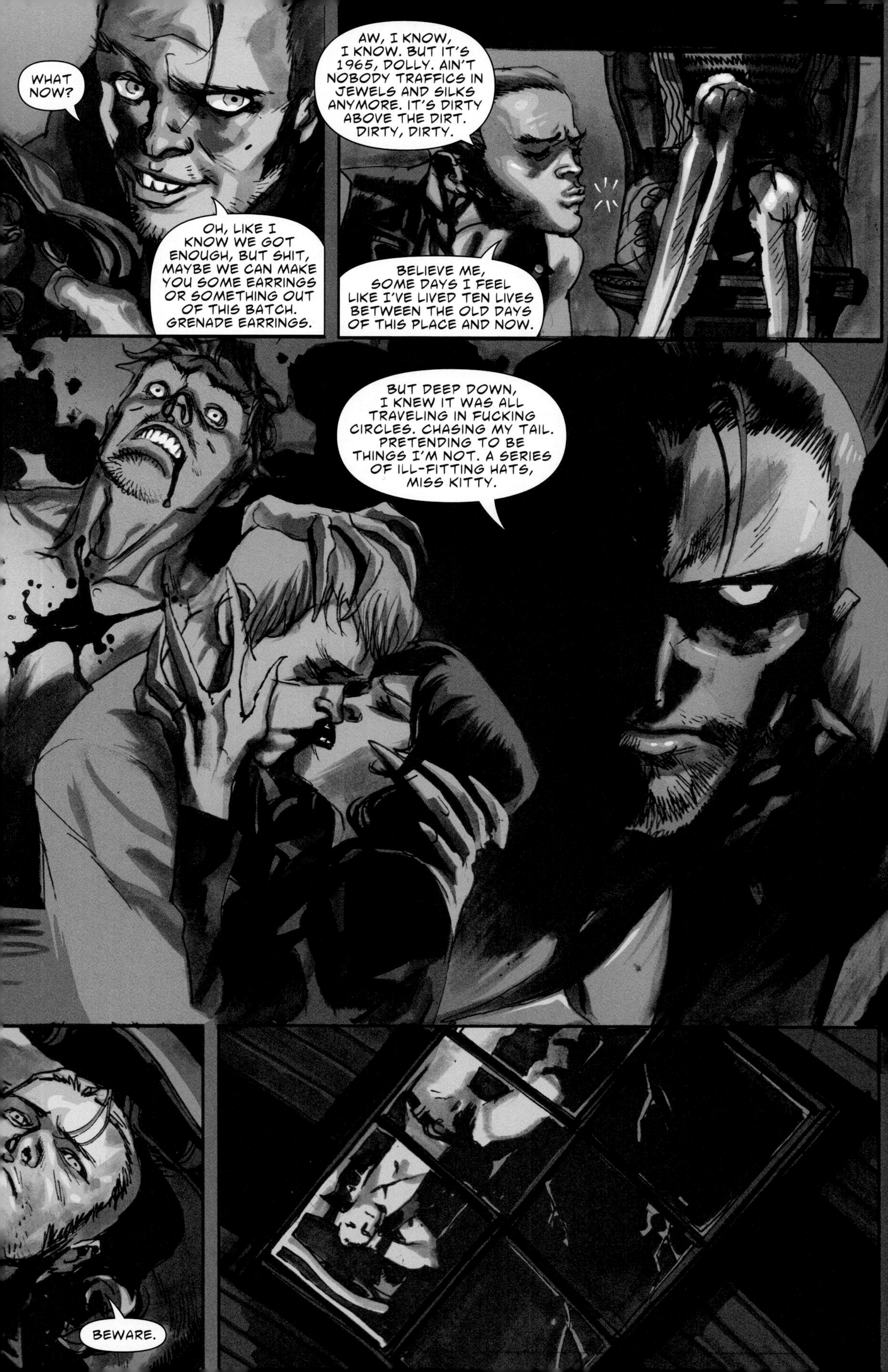
WHAT NOW?
OH, LIKE I KNOW WE GOT ENOUGH, BUT SHIT, MAYBE WE CAN MAKE YOU SOME EARRINGS OR SOMETHING OUT OF THIS BATCH. GRENADE EARRINGS.
AW, I KNOW, I KNOW. BUT IT'S 1965, DOLLY. AIN'T NOBODY TRAFFICS IN JEWELS AND SILKS ANYMORE. IT'S DIRTY ABOVE THE DIRT. DIRTY, DIRTY.
BELIEVE ME, SOME DAYS I FEEL LIKE I'VE LIVED TEN LIVES BETWEEN THE OLD DAYS OF THIS PLACE AND NOW.
BUT DEEP DOWN, I KNEW IT WAS ALL TRAVELING IN FUCKING CIRCLES. CHASING MY TAIL. PRETENDING TO BE THINGS I'M NOT. A SERIES OF ILL-FITTING HATS, MISS KITTY.
BEWARE.

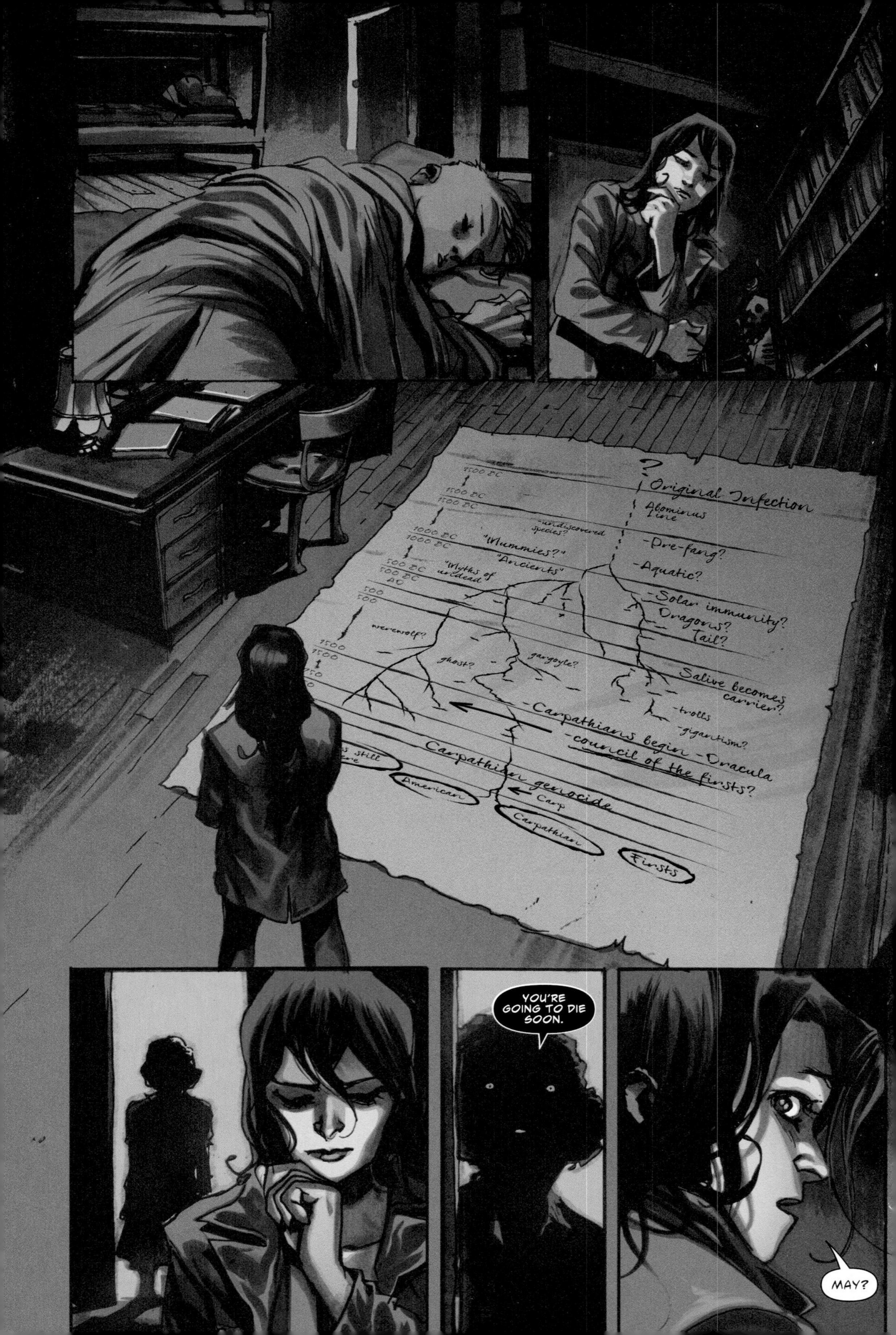
1500 BC
1500 BC
1000 BC
1000 BC
500 BC
500 BC
AD
500
500
1500
1500
Original Infection
Abominus Line
-undiscovered species?
"Mummies?"
"Ancients"
"Myths of undead"
-Pre-fang?
-Aquatic?
-Solar immunity?
Dragons?
Tail?
werewolf?
ghost?
gargoyle?
Salive becomes carrier?
-trolls
-gigantism?
-Carpathians begin -Dracula
-council of the firsts?
Carpathian genocide
Carp
American
Carpathian
Firsts
YOU'RE GOING TO DIE SOON.
MAY?

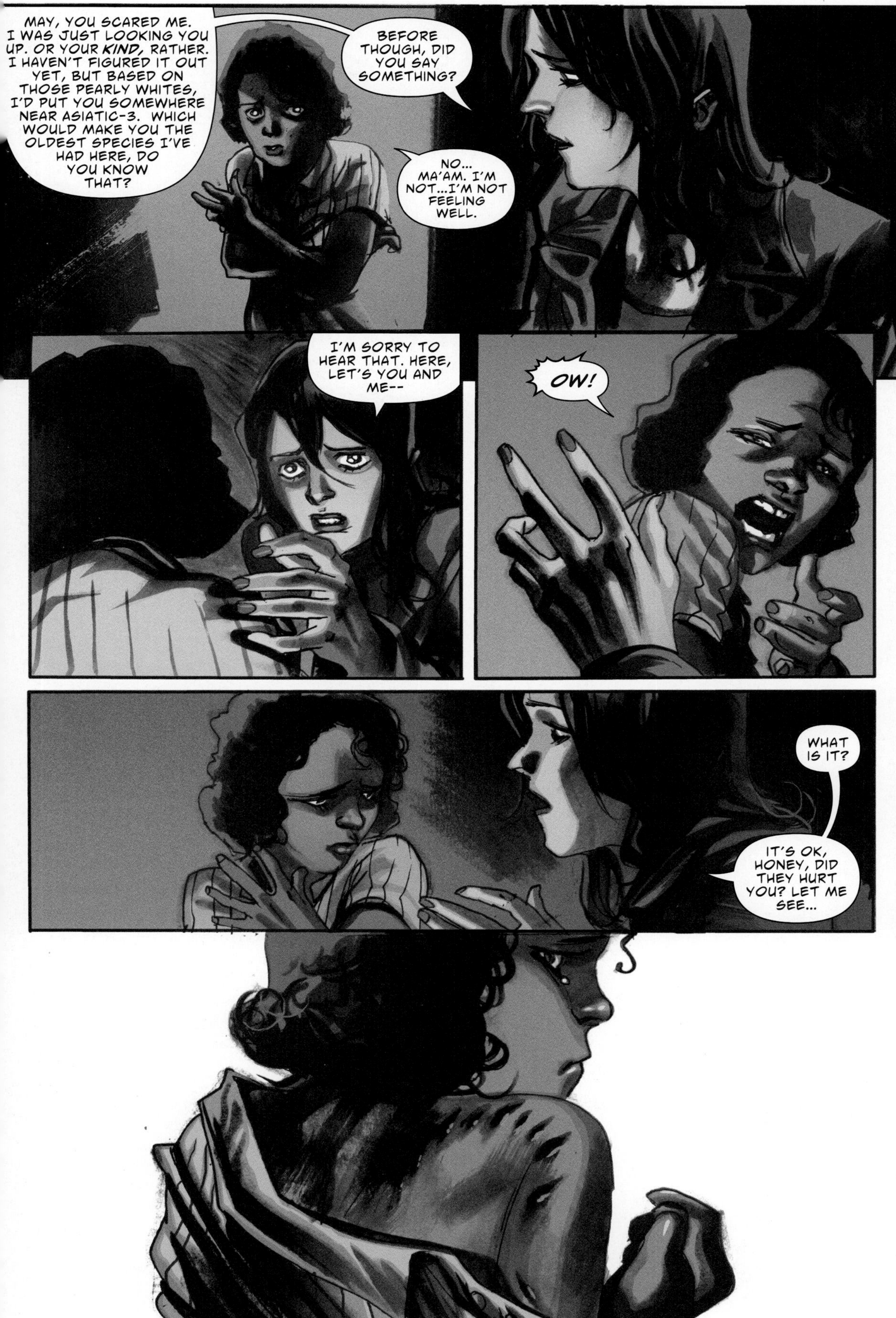
MAY, YOU SCARED ME. I WAS JUST LOOKING YOU UP. OR YOUR *KIND,* RATHER. I HAVEN'T FIGURED IT OUT YET, BUT BASED ON THOSE PEARLY WHITES, I'D PUT YOU SOMEWHERE NEAR ASIATIC-3. WHICH WOULD MAKE YOU THE OLDEST SPECIES I'VE HAD HERE, DO YOU KNOW THAT?
BEFORE THOUGH, DID YOU SAY SOMETHING?
NO... MA'AM. I'M NOT...I'M NOT FEELING WELL.
I'M SORRY TO HEAR THAT. HERE, LET'S YOU AND ME--
OW!
WHAT IS IT?
IT'S OK, HONEY, DID THEY HURT YOU? LET ME SEE...

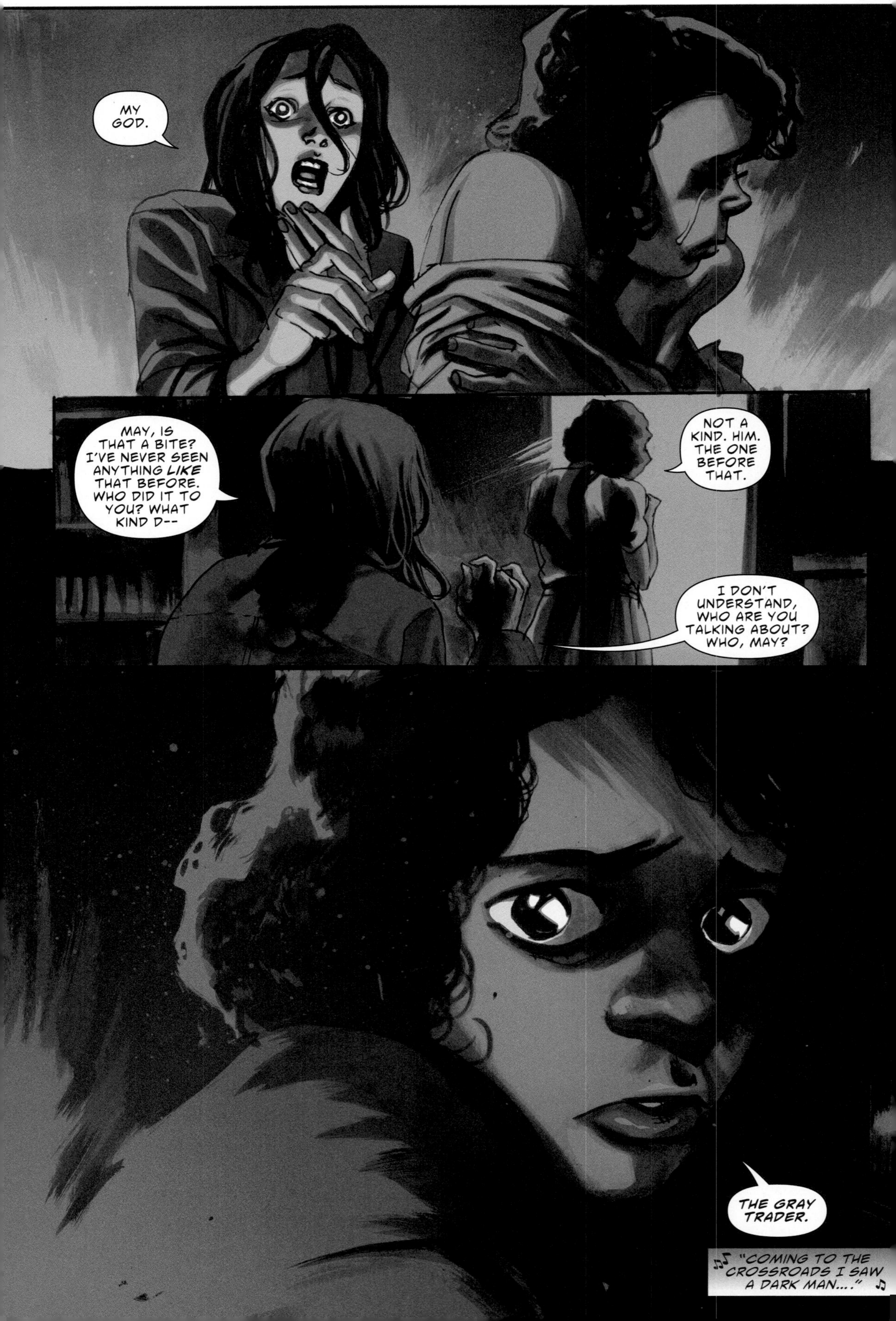
MY GOD.
MAY, IS THAT A BITE? I'VE NEVER SEEN ANYTHING LIKE THAT BEFORE. WHO DID IT TO YOU? WHAT KIND D--
NOT A KIND. HIM. THE ONE BEFORE THAT.
I DON'T UNDERSTAND, WHO ARE YOU TALKING ABOUT? WHO, MAY?
THE GRAY TRADER.
♫ "COMING TO THE CROSSROADS I SAW A DARK MAN..." ♫

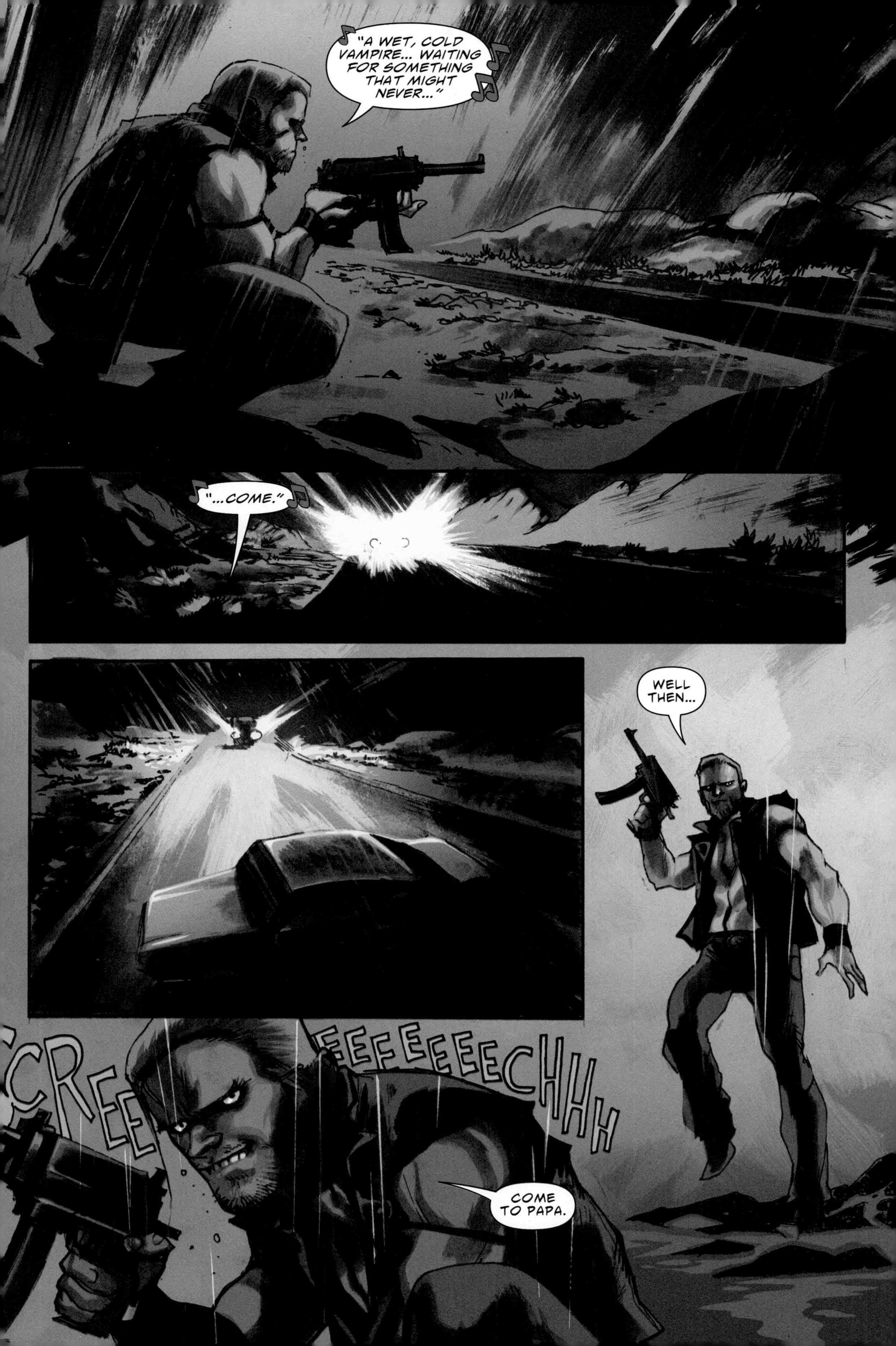
"A WET, COLD VAMPIRE... WAITING FOR SOMETHING THAT MIGHT NEVER..."
"...COME."
WELL THEN...
SCREEEEEEEEEEECHHH
COME TO PAPA.

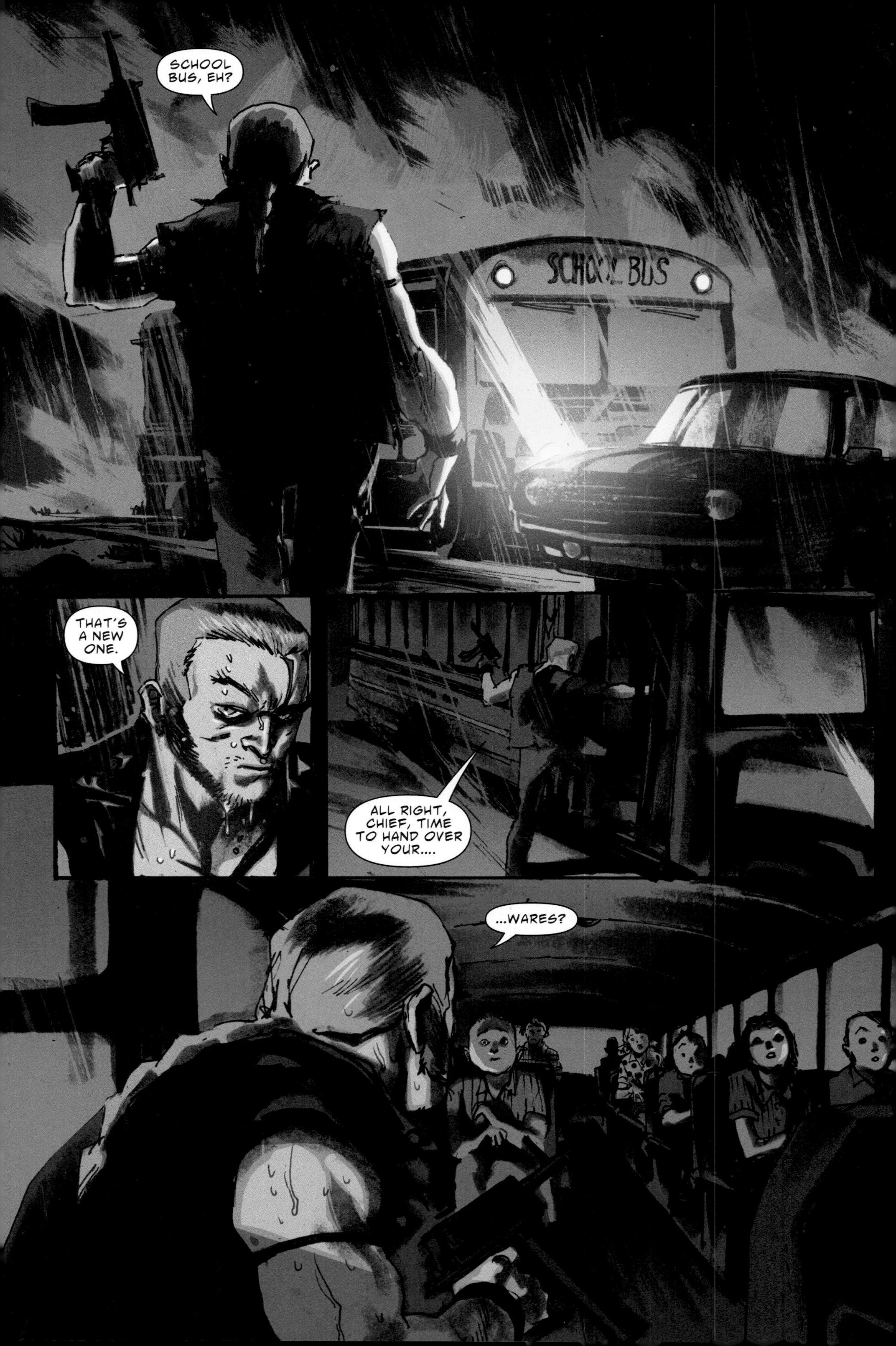
SCHOOL BUS, EH?
SCHOOL BUS
THAT'S A NEW ONE.
ALL RIGHT, CHIEF, TIME TO HAND OVER YOUR....
...WARES?

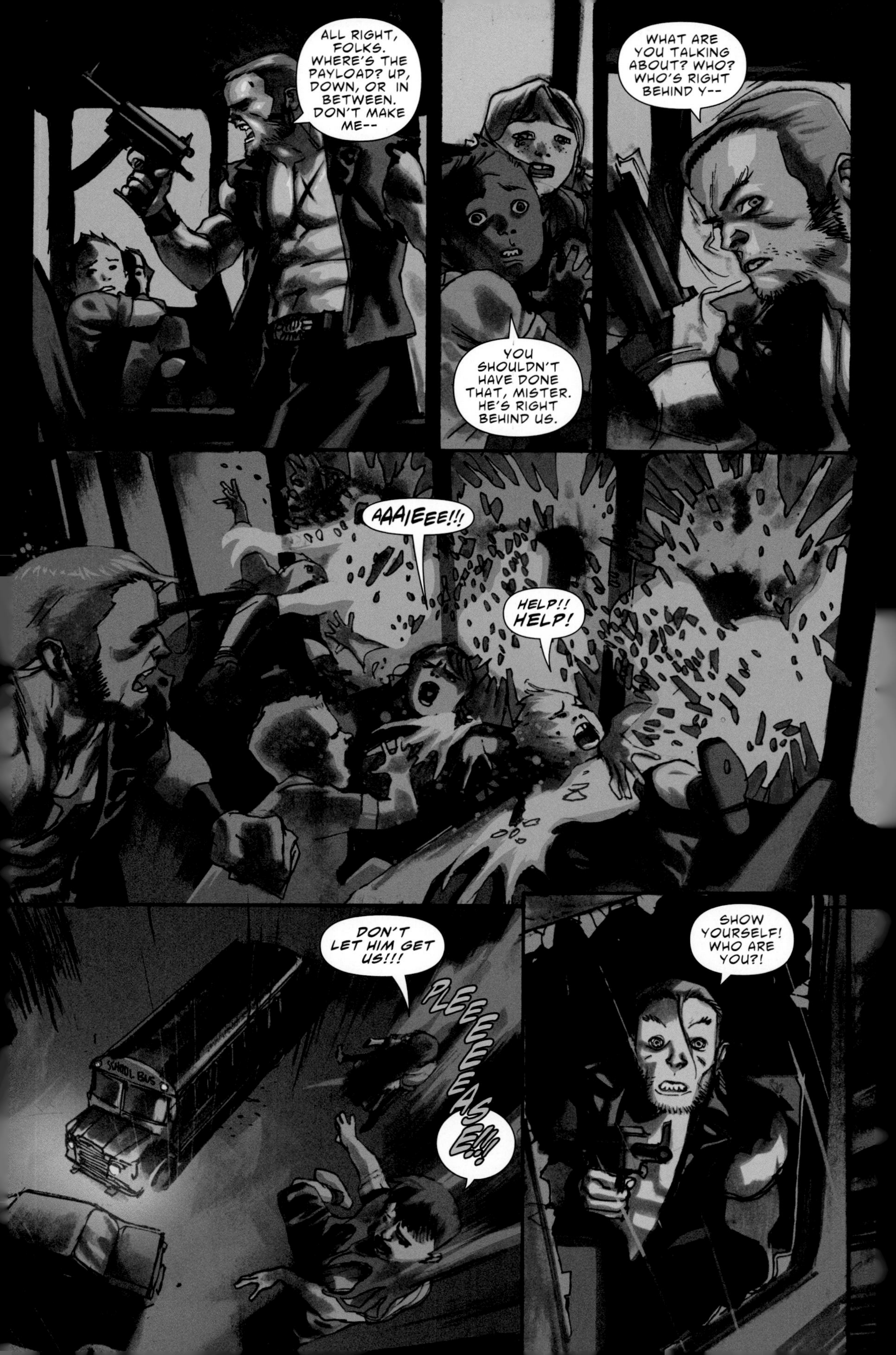
ALL RIGHT, FOLKS. WHERE'S THE PAYLOAD? UP, DOWN, OR IN BETWEEN. DON'T MAKE ME--
YOU SHOULDN'T HAVE DONE THAT, MISTER. HE'S RIGHT BEHIND US.
WHAT ARE YOU TALKING ABOUT? WHO? WHO'S RIGHT BEHIND Y--
AAAIEEE!!!
HELP!! HELP!
DON'T LET HIM GET US!!!
PLEEEEEEASE!!!
SCHOOL BUS
SHOW YOURSELF! WHO ARE YOU?!

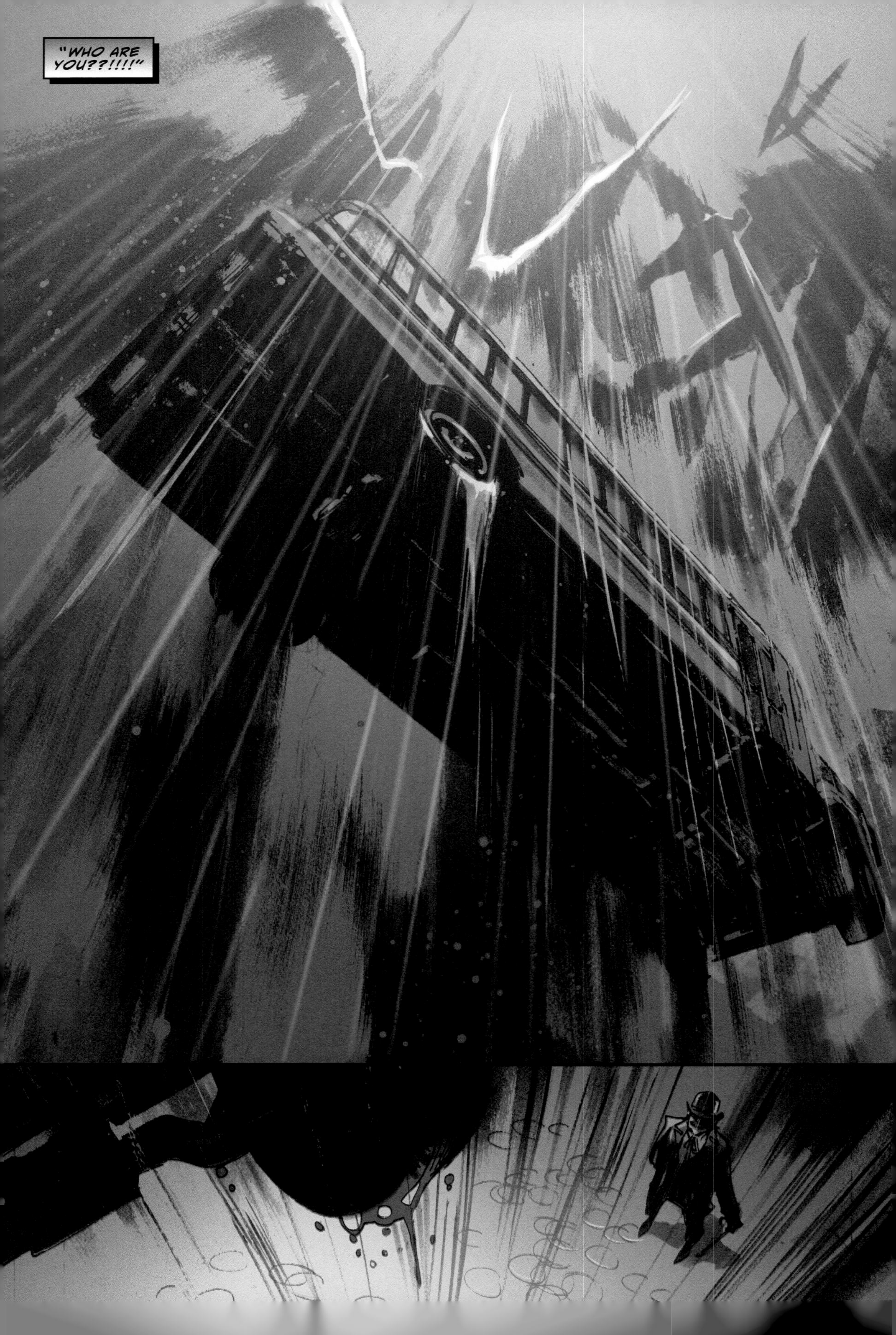
"WHO ARE YOU??!!!!"

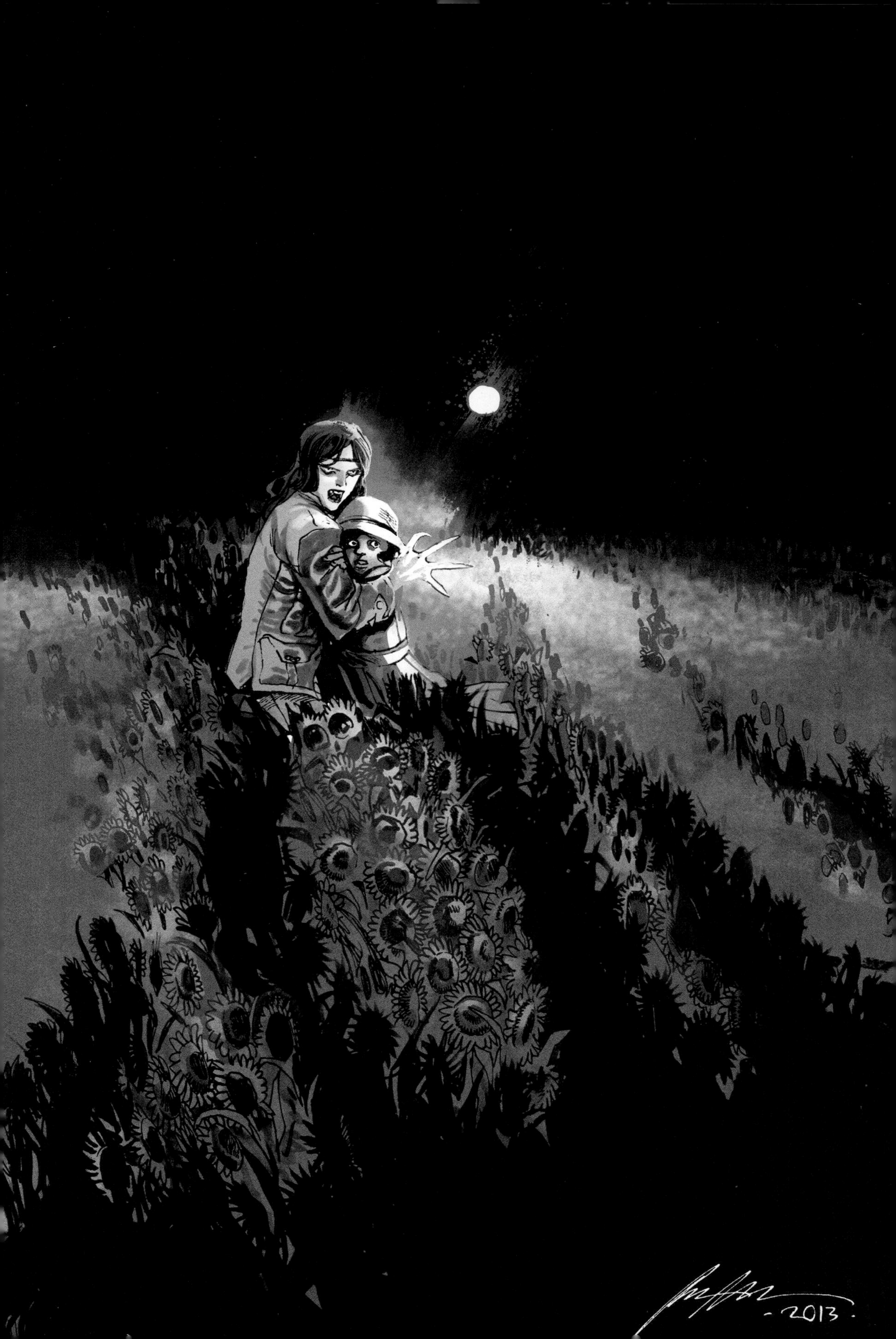
-2013-

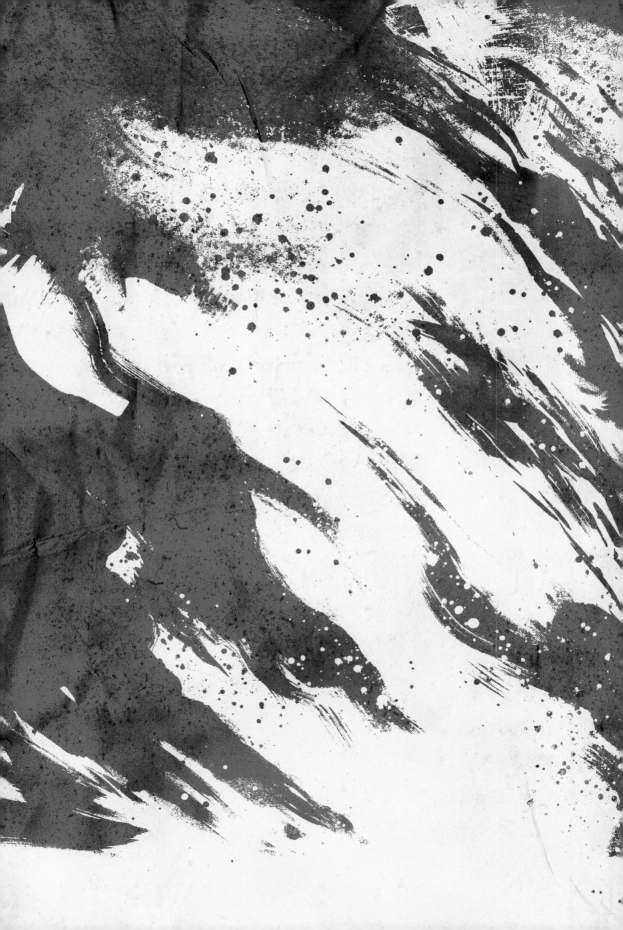

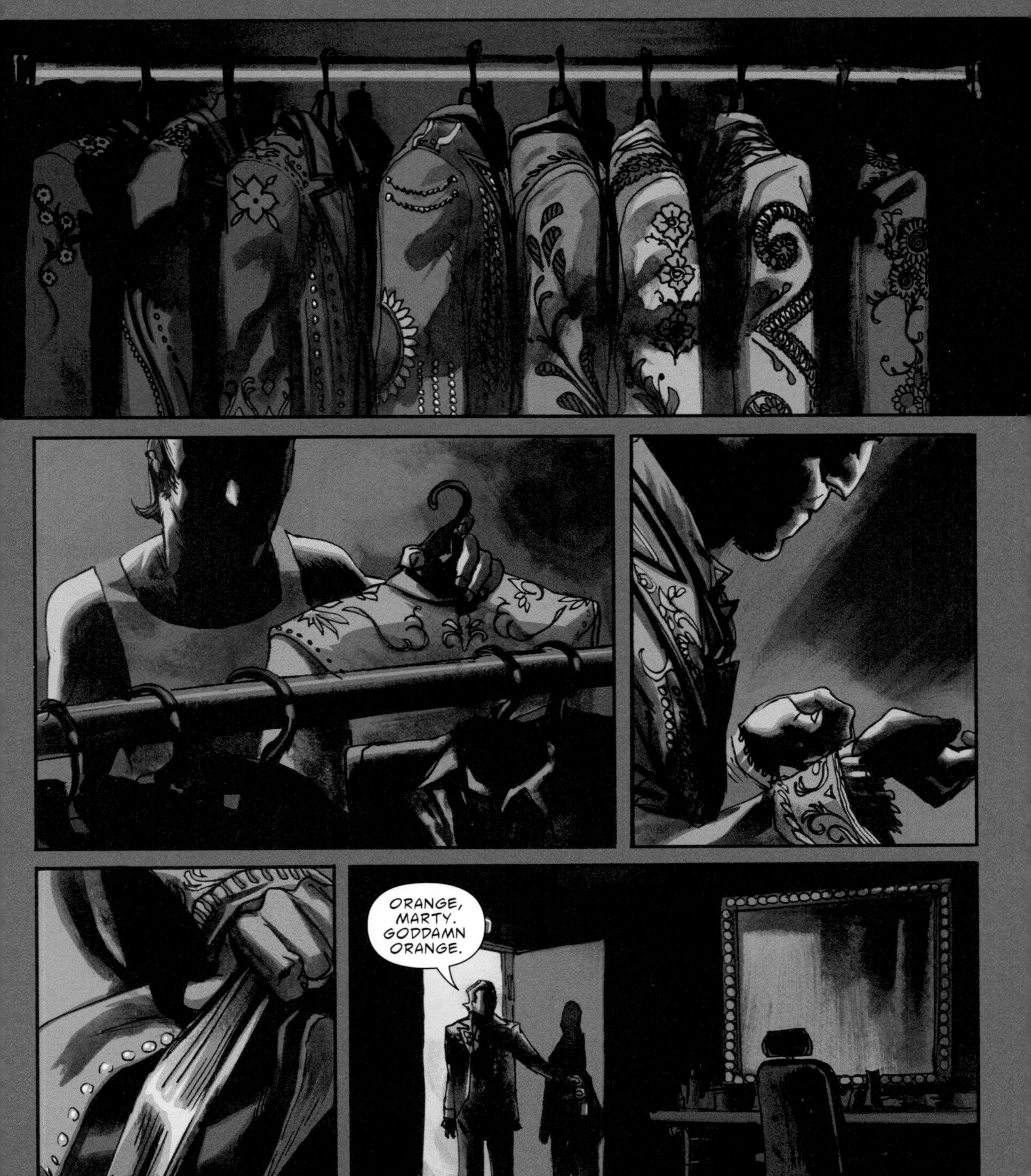
ORANGE, MARTY. GODDAMN ORANGE.

AMERICAN VAMPIRE SECOND CYCLE PART TWO

WRITER **SCOTT SNYDER** ARTIST **RAFAEL ALBUQUERQUE**
COLORS **DAVE McCAIG** LETTERS **STEVE WANDS**
COVER BY **RAFAEL ALBUQUERQUE**

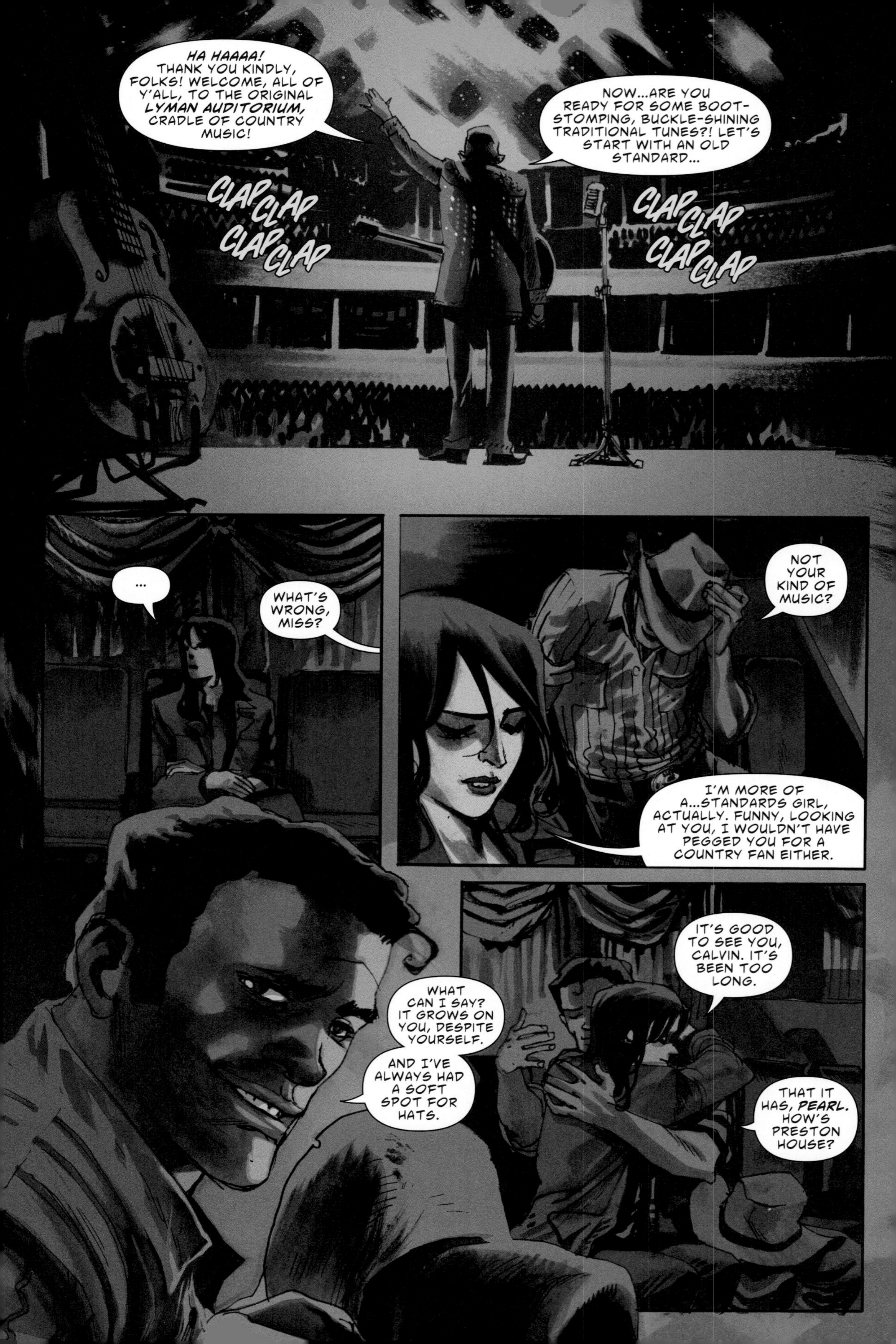
HA HAAAA! THANK YOU KINDLY, FOLKS! WELCOME, ALL OF Y'ALL, TO THE ORIGINAL LYMAN AUDITORIUM, CRADLE OF COUNTRY MUSIC!
NOW...ARE YOU READY FOR SOME BOOT-STOMPING, BUCKLE-SHINING TRADITIONAL TUNES?! LET'S START WITH AN OLD STANDARD...
CLAP CLAP CLAP CLAP
CLAP CLAP CLAP CLAP
...
WHAT'S WRONG, MISS?
NOT YOUR KIND OF MUSIC?
I'M MORE OF A...STANDARDS GIRL, ACTUALLY. FUNNY, LOOKING AT YOU, I WOULDN'T HAVE PEGGED YOU FOR A COUNTRY FAN EITHER.
WHAT CAN I SAY? IT GROWS ON YOU, DESPITE YOURSELF.
AND I'VE ALWAYS HAD A SOFT SPOT FOR HATS.
IT'S GOOD TO SEE YOU, CALVIN. IT'S BEEN TOO LONG.
THAT IT HAS, PEARL. HOW'S PRESTON HOUSE?

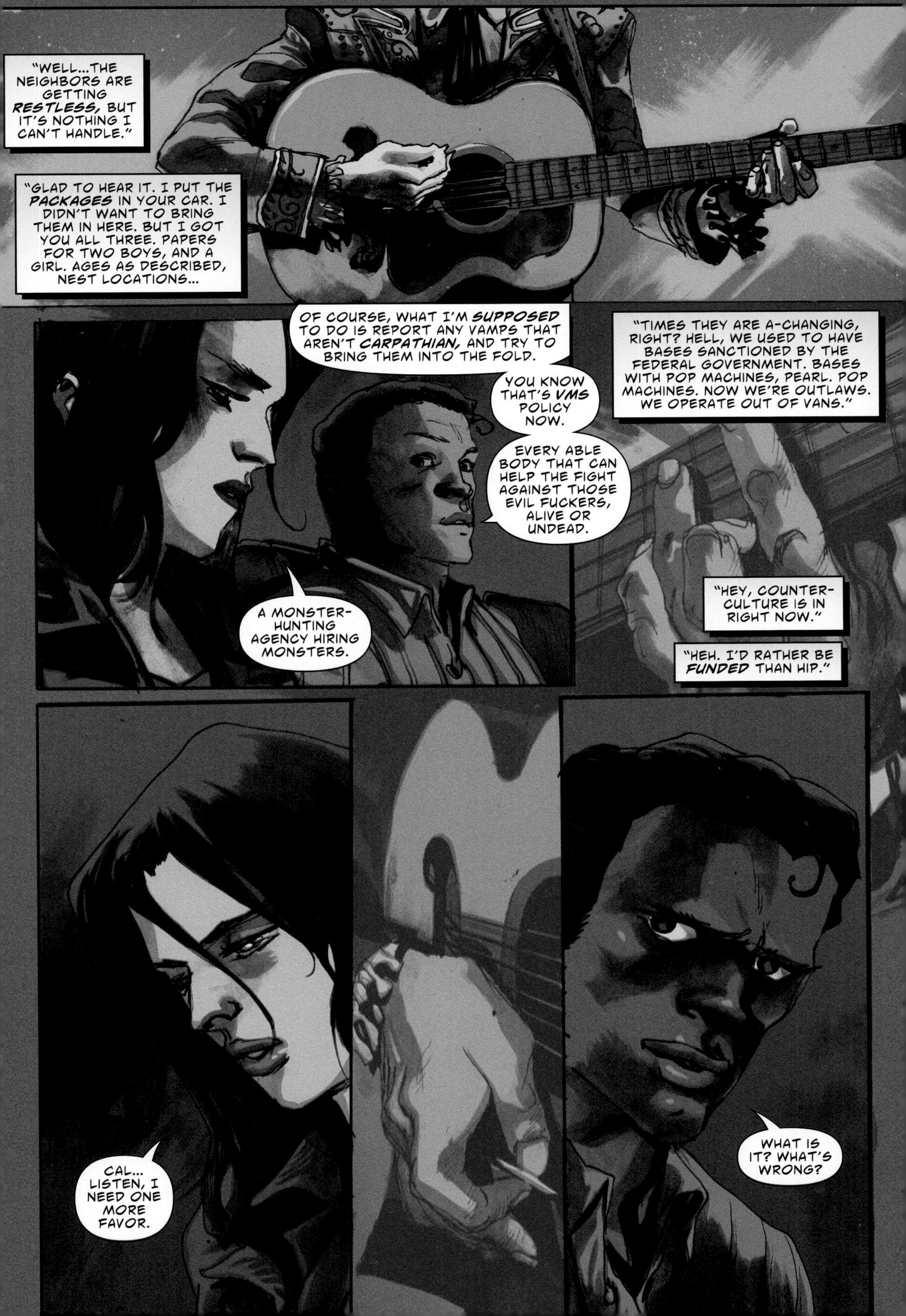
"WELL...THE NEIGHBORS ARE GETTING RESTLESS, BUT IT'S NOTHING I CAN'T HANDLE."
"GLAD TO HEAR IT. I PUT THE PACKAGES IN YOUR CAR. I DIDN'T WANT TO BRING THEM IN HERE. BUT I GOT YOU ALL THREE. PAPERS FOR TWO BOYS, AND A GIRL. AGES AS DESCRIBED, NEST LOCATIONS...
OF COURSE, WHAT I'M SUPPOSED TO DO IS REPORT ANY VAMPS THAT AREN'T CARPATHIAN, AND TRY TO BRING THEM INTO THE FOLD.
YOU KNOW THAT'S VMS POLICY NOW.
EVERY ABLE BODY THAT CAN HELP THE FIGHT AGAINST THOSE EVIL FUCKERS, ALIVE OR UNDEAD.
A MONSTER-HUNTING AGENCY HIRING MONSTERS.
"TIMES THEY ARE A-CHANGING, RIGHT? HELL, WE USED TO HAVE BASES SANCTIONED BY THE FEDERAL GOVERNMENT. BASES WITH POP MACHINES, PEARL. POP MACHINES. NOW WE'RE OUTLAWS. WE OPERATE OUT OF VANS."
"HEY, COUNTER-CULTURE IS IN RIGHT NOW."
"HEH. I'D RATHER BE FUNDED THAN HIP."
CAL... LISTEN, I NEED ONE MORE FAVOR.
WHAT IS IT? WHAT'S WRONG?

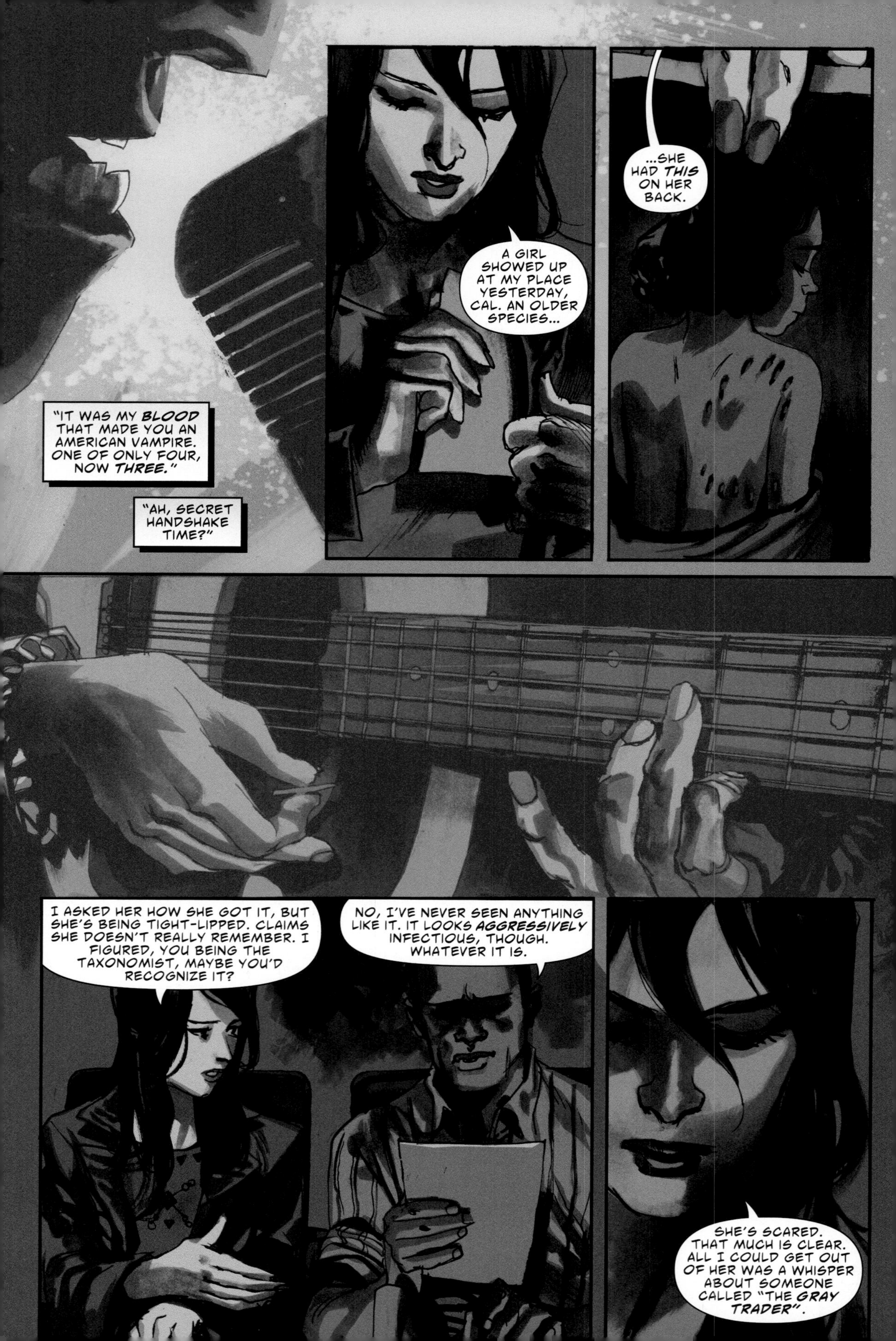
"IT WAS MY BLOOD THAT MADE YOU AN AMERICAN VAMPIRE. ONE OF ONLY FOUR, NOW THREE."
"AH, SECRET HANDSHAKE TIME?"
A GIRL SHOWED UP AT MY PLACE YESTERDAY, CAL. AN OLDER SPECIES...
...SHE HAD THIS ON HER BACK.
I ASKED HER HOW SHE GOT IT, BUT SHE'S BEING TIGHT-LIPPED. CLAIMS SHE DOESN'T REALLY REMEMBER. I FIGURED, YOU BEING THE TAXONOMIST, MAYBE YOU'D RECOGNIZE IT?
NO, I'VE NEVER SEEN ANYTHING LIKE IT. IT LOOKS AGGRESSIVELY INFECTIOUS, THOUGH. WHATEVER IT IS.
SHE'S SCARED. THAT MUCH IS CLEAR. ALL I COULD GET OUT OF HER WAS A WHISPER ABOUT SOMEONE CALLED "THE GRAY TRADER".

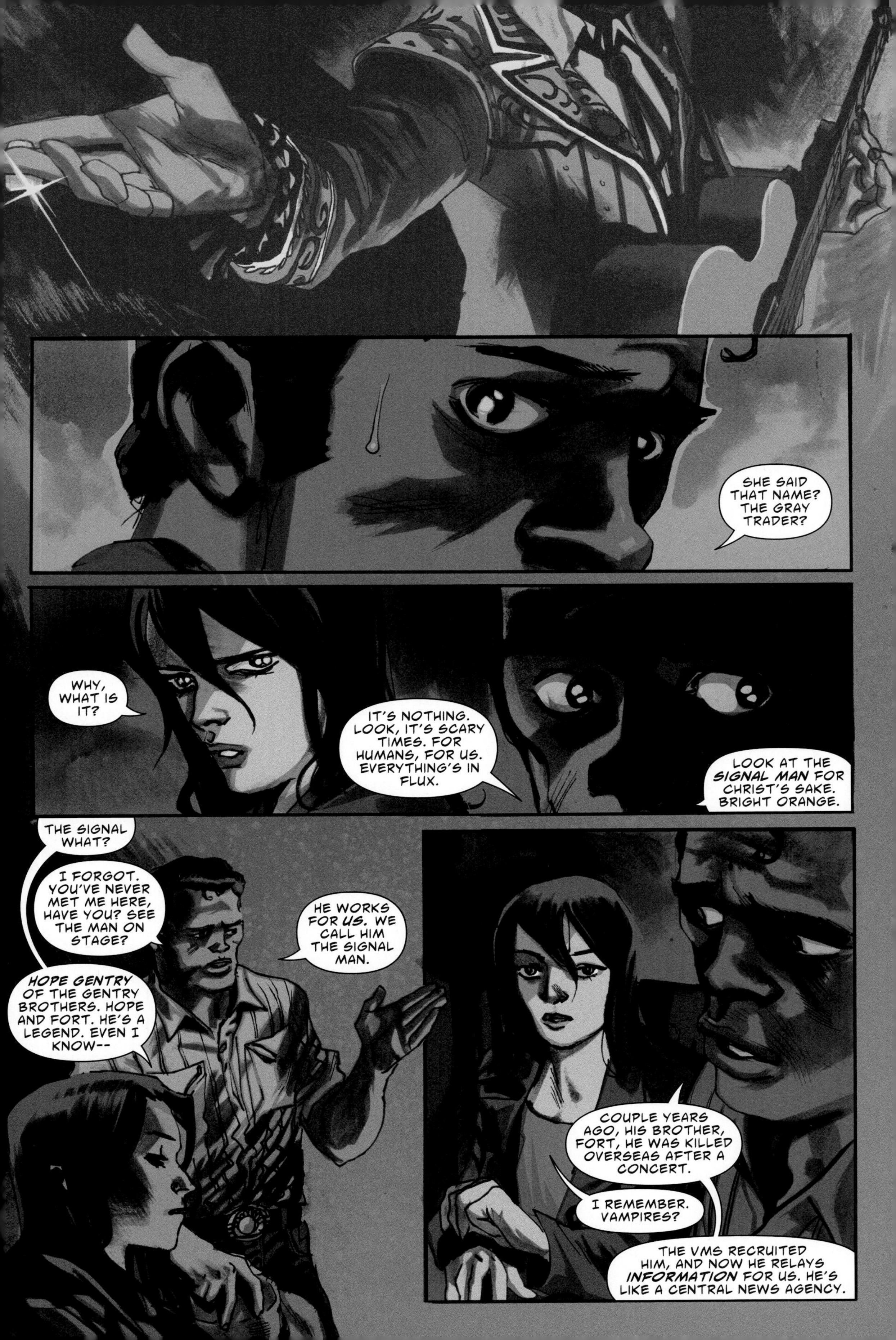
SHE SAID THAT NAME? THE GRAY TRADER?
WHY, WHAT IS IT?
IT'S NOTHING. LOOK, IT'S SCARY TIMES. FOR HUMANS, FOR US. EVERYTHING'S IN FLUX.
LOOK AT THE SIGNAL MAN FOR CHRIST'S SAKE. BRIGHT ORANGE.
THE SIGNAL WHAT?
I FORGOT. YOU'VE NEVER MET ME HERE, HAVE YOU? SEE THE MAN ON STAGE?
HOPE GENTRY OF THE GENTRY BROTHERS. HOPE AND FORT. HE'S A LEGEND. EVEN I KNOW--
HE WORKS FOR US. WE CALL HIM THE SIGNAL MAN.
COUPLE YEARS AGO, HIS BROTHER, FORT, HE WAS KILLED OVERSEAS AFTER A CONCERT.
I REMEMBER. VAMPIRES?
THE VMS RECRUITED HIM, AND NOW HE RELAYS INFORMATION FOR US. HE'S LIKE A CENTRAL NEWS AGENCY.

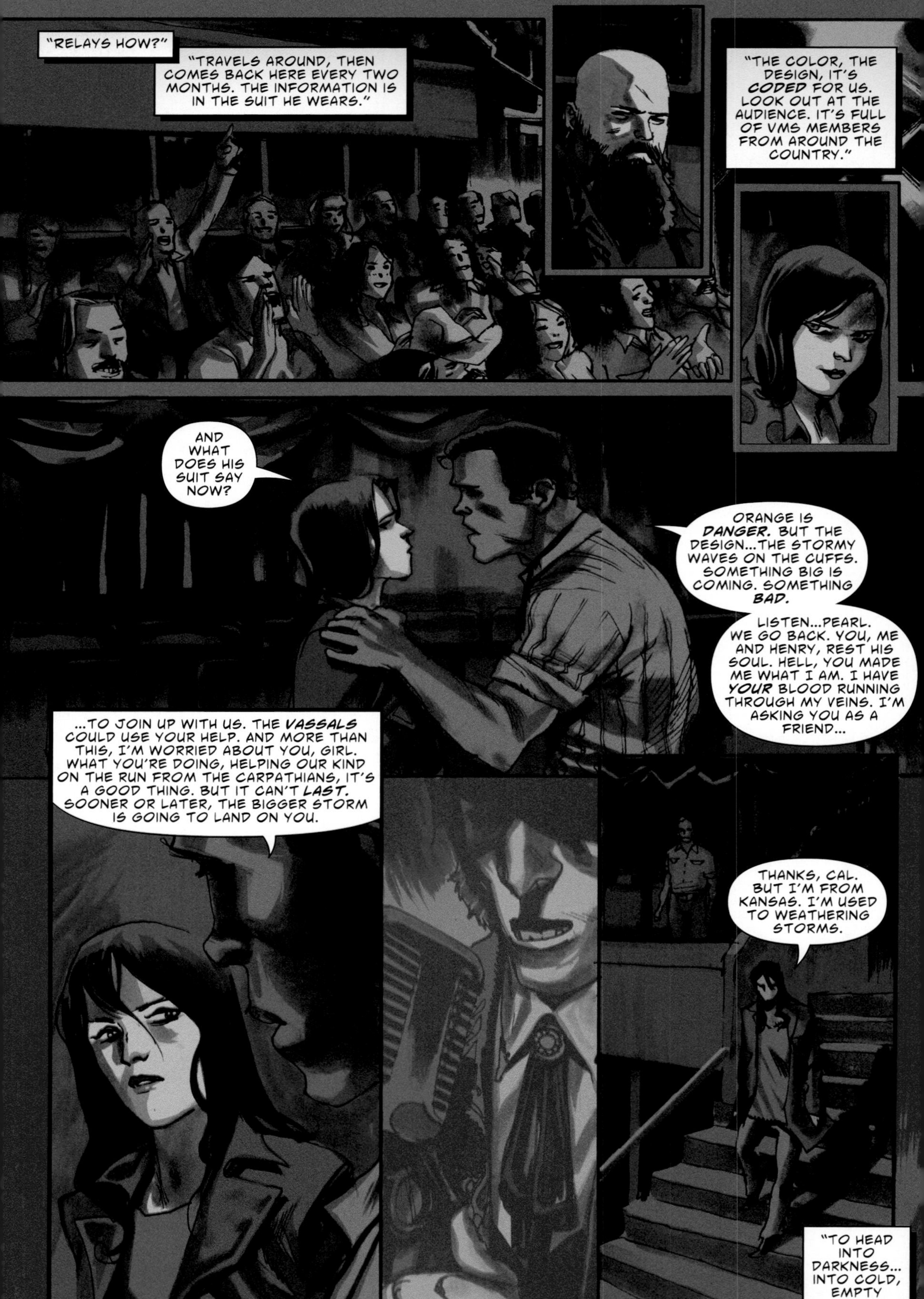
"RELAYS HOW?"
"TRAVELS AROUND, THEN COMES BACK HERE EVERY TWO MONTHS. THE INFORMATION IS IN THE SUIT HE WEARS."
"THE COLOR, THE DESIGN, IT'S *CODED* FOR US. LOOK OUT AT THE AUDIENCE. IT'S FULL OF VMS MEMBERS FROM AROUND THE COUNTRY."
AND WHAT DOES HIS SUIT SAY NOW?
ORANGE IS *DANGER.* BUT THE DESIGN...THE STORMY WAVES ON THE CUFFS. SOMETHING BIG IS COMING. SOMETHING *BAD.*
LISTEN...PEARL. WE GO BACK. YOU, ME AND HENRY, REST HIS SOUL. HELL, YOU MADE ME WHAT I AM. I HAVE *YOUR* BLOOD RUNNING THROUGH MY VEINS. I'M ASKING YOU AS A FRIEND...
...TO JOIN UP WITH US. THE *VASSALS* COULD USE YOUR HELP. AND MORE THAN THIS, I'M WORRIED ABOUT YOU, GIRL. WHAT YOU'RE DOING, HELPING OUR KIND ON THE RUN FROM THE CARPATHIANS, IT'S A GOOD THING. BUT IT CAN'T *LAST.* SOONER OR LATER, THE BIGGER STORM IS GOING TO LAND ON YOU.
THANKS, CAL. BUT I'M FROM KANSAS. I'M USED TO WEATHERING STORMS.
"TO HEAD INTO DARKNESS... INTO COLD, EMPTY DARKNESS..."

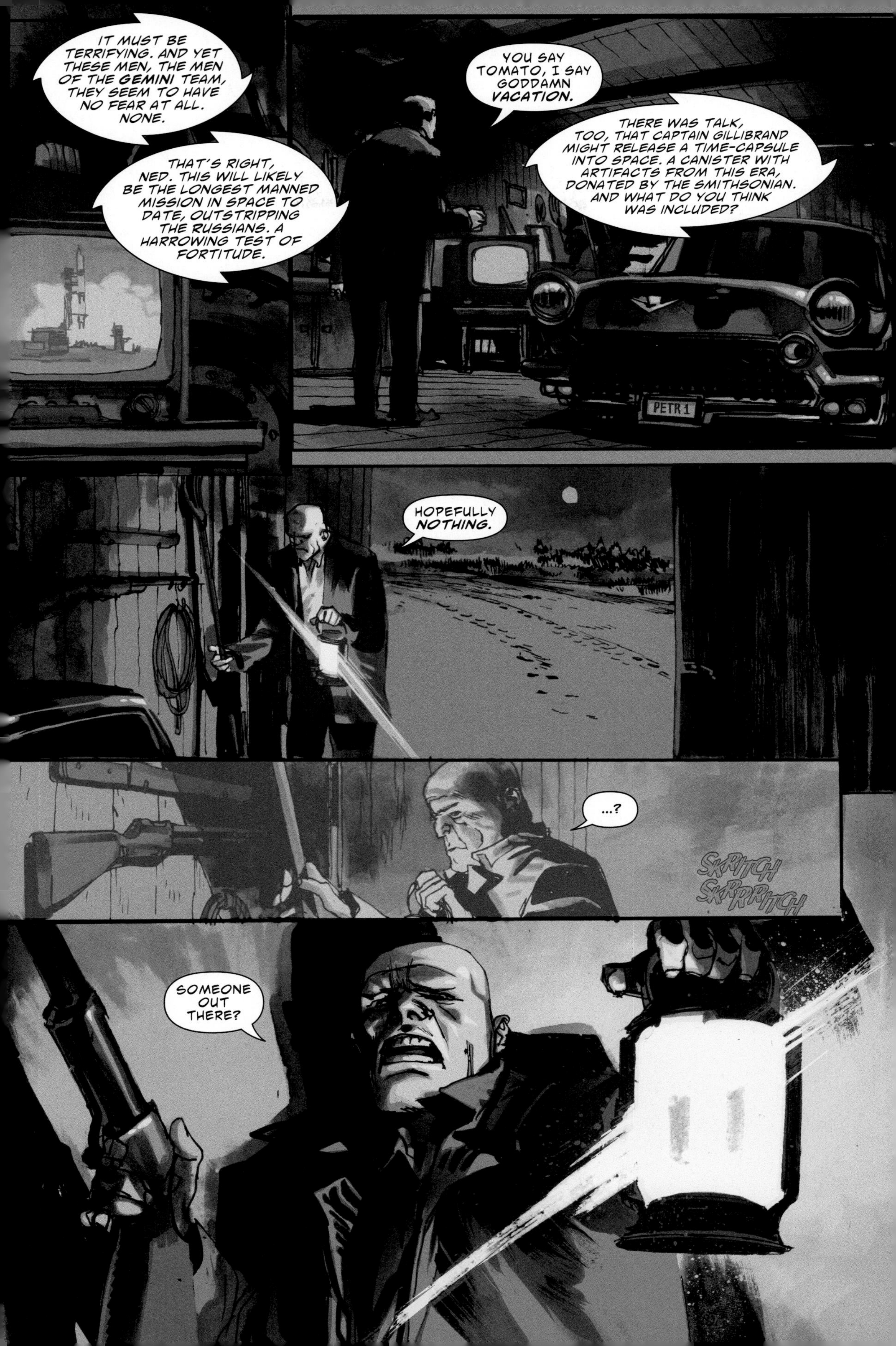
IT MUST BE TERRIFYING. AND YET THESE MEN, THE MEN OF THE GEMINI TEAM, THEY SEEM TO HAVE NO FEAR AT ALL. NONE.
THAT'S RIGHT, NED. THIS WILL LIKELY BE THE LONGEST MANNED MISSION IN SPACE TO DATE, OUTSTRIPPING THE RUSSIANS. A HARROWING TEST OF FORTITUDE.
YOU SAY TOMATO, I SAY GODDAMN VACATION.
THERE WAS TALK, TOO, THAT CAPTAIN GILLIBRAND MIGHT RELEASE A TIME-CAPSULE INTO SPACE. A CANISTER WITH ARTIFACTS FROM THIS ERA, DONATED BY THE SMITHSONIAN. AND WHAT DO YOU THINK WAS INCLUDED?
PETR 1
HOPEFULLY NOTHING.
...?
SKRITCH
SKRRRITCH
SOMEONE OUT THERE?

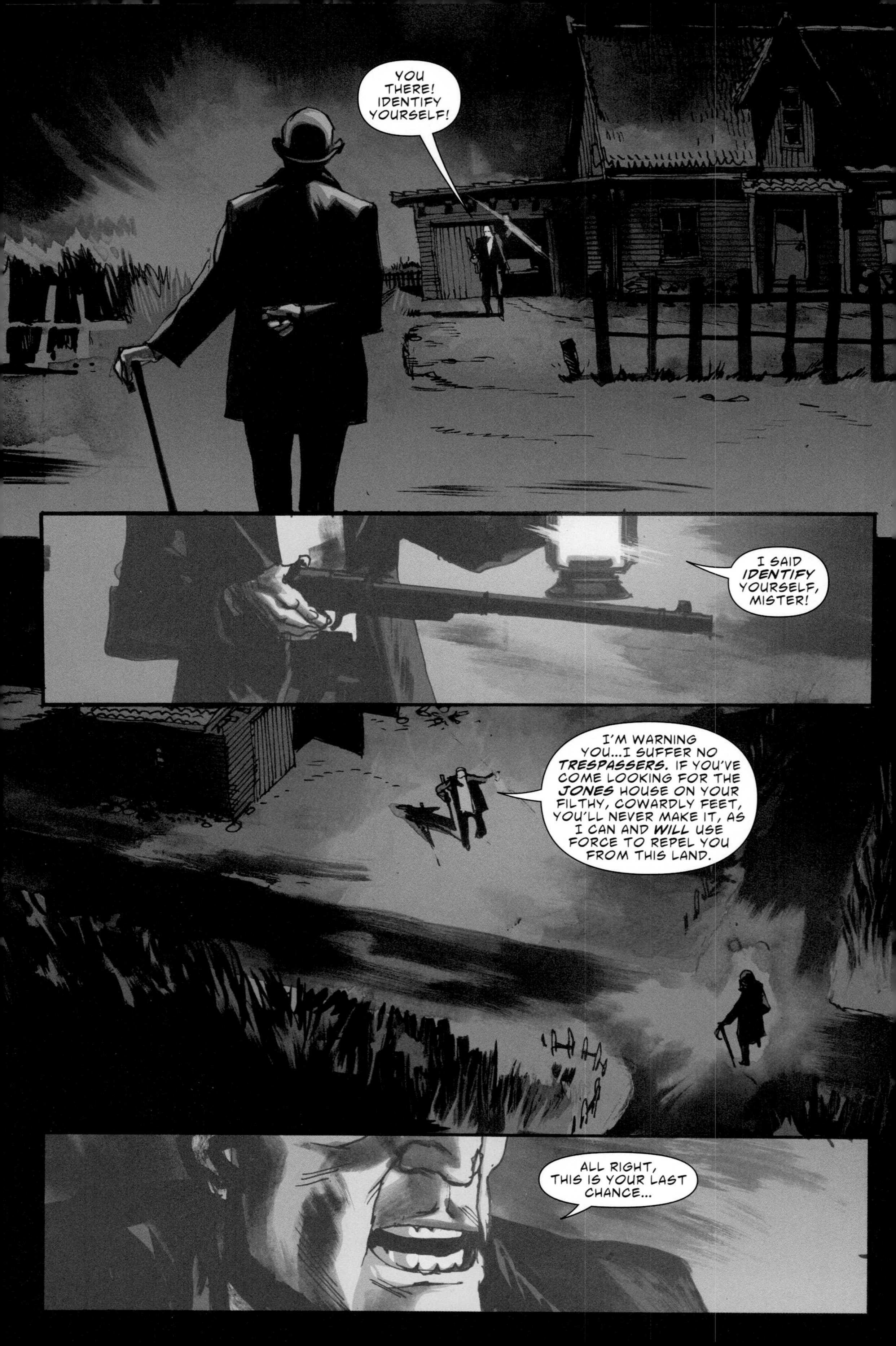
YOU THERE! IDENTIFY YOURSELF!
I SAID *IDENTIFY* YOURSELF, MISTER!
I'M WARNING YOU...I SUFFER NO ***TRESPASSERS.*** IF YOU'VE COME LOOKING FOR THE ***JONES*** HOUSE ON YOUR FILTHY, COWARDLY FEET, YOU'LL NEVER MAKE IT, AS I CAN AND ***WILL*** USE FORCE TO REPEL YOU FROM THIS LAND.
ALL RIGHT, THIS IS YOUR LAST CHANCE...

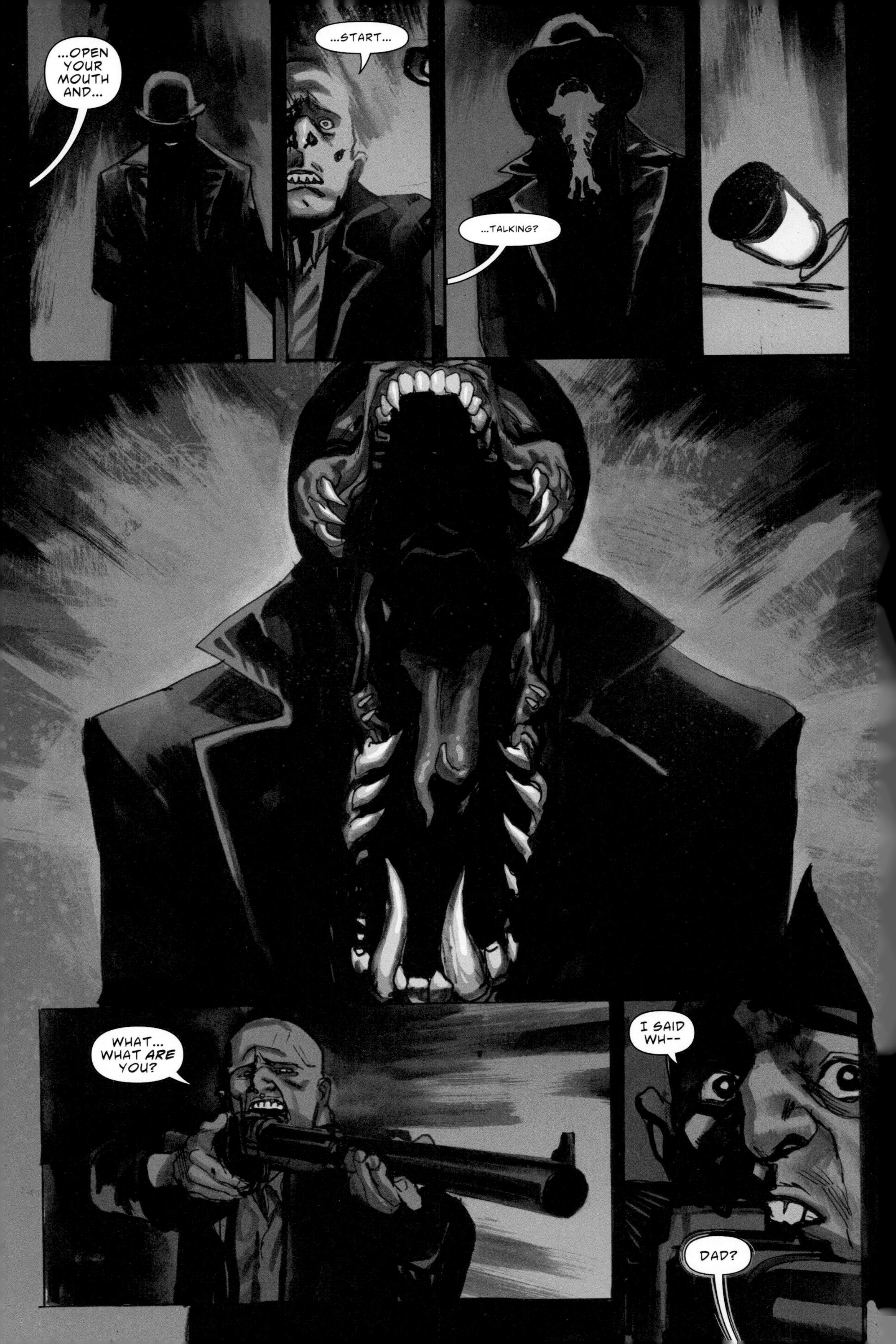
...OPEN YOUR MOUTH AND...
...START...
...TALKING?
WHAT... WHAT ARE YOU?
I SAID WH--
DAD?

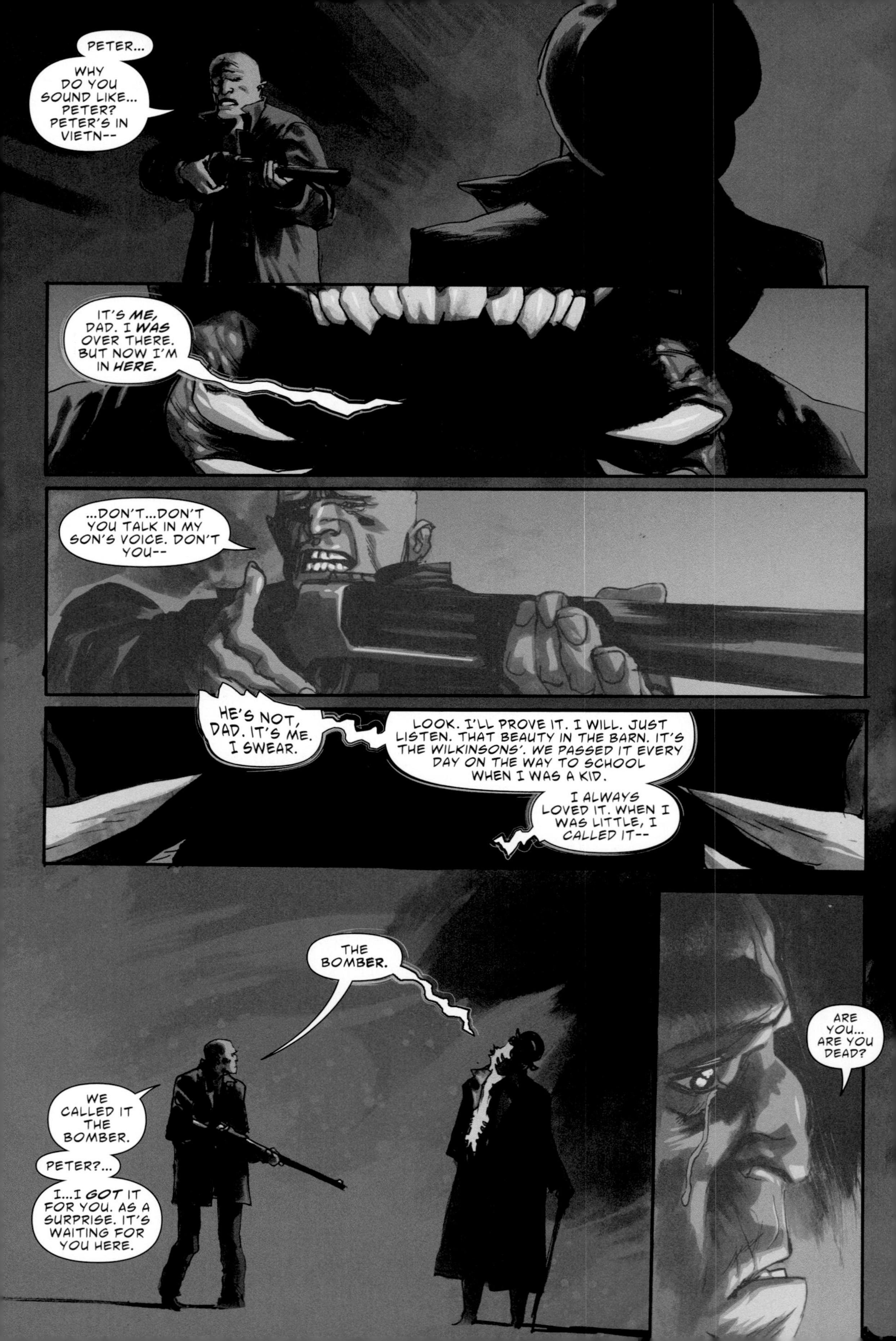
PETER...
WHY DO YOU SOUND LIKE... PETER? PETER'S IN VIETN--
IT'S ME, DAD. I WAS OVER THERE. BUT NOW I'M IN HERE.
...DON'T...DON'T YOU TALK IN MY SON'S VOICE. DON'T YOU--
HE'S NOT, DAD. IT'S ME. I SWEAR.
LOOK. I'LL PROVE IT. I WILL. JUST LISTEN. THAT BEAUTY IN THE BARN. IT'S THE WILKINSONS'. WE PASSED IT EVERY DAY ON THE WAY TO SCHOOL WHEN I WAS A KID.
I ALWAYS LOVED IT. WHEN I WAS LITTLE, I CALLED IT--
THE BOMBER.
WE CALLED IT THE BOMBER.
PETER?...
I...I GOT IT FOR YOU. AS A SURPRISE. IT'S WAITING FOR YOU HERE.
ARE YOU... ARE YOU DEAD?

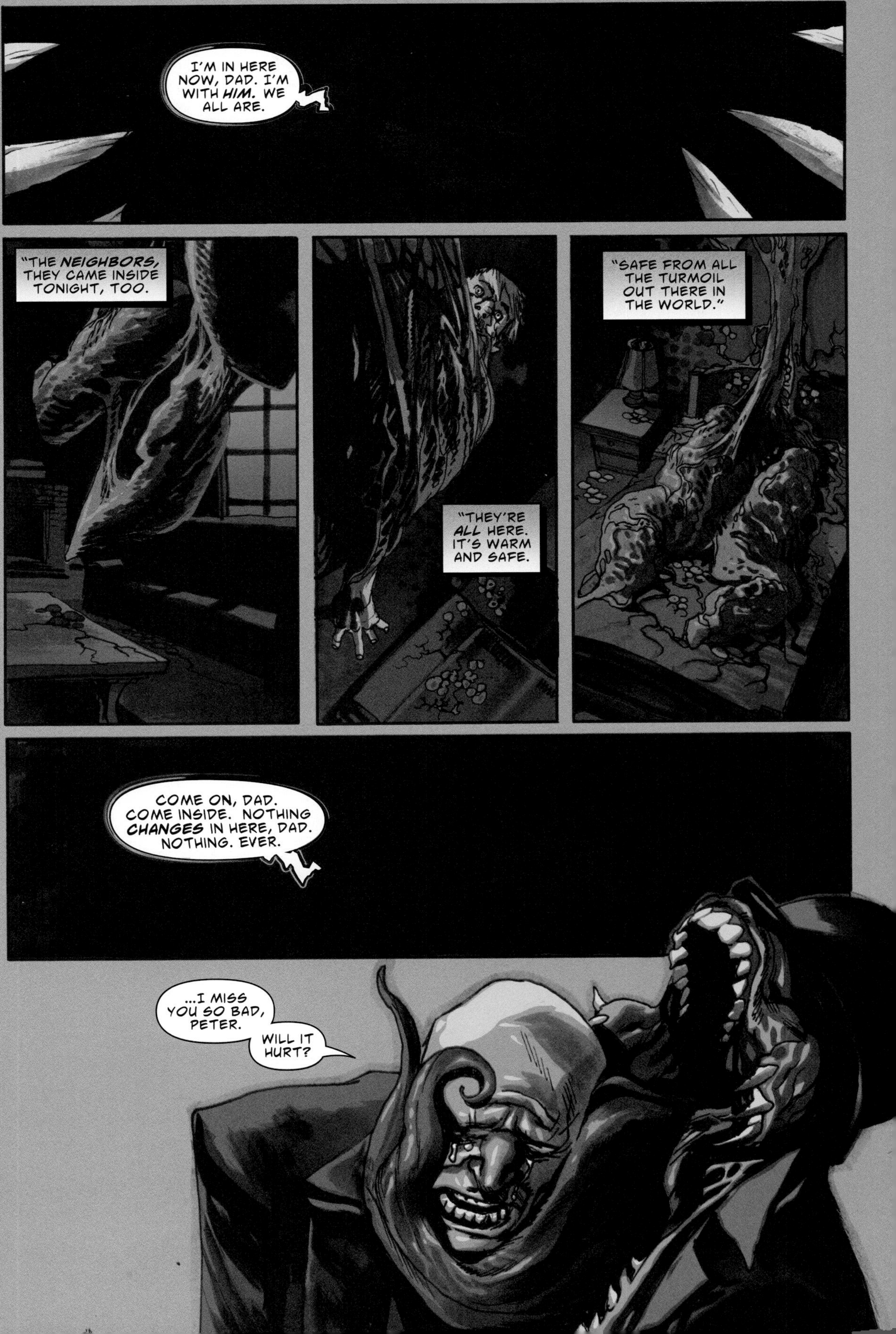

I'M IN HERE NOW, DAD. I'M WITH HIM. WE ALL ARE.
"THE NEIGHBORS, THEY CAME INSIDE TONIGHT, TOO.
"THEY'RE ALL HERE. IT'S WARM AND SAFE.
"SAFE FROM ALL THE TURMOIL OUT THERE IN THE WORLD."
COME ON, DAD. COME INSIDE. NOTHING CHANGES IN HERE, DAD. NOTHING. EVER.
...I MISS YOU SO BAD, PETER.
WILL IT HURT?

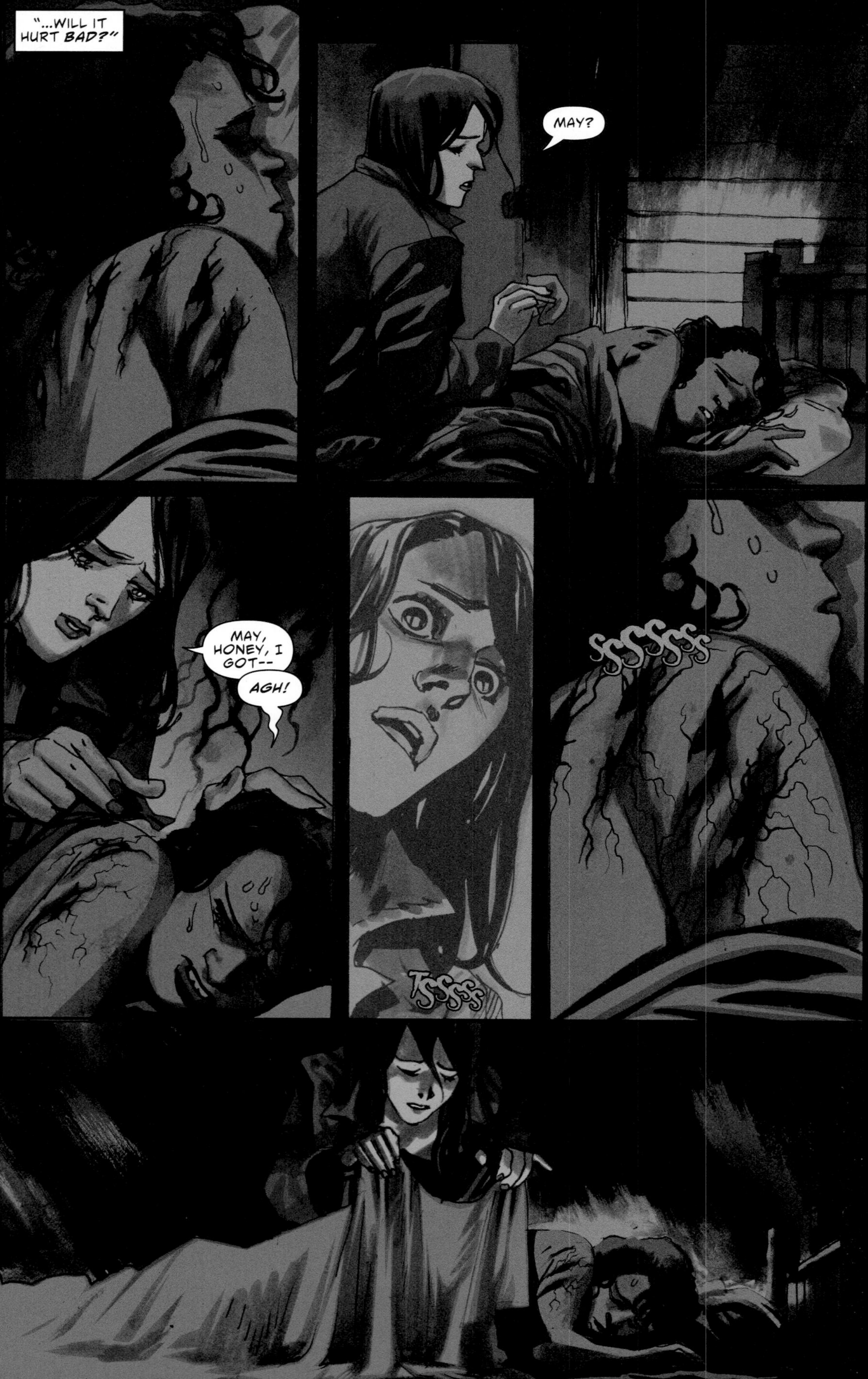
"...WILL IT HURT BAD?"
MAY?
MAY, HONEY, I GOT--
AGH!
TSSSSS
SSSSSSS

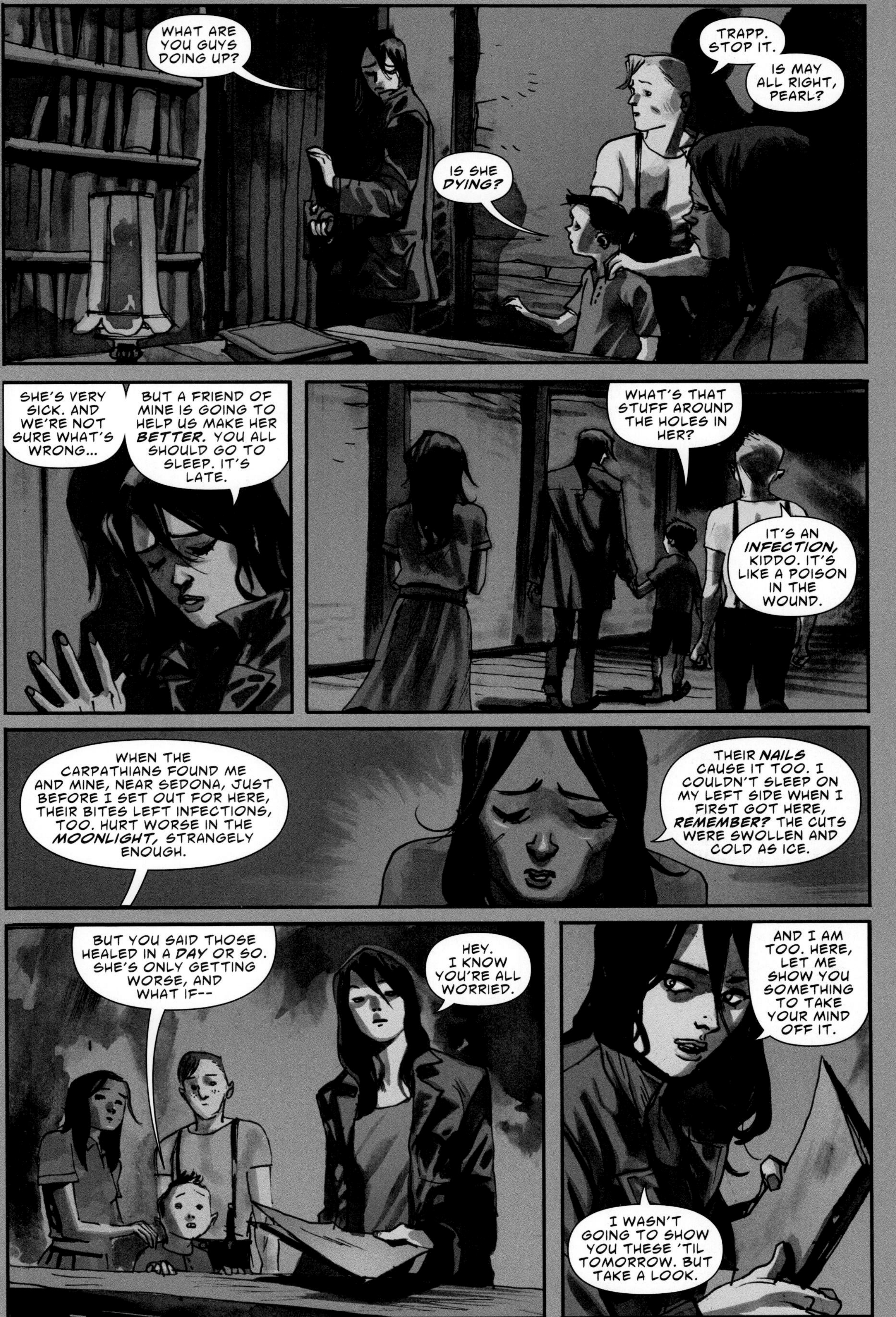
WHAT ARE YOU GUYS DOING UP?
TRAPP. STOP IT.
IS MAY ALL RIGHT, PEARL?
IS SHE *DYING?*
SHE'S VERY SICK. AND WE'RE NOT SURE WHAT'S WRONG...
BUT A FRIEND OF MINE IS GOING TO HELP US MAKE HER *BETTER.* YOU ALL SHOULD GO TO SLEEP. IT'S LATE.
WHAT'S THAT STUFF AROUND THE HOLES IN HER?
IT'S AN *INFECTION,* KIDDO. IT'S LIKE A POISON IN THE WOUND.
WHEN THE CARPATHIANS FOUND ME AND MINE, NEAR SEDONA, JUST BEFORE I SET OUT FOR HERE, THEIR BITES LEFT INFECTIONS, TOO. HURT WORSE IN THE *MOONLIGHT,* STRANGELY ENOUGH.
THEIR *NAILS* CAUSE IT TOO. I COULDN'T SLEEP ON MY LEFT SIDE WHEN I FIRST GOT HERE, *REMEMBER?* THE CUTS WERE SWOLLEN AND COLD AS ICE.
BUT YOU SAID THOSE HEALED IN A *DAY* OR SO. SHE'S ONLY GETTING WORSE, AND WHAT IF--
HEY. I KNOW YOU'RE ALL WORRIED.
AND I AM TOO. HERE, LET ME SHOW YOU SOMETHING TO TAKE YOUR MIND OFF IT.
I WASN'T GOING TO SHOW YOU THESE 'TIL TOMORROW. BUT TAKE A LOOK.

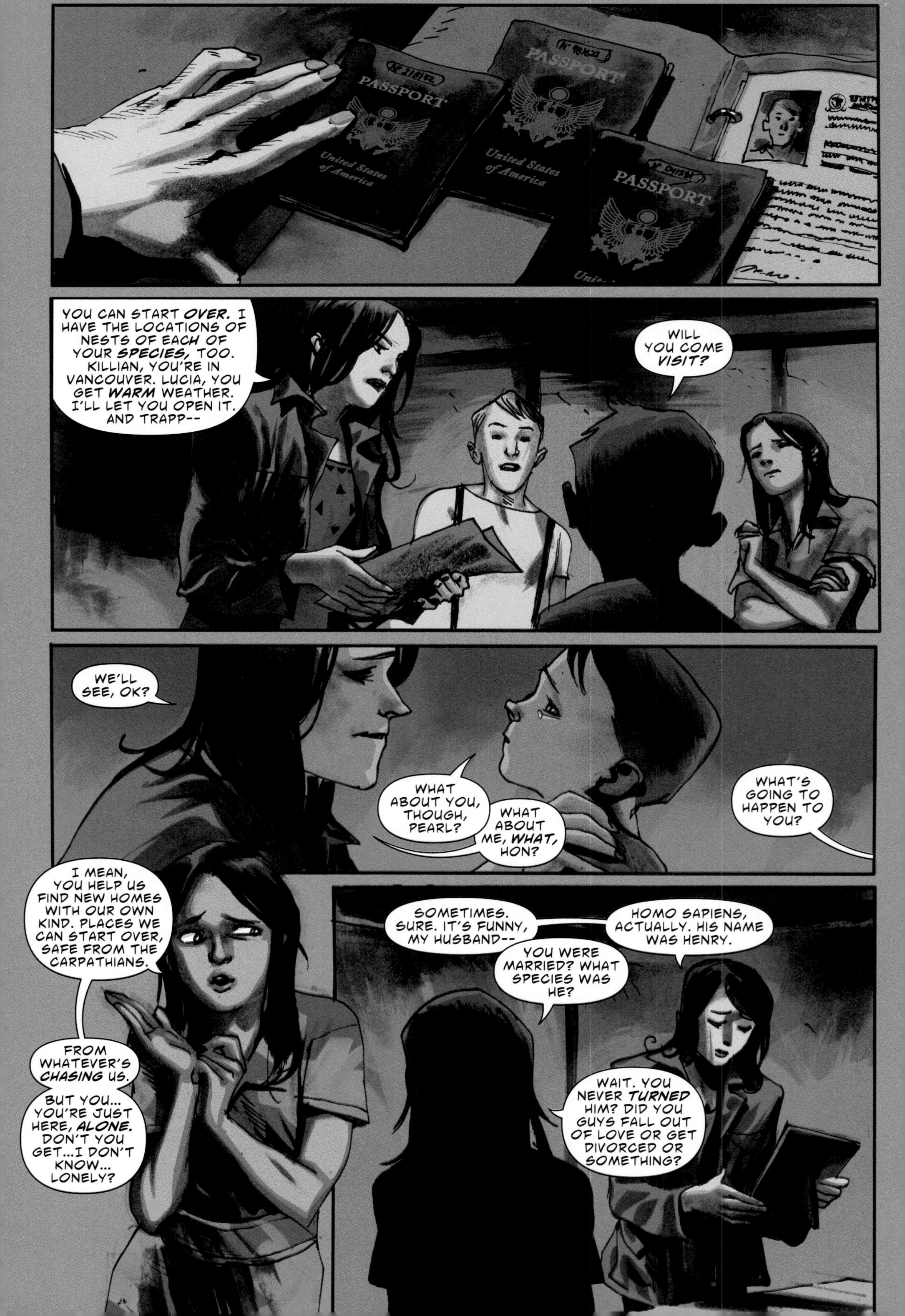
PASSPORT
United States of America
PASSPORT
United States of America
PASSPORT
YOU CAN START OVER. I HAVE THE LOCATIONS OF NESTS OF EACH OF YOUR SPECIES, TOO. KILLIAN, YOU'RE IN VANCOUVER. LUCIA, YOU GET WARM WEATHER. I'LL LET YOU OPEN IT. AND TRAPP--
WILL YOU COME VISIT?
WE'LL SEE, OK?
WHAT ABOUT YOU, THOUGH, PEARL?
WHAT ABOUT ME, WHAT, HON?
WHAT'S GOING TO HAPPEN TO YOU?
I MEAN, YOU HELP US FIND NEW HOMES WITH OUR OWN KIND. PLACES WE CAN START OVER, SAFE FROM THE CARPATHIANS.
FROM WHATEVER'S CHASING US.
BUT YOU... YOU'RE JUST HERE, ALONE. DON'T YOU GET...I DON'T KNOW... LONELY?
SOMETIMES. SURE. IT'S FUNNY, MY HUSBAND--
YOU WERE MARRIED? WHAT SPECIES WAS HE?
HOMO SAPIENS, ACTUALLY. HIS NAME WAS HENRY.
WAIT. YOU NEVER TURNED HIM? DID YOU GUYS FALL OUT OF LOVE OR GET DIVORCED OR SOMETHING?

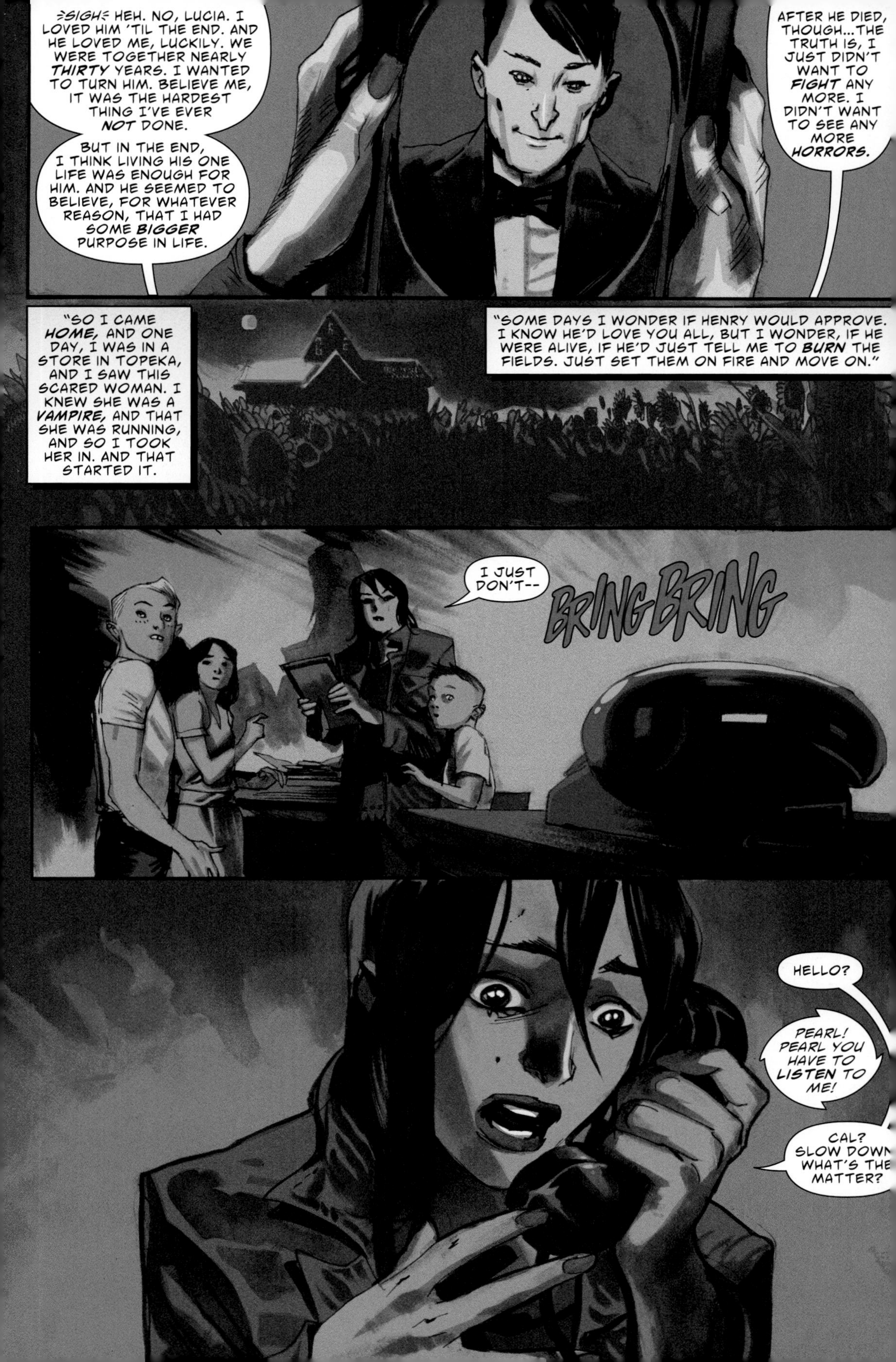

=SIGH= HEH. NO, LUCIA. I LOVED HIM 'TIL THE END. AND HE LOVED ME, LUCKILY. WE WERE TOGETHER NEARLY THIRTY YEARS. I WANTED TO TURN HIM. BELIEVE ME, IT WAS THE HARDEST THING I'VE EVER NOT DONE.
BUT IN THE END, I THINK LIVING HIS ONE LIFE WAS ENOUGH FOR HIM. AND HE SEEMED TO BELIEVE, FOR WHATEVER REASON, THAT I HAD SOME BIGGER PURPOSE IN LIFE.
AFTER HE DIED, THOUGH...THE TRUTH IS, I JUST DIDN'T WANT TO FIGHT ANY MORE. I DIDN'T WANT TO SEE ANY MORE HORRORS.
"SO I CAME HOME, AND ONE DAY, I WAS IN A STORE IN TOPEKA, AND I SAW THIS SCARED WOMAN. I KNEW SHE WAS A VAMPIRE, AND THAT SHE WAS RUNNING, AND SO I TOOK HER IN. AND THAT STARTED IT.
"SOME DAYS I WONDER IF HENRY WOULD APPROVE. I KNOW HE'D LOVE YOU ALL, BUT I WONDER, IF HE WERE ALIVE, IF HE'D JUST TELL ME TO BURN THE FIELDS. JUST SET THEM ON FIRE AND MOVE ON."
I JUST DON'T--
BRING BRING
HELLO?
PEARL! PEARL YOU HAVE TO LISTEN TO ME!
CAL? SLOW DOWN WHAT'S THE MATTER?

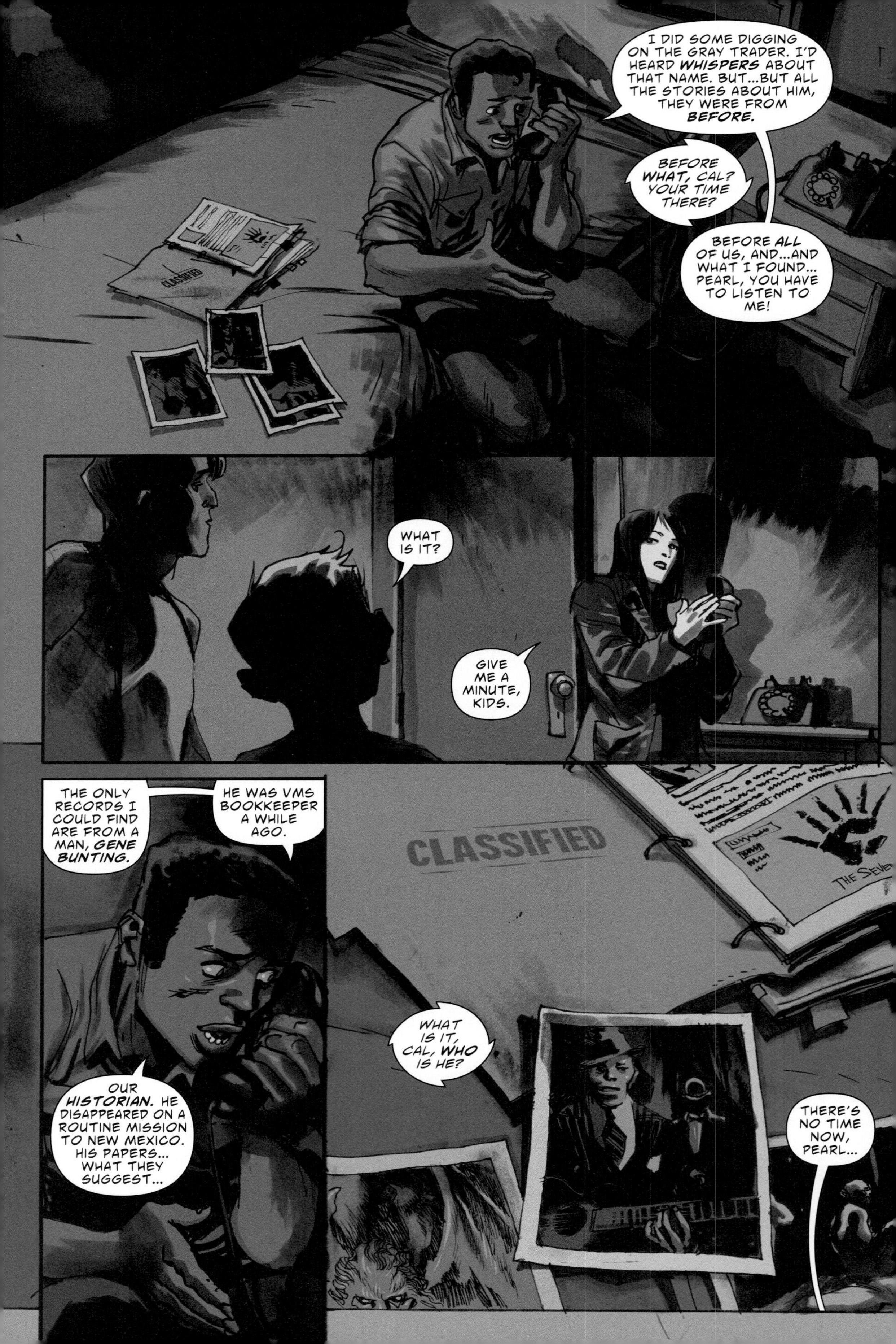
I DID SOME DIGGING ON THE GRAY TRADER. I'D HEARD **WHISPERS** ABOUT THAT NAME. BUT...BUT ALL THE STORIES ABOUT HIM, THEY WERE FROM **BEFORE.**
CLASSIFIED
BEFORE ***WHAT,*** *CAL? YOUR TIME THERE?*
BEFORE ***ALL*** OF US, AND...AND WHAT I FOUND... PEARL, YOU HAVE TO LISTEN TO ME!
WHAT IS IT?
GIVE ME A MINUTE, KIDS.
THE ONLY RECORDS I COULD FIND ARE FROM A MAN, ***GENE BUNTING.***
HE WAS VMS BOOKKEEPER A WHILE AGO.
CLASSIFIED
OUR ***HISTORIAN.*** HE DISAPPEARED ON A ROUTINE MISSION TO NEW MEXICO. HIS PAPERS... WHAT THEY SUGGEST...
WHAT IS IT, CAL, ***WHO*** *IS HE?*
THERE'S NO TIME NOW, PEARL...

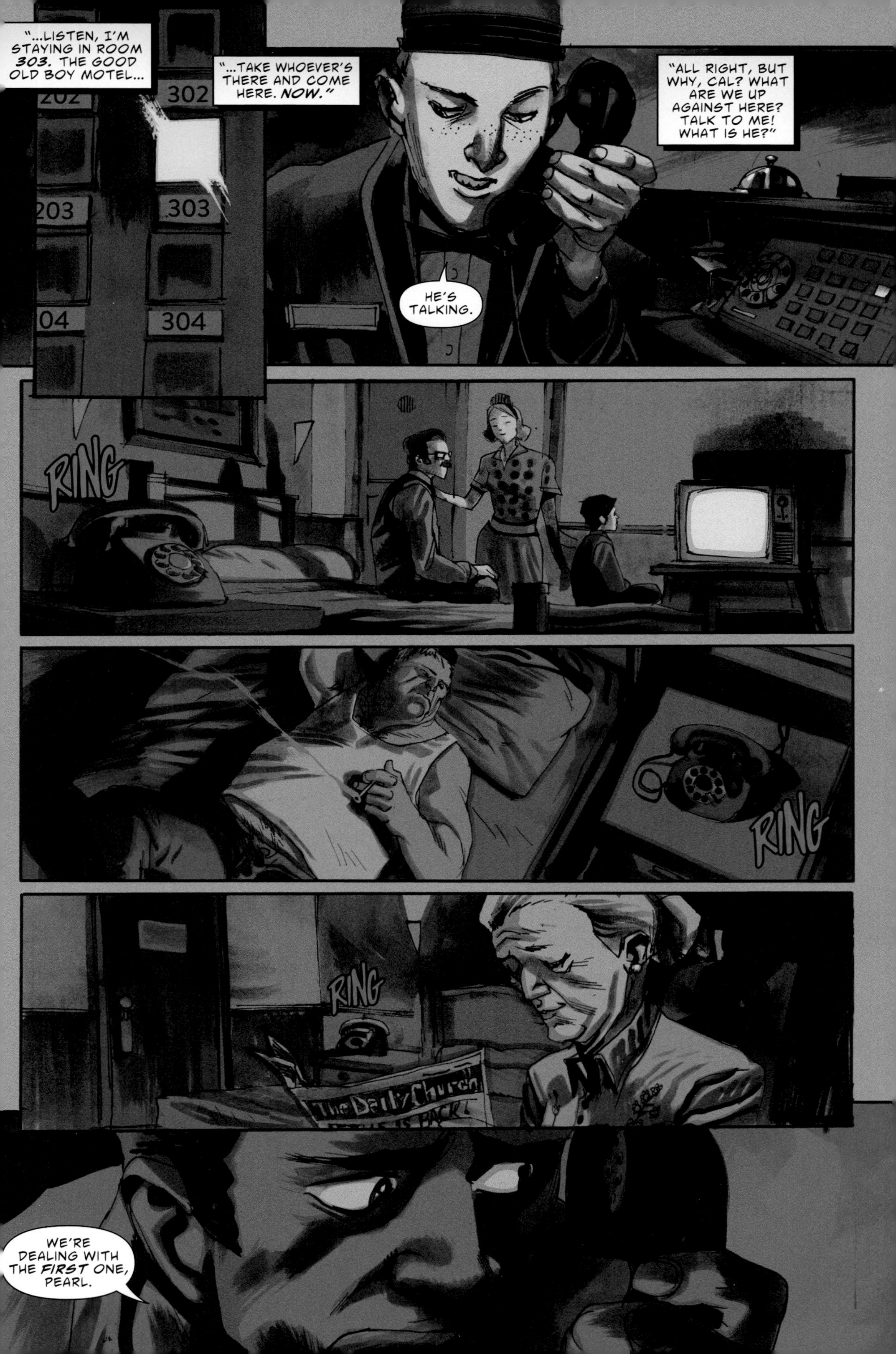
"...LISTEN, I'M STAYING IN ROOM 303. THE GOOD OLD BOY MOTEL...
"...TAKE WHOEVER'S THERE AND COME HERE. NOW."
"ALL RIGHT, BUT WHY, CAL? WHAT ARE WE UP AGAINST HERE? TALK TO ME! WHAT IS HE?"
302
202
203
303
04
304
HE'S TALKING.
RING
RING
RING
The Daily Church
WE'RE DEALING WITH THE FIRST ONE, PEARL.

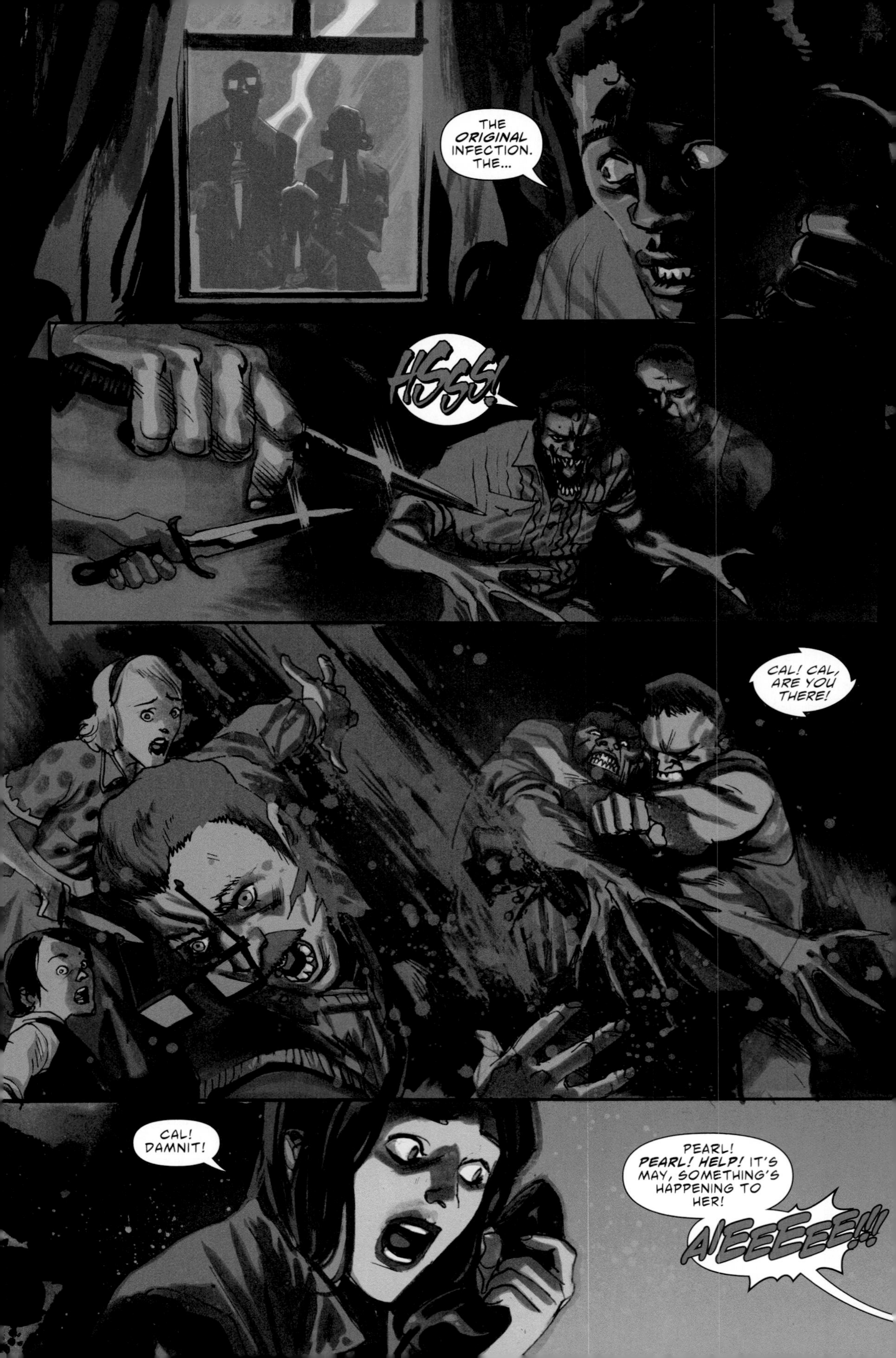
THE ORIGINAL INFECTION. THE...
HSSS!
CAL! CAL, ARE YOU THERE!
CAL! DAMNIT!
PEARL! PEARL! HELP! IT'S MAY, SOMETHING'S HAPPENING TO HER!
AIEEEEEE!!!

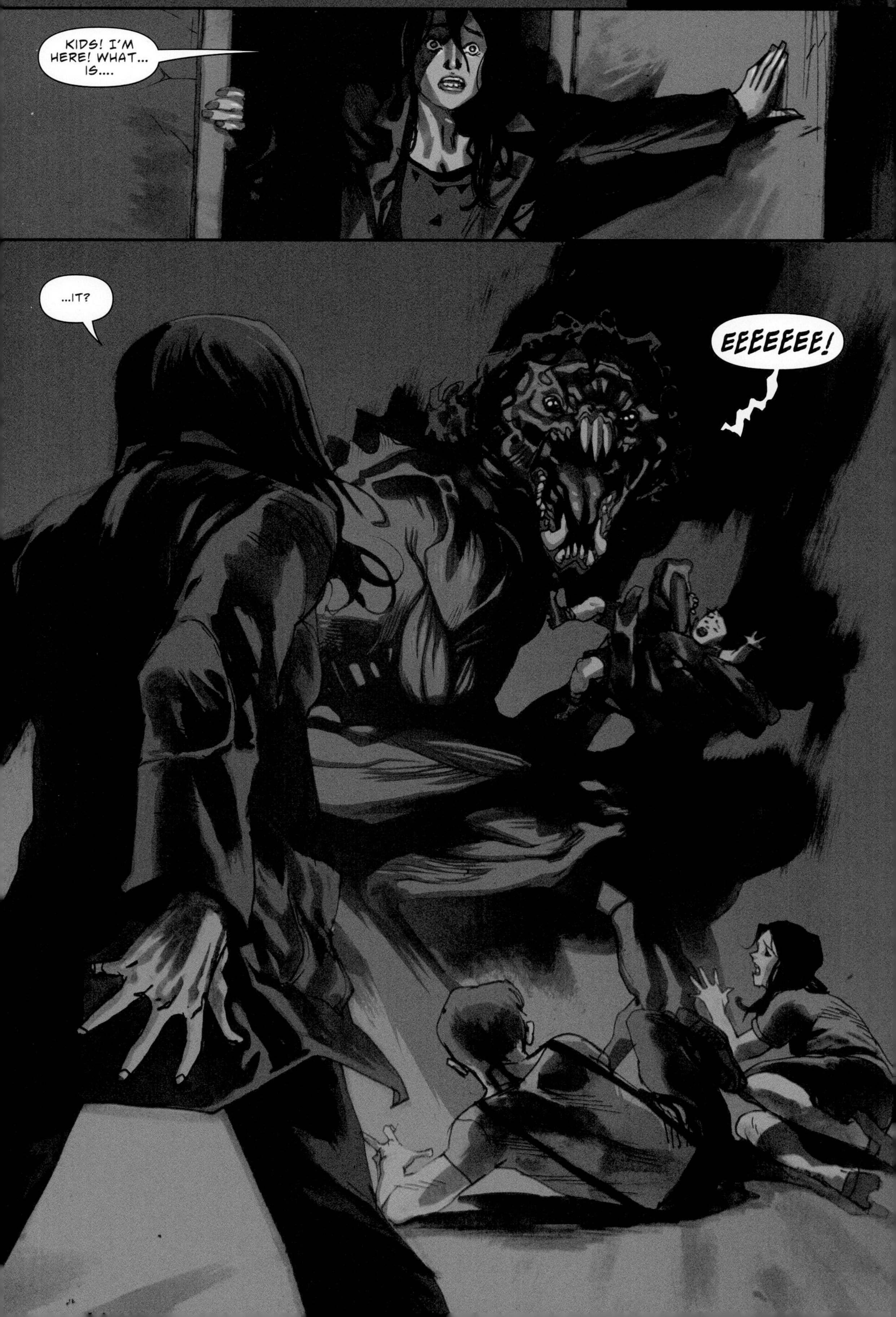
KIDS! I'M HERE! WHAT... IS....
...IT?
EEEEEEE!

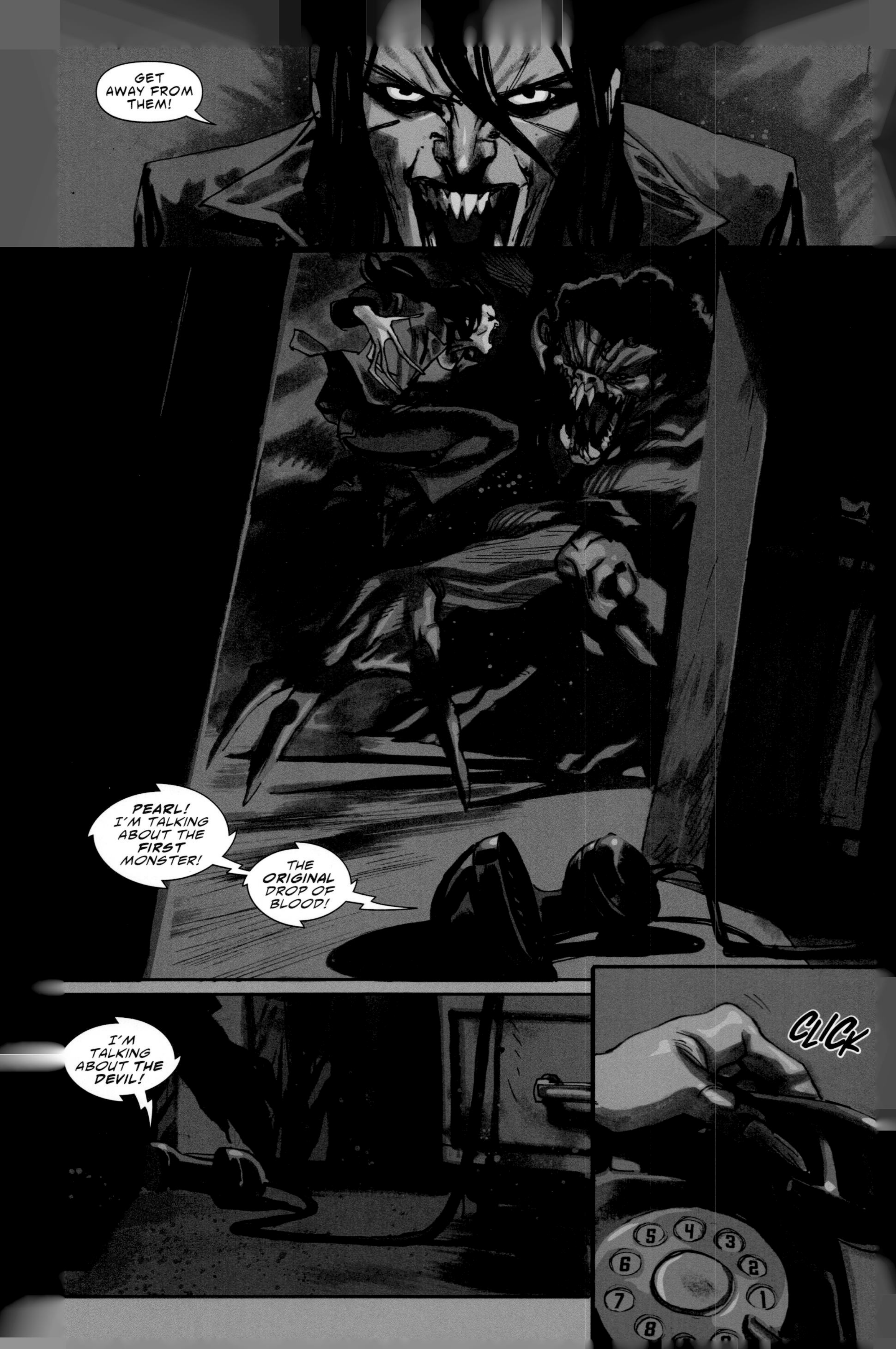
GET AWAY FROM THEM!
PEARL! I'M TALKING ABOUT THE FIRST MONSTER!
THE ORIGINAL DROP OF BLOOD!
I'M TALKING ABOUT THE DEVIL!
CLICK

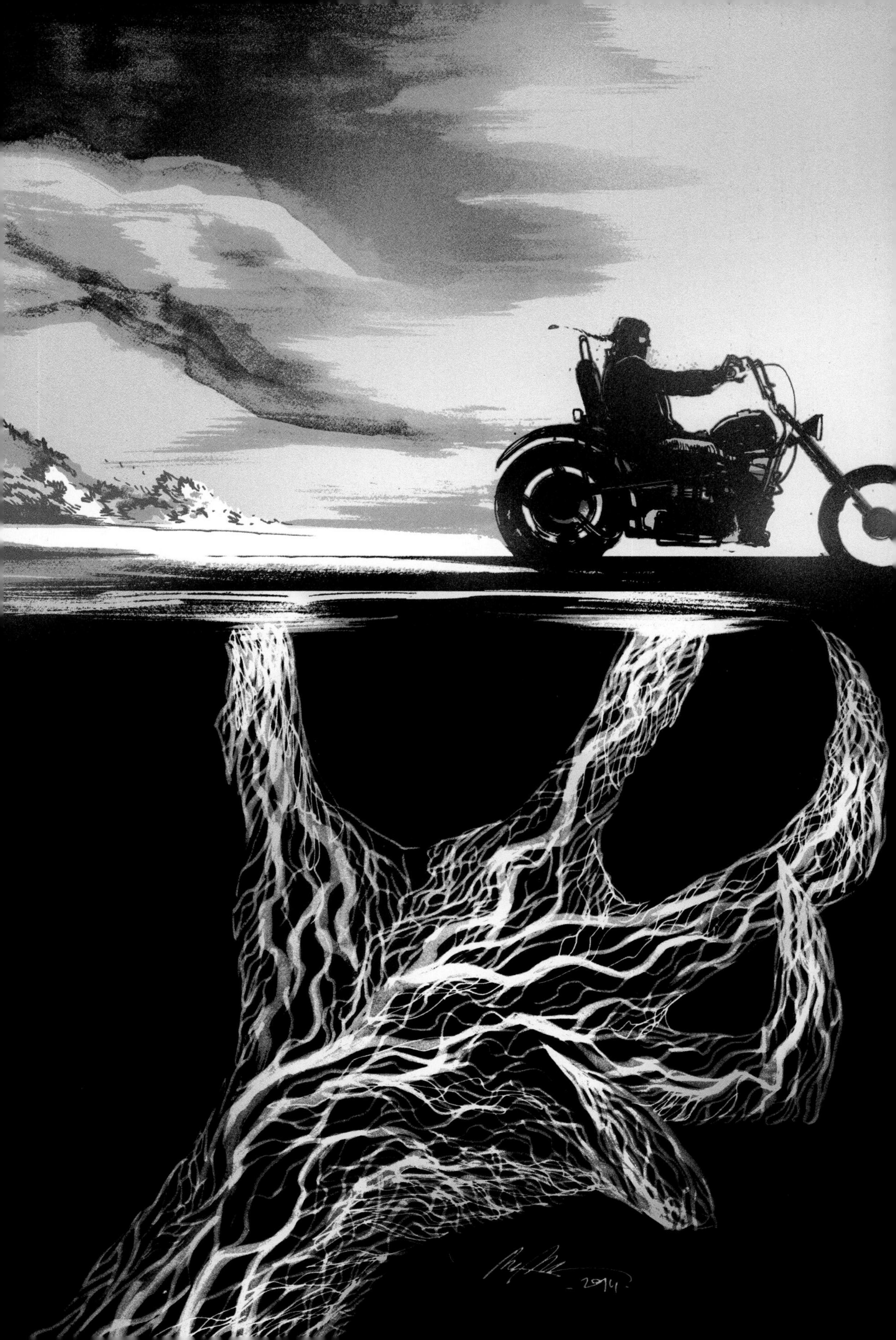

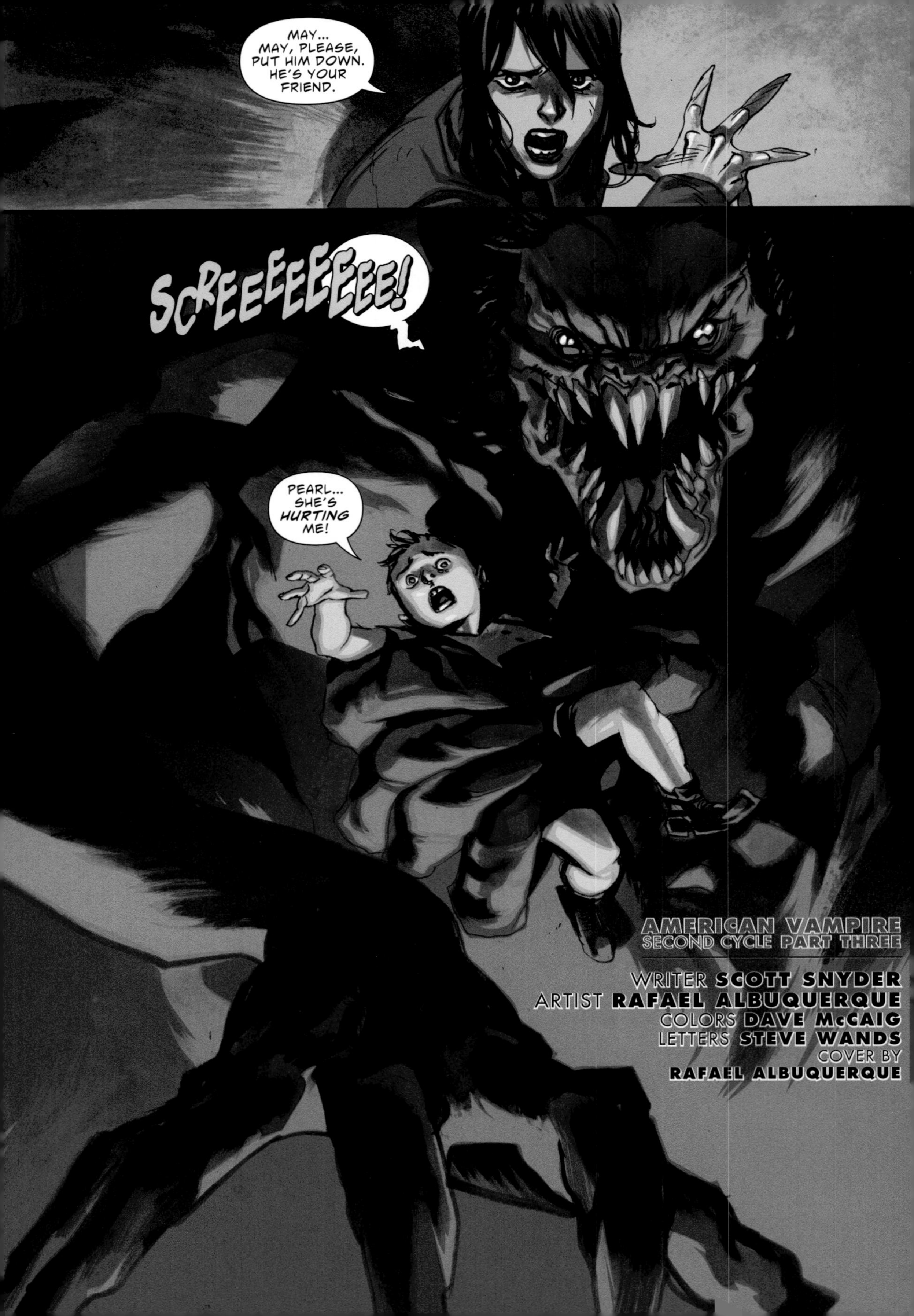
MAY... MAY, PLEASE, PUT HIM DOWN. HE'S YOUR FRIEND.
SCREEEEEEEEEE!
PEARL... SHE'S HURTING ME!
AMERICAN VAMPIRE
SECOND CYCLE PART THREE
WRITER SCOTT SNYDER
ARTIST RAFAEL ALBUQUERQUE
COLORS DAVE McCAIG
LETTERS STEVE WANDS
COVER BY
RAFAEL ALBUQUERQUE

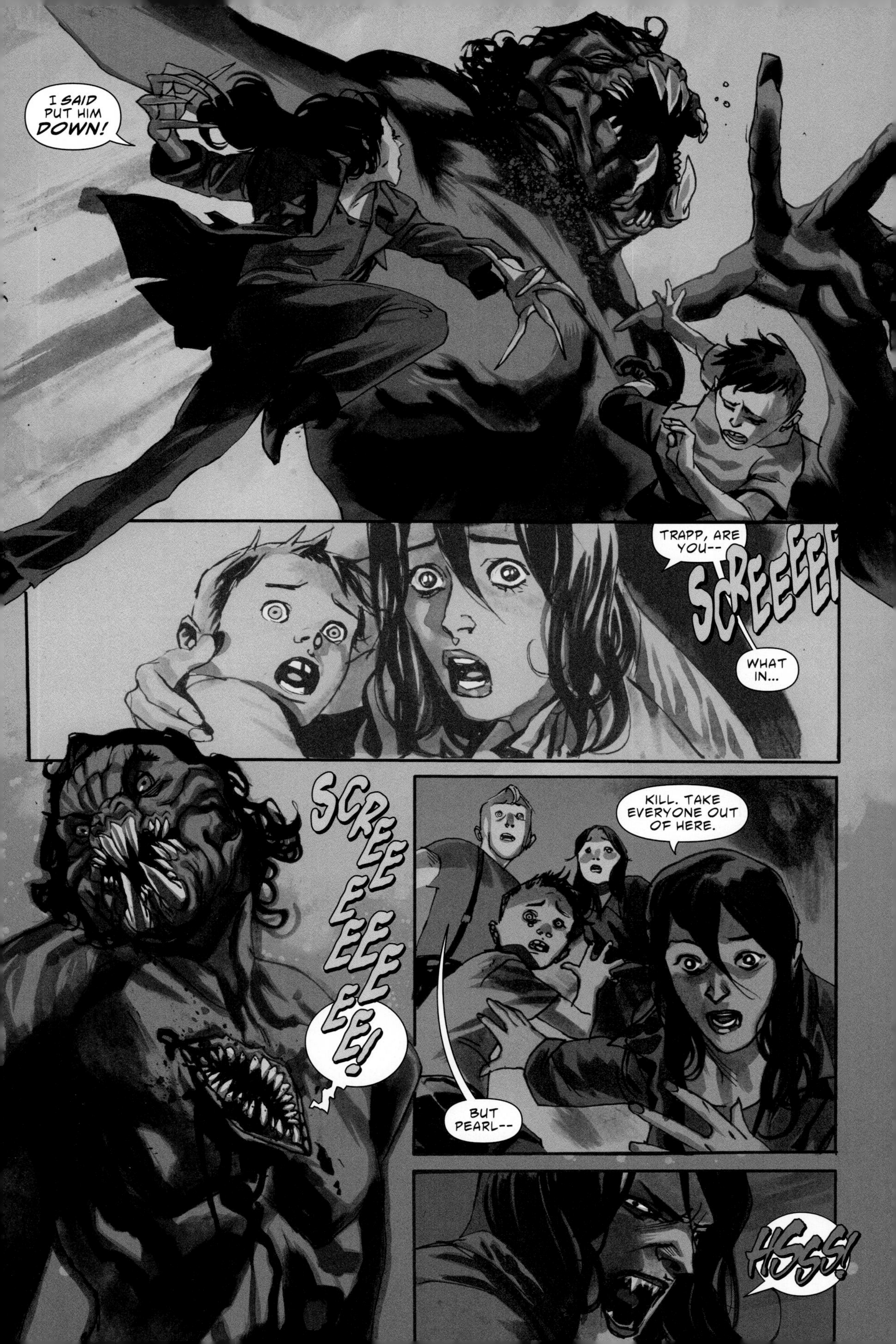
I SAID PUT HIM DOWN!
TRAPP, ARE YOU--
SCREEEEE
WHAT IN...
SCREEEEEEEEE!
KILL. TAKE EVERYONE OUT OF HERE.
BUT PEARL--
HSSS!

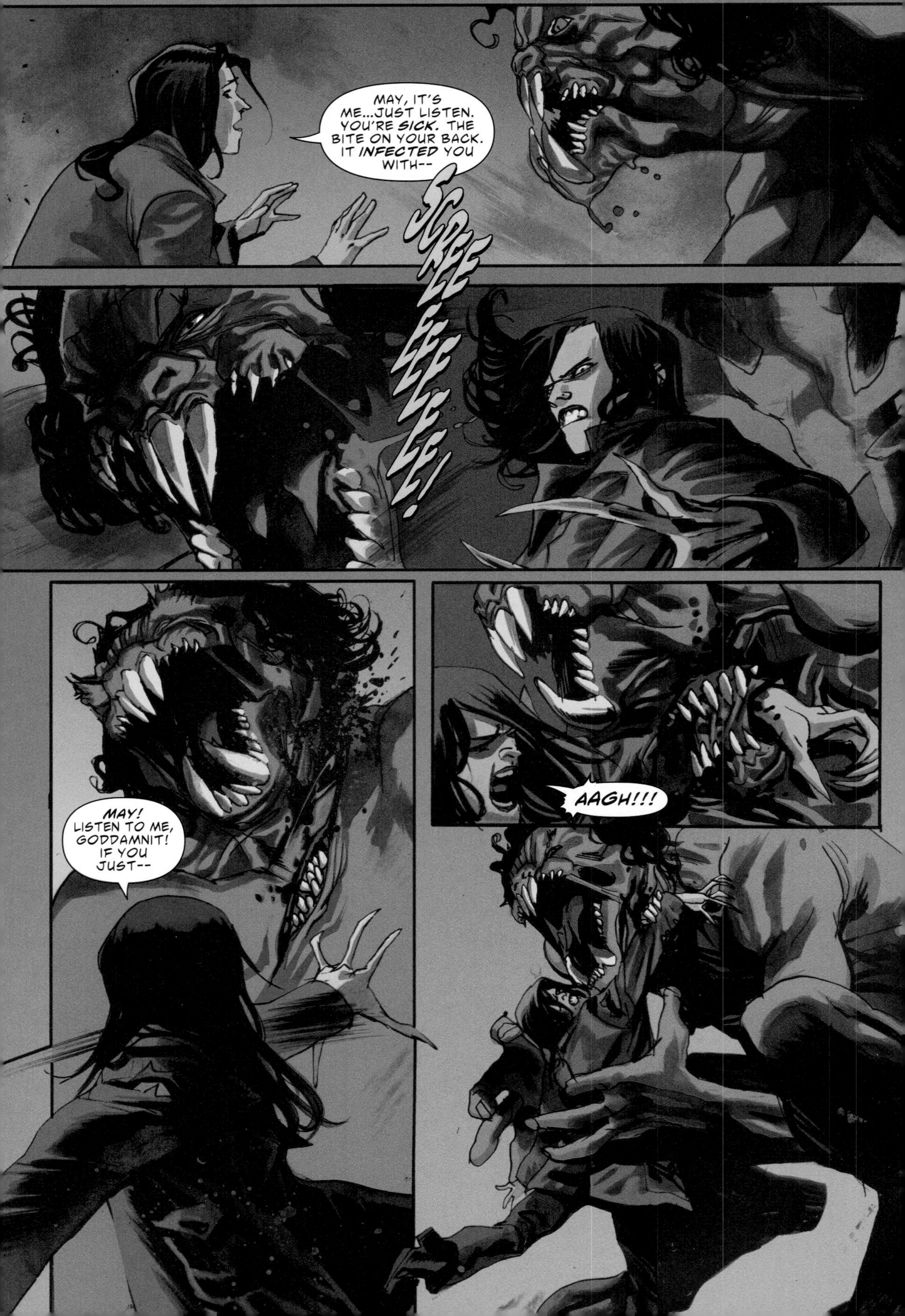
MAY, IT'S ME...JUST LISTEN. YOU'RE SICK. THE BITE ON YOUR BACK. IT INFECTED YOU WITH--
SCREEEEEEEE!
MAY! LISTEN TO ME, GODDAMNIT! IF YOU JUST--
AAGH!!!

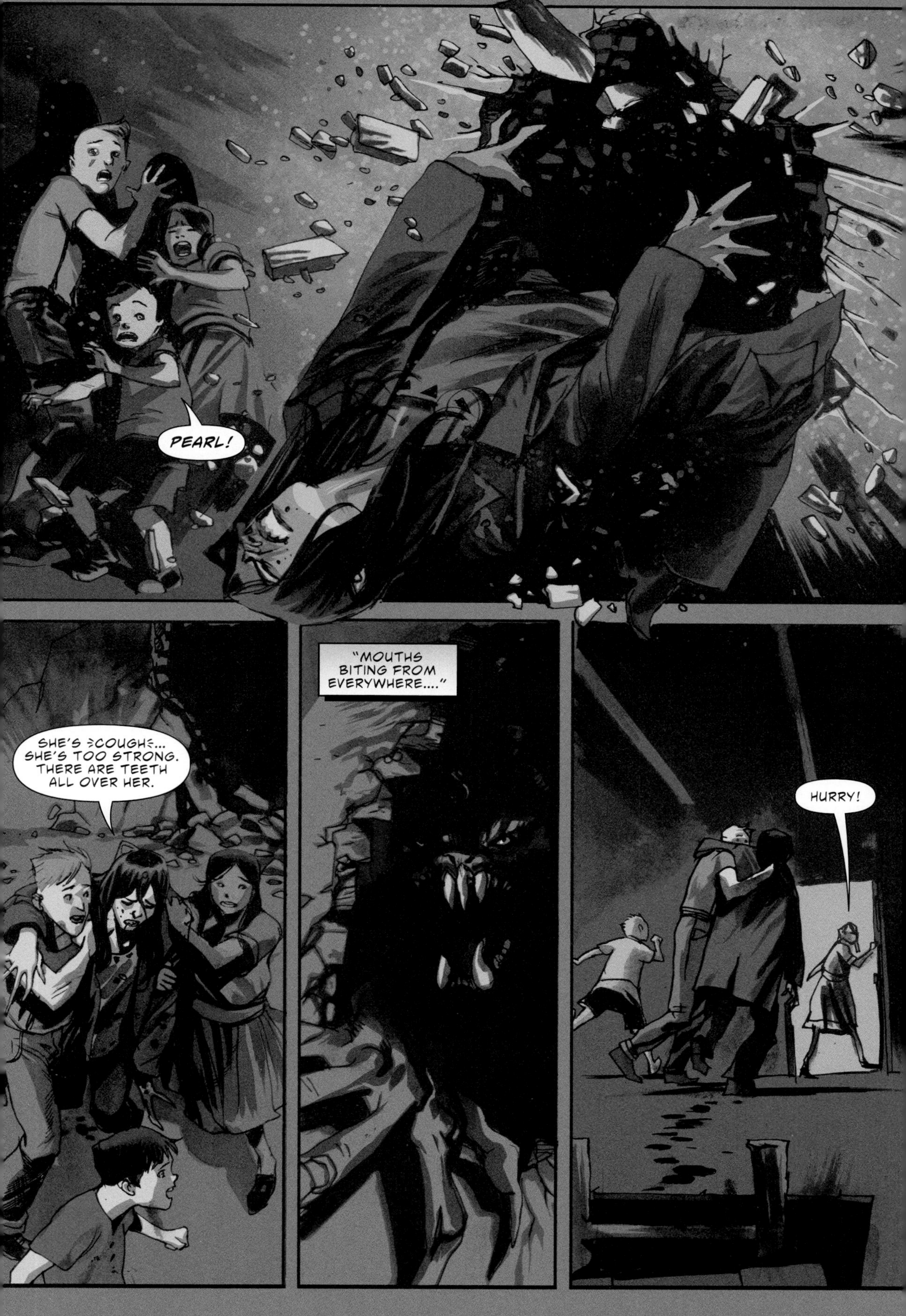
PEARL!
SHE'S ≈COUGH≈... SHE'S TOO STRONG. THERE ARE TEETH ALL OVER HER.
"MOUTHS BITING FROM EVERYWHERE...."
HURRY!

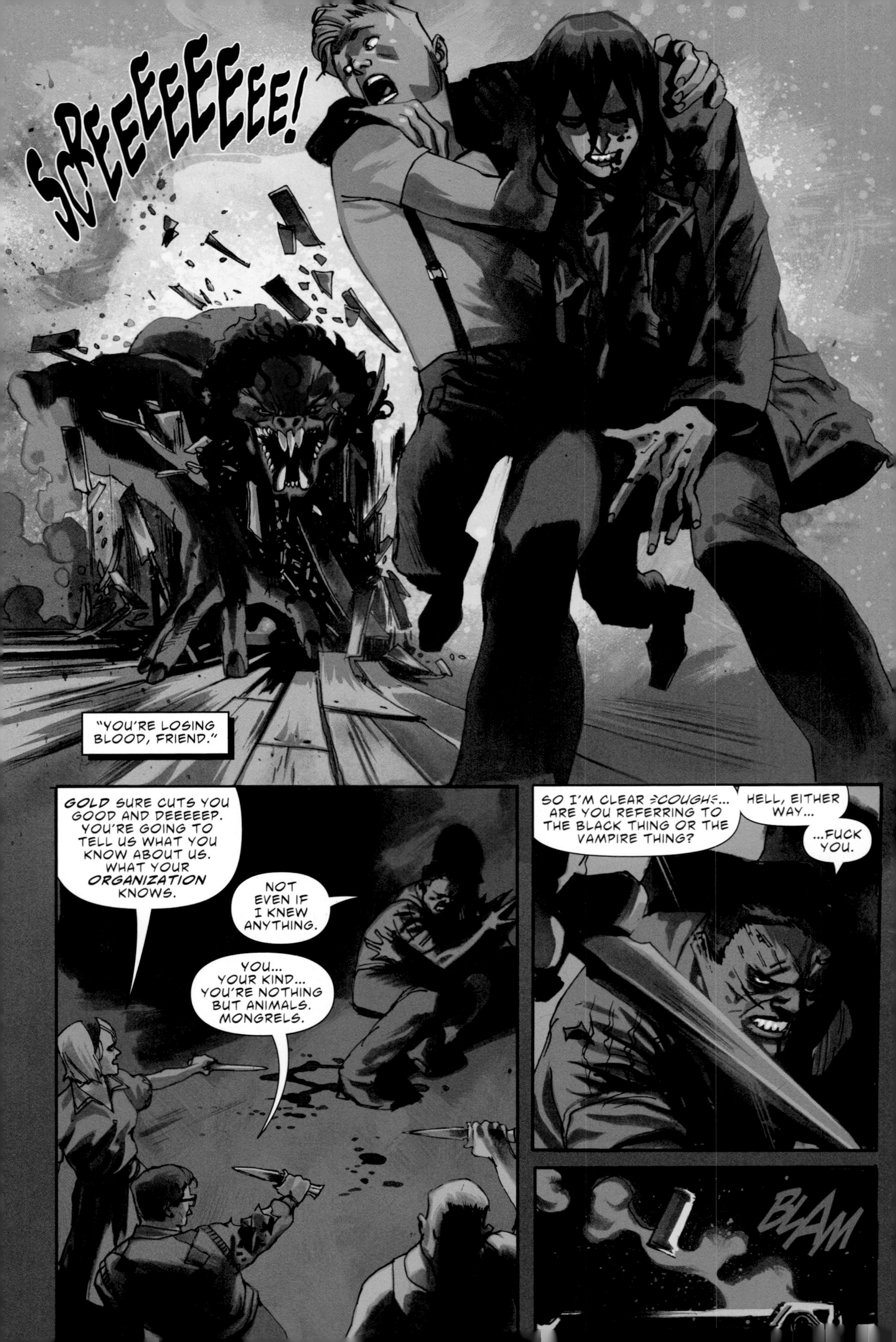
SCREEEEEEEEE!
"YOU'RE LOSING BLOOD, FRIEND."
GOLD SURE CUTS YOU GOOD AND DEEEEEP. YOU'RE GOING TO TELL US WHAT YOU KNOW ABOUT US. WHAT YOUR ORGANIZATION KNOWS.
NOT EVEN IF I KNEW ANYTHING.
YOU... YOUR KIND... YOU'RE NOTHING BUT ANIMALS. MONGRELS.
SO I'M CLEAR =COUGH=... ARE YOU REFERRING TO THE BLACK THING OR THE VAMPIRE THING?
HELL, EITHER WAY...
...FUCK YOU.
BLAM

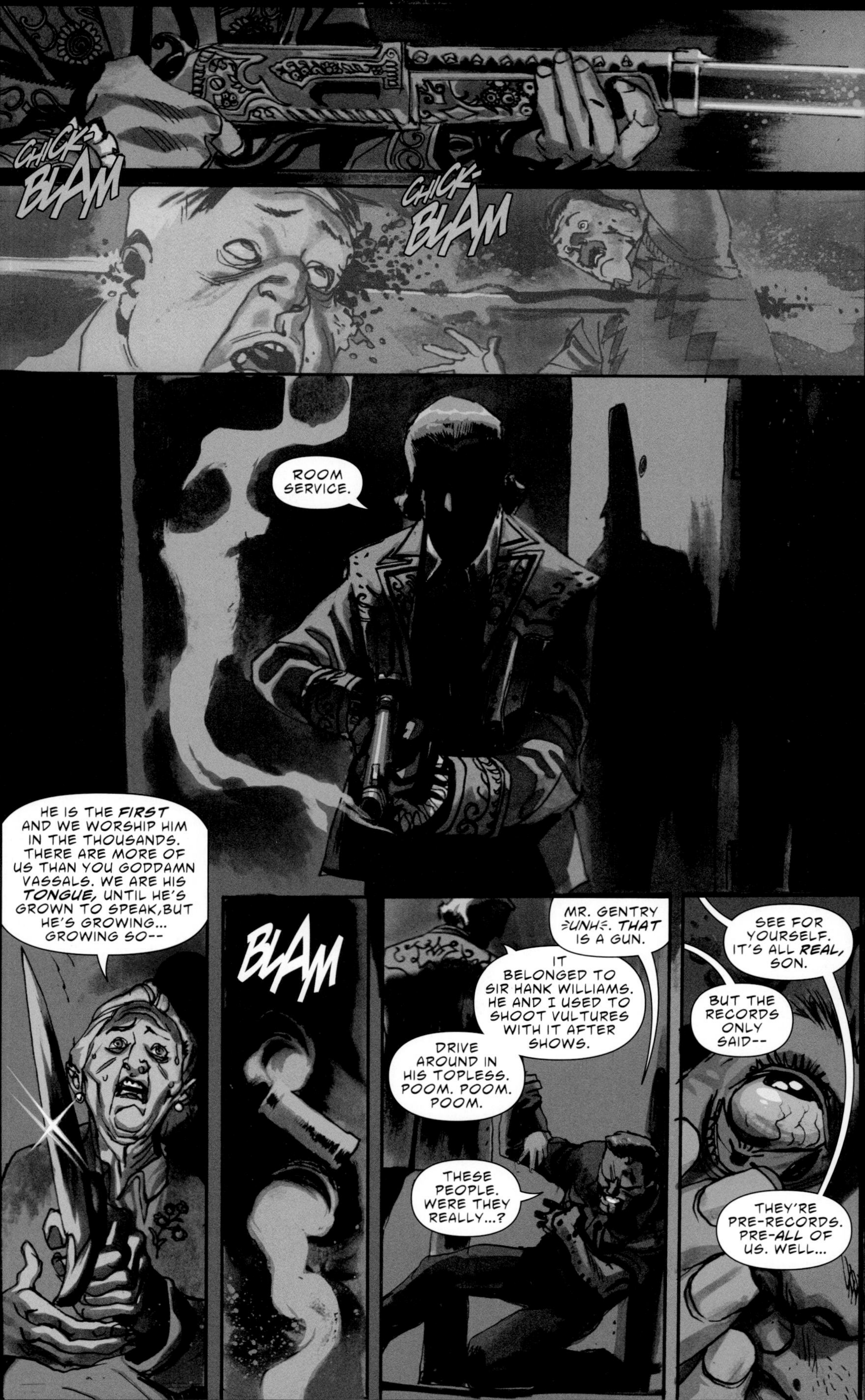
CHICK-BLAM
CHICK-BLAM
ROOM SERVICE.
HE IS THE FIRST AND WE WORSHIP HIM IN THE THOUSANDS. THERE ARE MORE OF US THAN YOU GODDAMN VASSALS. WE ARE HIS TONGUE, UNTIL HE'S GROWN TO SPEAK, BUT HE'S GROWING... GROWING SO--
BLAM
MR. GENTRY =UNH=. THAT IS A GUN.
IT BELONGED TO SIR HANK WILLIAMS. HE AND I USED TO SHOOT VULTURES WITH IT AFTER SHOWS.
DRIVE AROUND IN HIS TOPLESS. POOM. POOM. POOM.
THESE PEOPLE. WERE THEY REALLY...?
SEE FOR YOURSELF. IT'S ALL REAL, SON.
BUT THE RECORDS ONLY SAID--
THEY'RE PRE-RECORDS. PRE-ALL OF US. WELL...

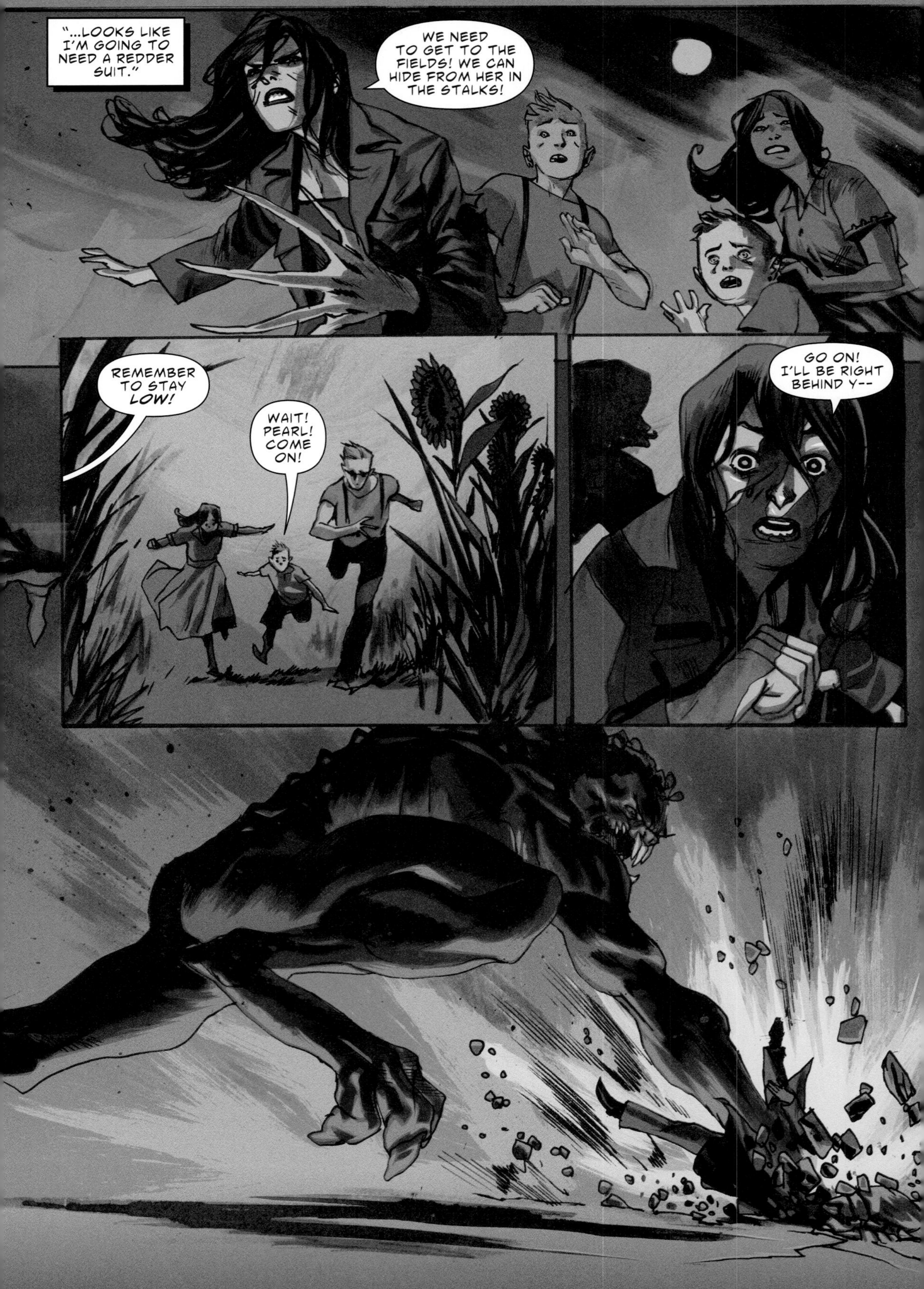
"...LOOKS LIKE I'M GOING TO NEED A REDDER SUIT."
WE NEED TO GET TO THE FIELDS! WE CAN HIDE FROM HER IN THE STALKS!
REMEMBER TO STAY *LOW!*
WAIT! PEARL! COME ON!
GO ON! I'LL BE RIGHT BEHIND Y--

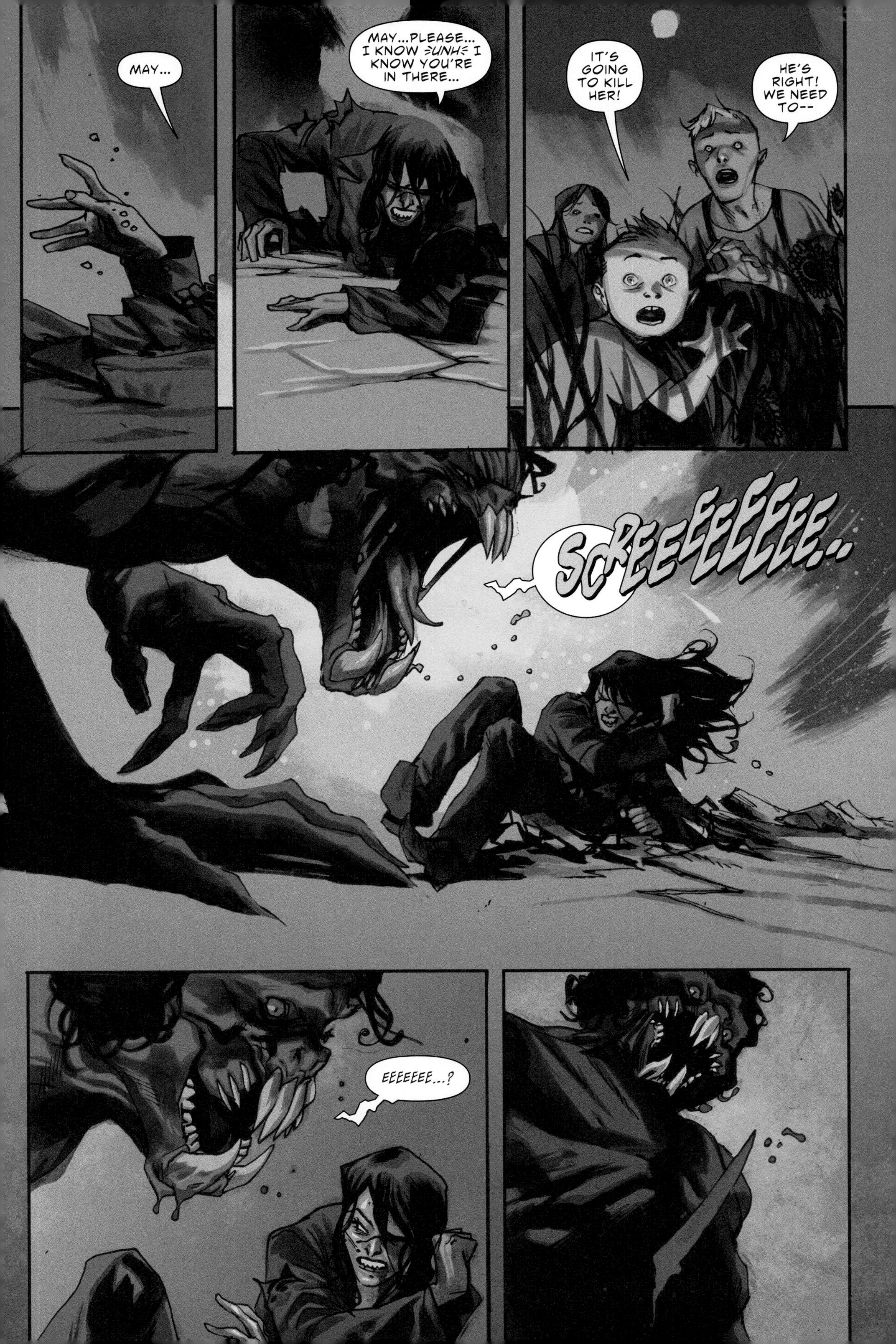
MAY...
MAY...PLEASE... I KNOW =UNH= I KNOW YOU'RE IN THERE...
IT'S GOING TO KILL HER!
HE'S RIGHT! WE NEED TO--
SCREEEEEEEE...
EEEEEEE...?

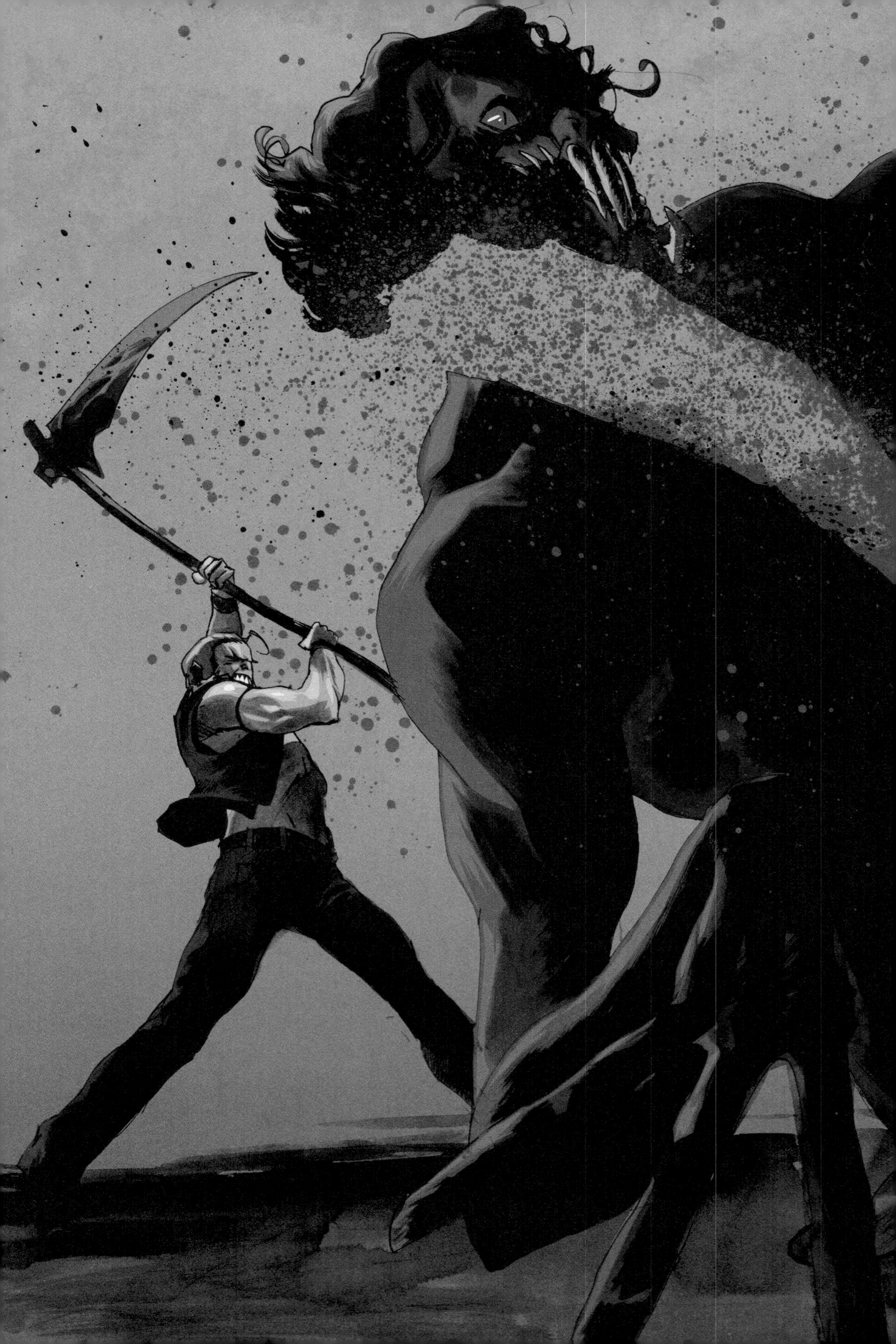

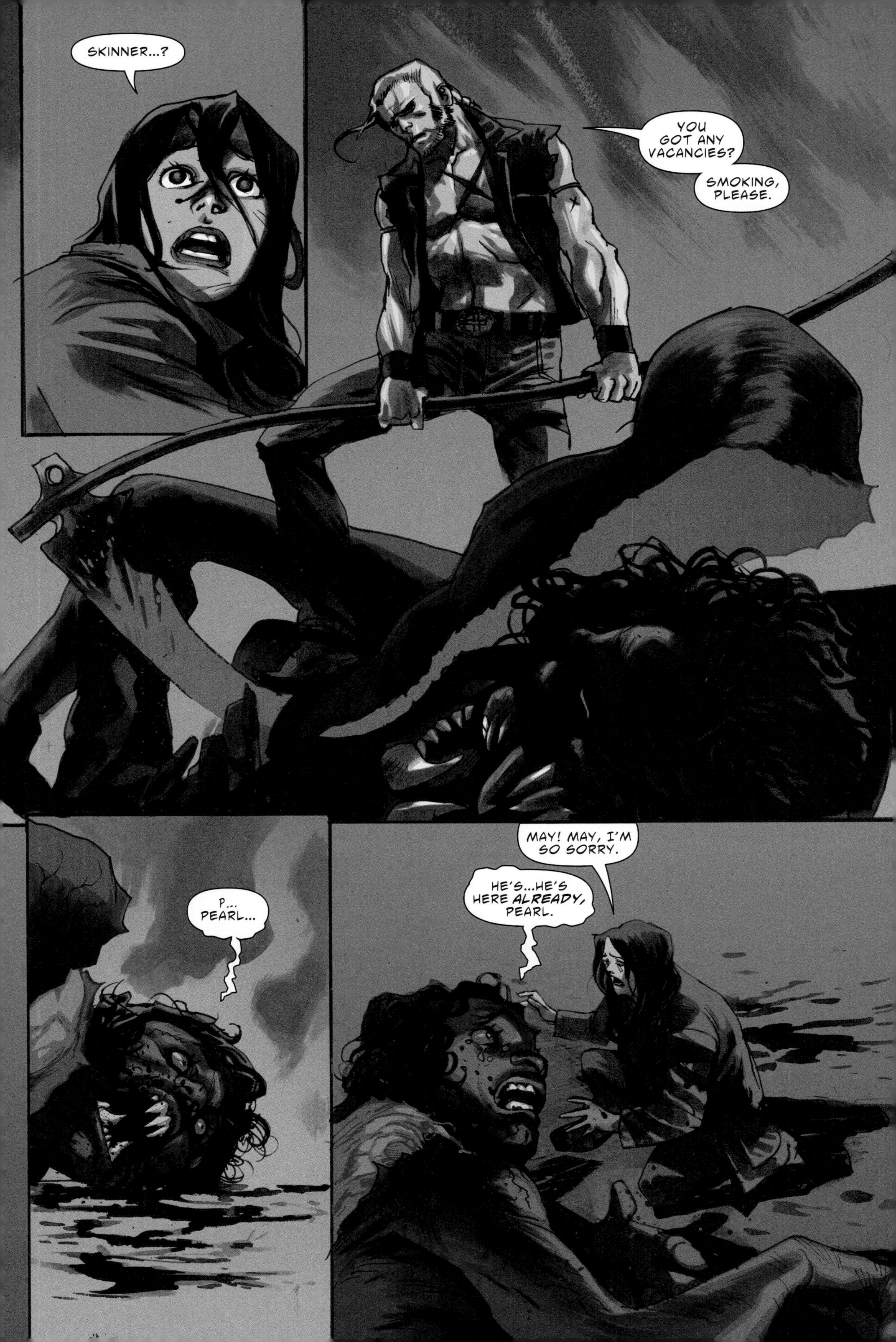
SKINNER...?
YOU GOT ANY VACANCIES?
SMOKING, PLEASE.
P... PEARL...
MAY! MAY, I'M SO SORRY.
HE'S...HE'S HERE ALREADY, PEARL.

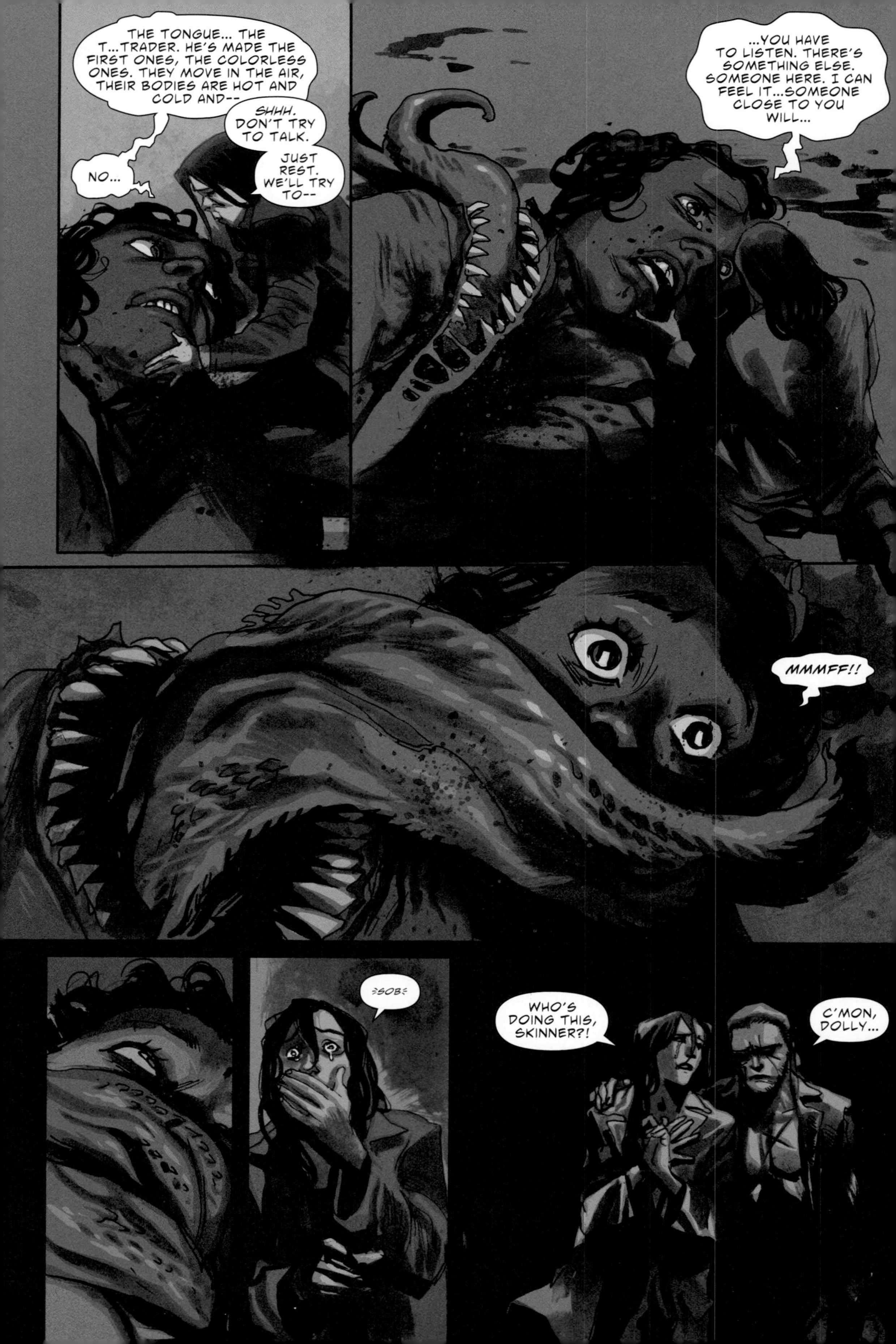
THE TONGUE... THE T...TRADER. HE'S MADE THE FIRST ONES, THE COLORLESS ONES. THEY MOVE IN THE AIR, THEIR BODIES ARE HOT AND COLD AND--
SHHH. DON'T TRY TO TALK.
NO...
JUST REST. WE'LL TRY TO--
...YOU HAVE TO LISTEN. THERE'S SOMETHING ELSE. SOMEONE HERE. I CAN FEEL IT...SOMEONE CLOSE TO YOU WILL...
MMMFF!!
SOB
WHO'S DOING THIS, SKINNER?!
C'MON, DOLLY...

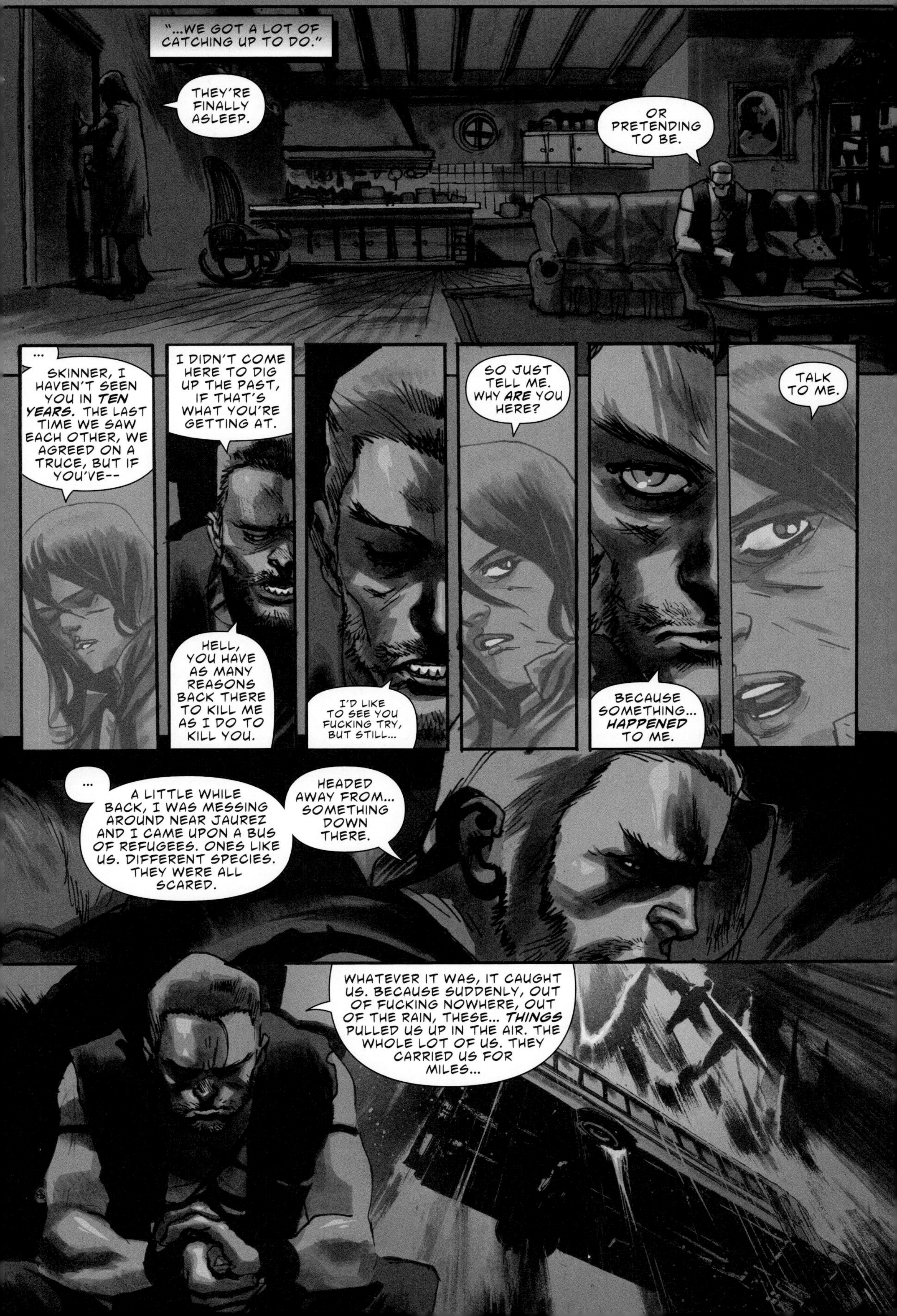
"...WE GOT A LOT OF CATCHING UP TO DO."
THEY'RE FINALLY ASLEEP.
OR PRETENDING TO BE.
... SKINNER, I HAVEN'T SEEN YOU IN *TEN YEARS.* THE LAST TIME WE SAW EACH OTHER, WE AGREED ON A TRUCE, BUT IF YOU'VE--
I DIDN'T COME HERE TO DIG UP THE PAST, IF THAT'S WHAT YOU'RE GETTING AT.
HELL, YOU HAVE AS MANY REASONS BACK THERE TO KILL ME AS I DO TO KILL YOU.
I'D LIKE TO SEE YOU FUCKING TRY, BUT STILL...
SO JUST TELL ME. WHY *ARE* YOU HERE?
BECAUSE SOMETHING... *HAPPENED* TO ME.
TALK TO ME.
... A LITTLE WHILE BACK, I WAS MESSING AROUND NEAR JAUREZ AND I CAME UPON A BUS OF REFUGEES. ONES LIKE US. DIFFERENT SPECIES. THEY WERE ALL SCARED.
HEADED AWAY FROM... SOMETHING DOWN THERE.
WHATEVER IT WAS, IT CAUGHT US. BECAUSE SUDDENLY, OUT OF FUCKING NOWHERE, OUT OF THE RAIN, THESE... *THINGS* PULLED US UP IN THE AIR. THE WHOLE LOT OF US. THEY CARRIED US FOR MILES...

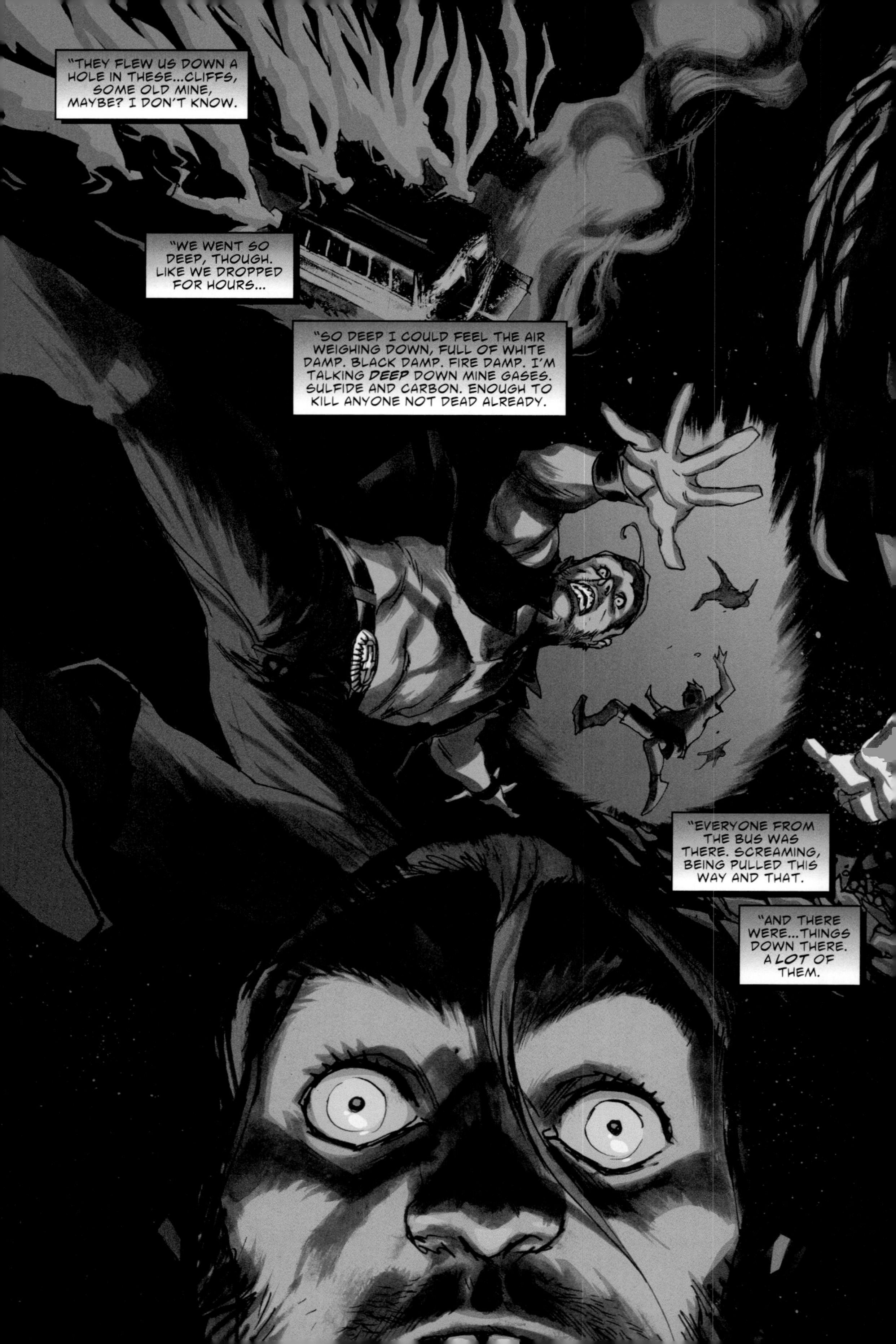
"THEY FLEW US DOWN A HOLE IN THESE...CLIFFS, SOME OLD MINE, MAYBE? I DON'T KNOW.
"WE WENT SO DEEP, THOUGH. LIKE WE DROPPED FOR HOURS...
"SO DEEP I COULD FEEL THE AIR WEIGHING DOWN, FULL OF WHITE DAMP. BLACK DAMP. FIRE DAMP. I'M TALKING DEEP DOWN MINE GASES. SULFIDE AND CARBON. ENOUGH TO KILL ANYONE NOT DEAD ALREADY.
"EVERYONE FROM THE BUS WAS THERE. SCREAMING, BEING PULLED THIS WAY AND THAT.
"AND THERE WERE...THINGS DOWN THERE. A LOT OF THEM.

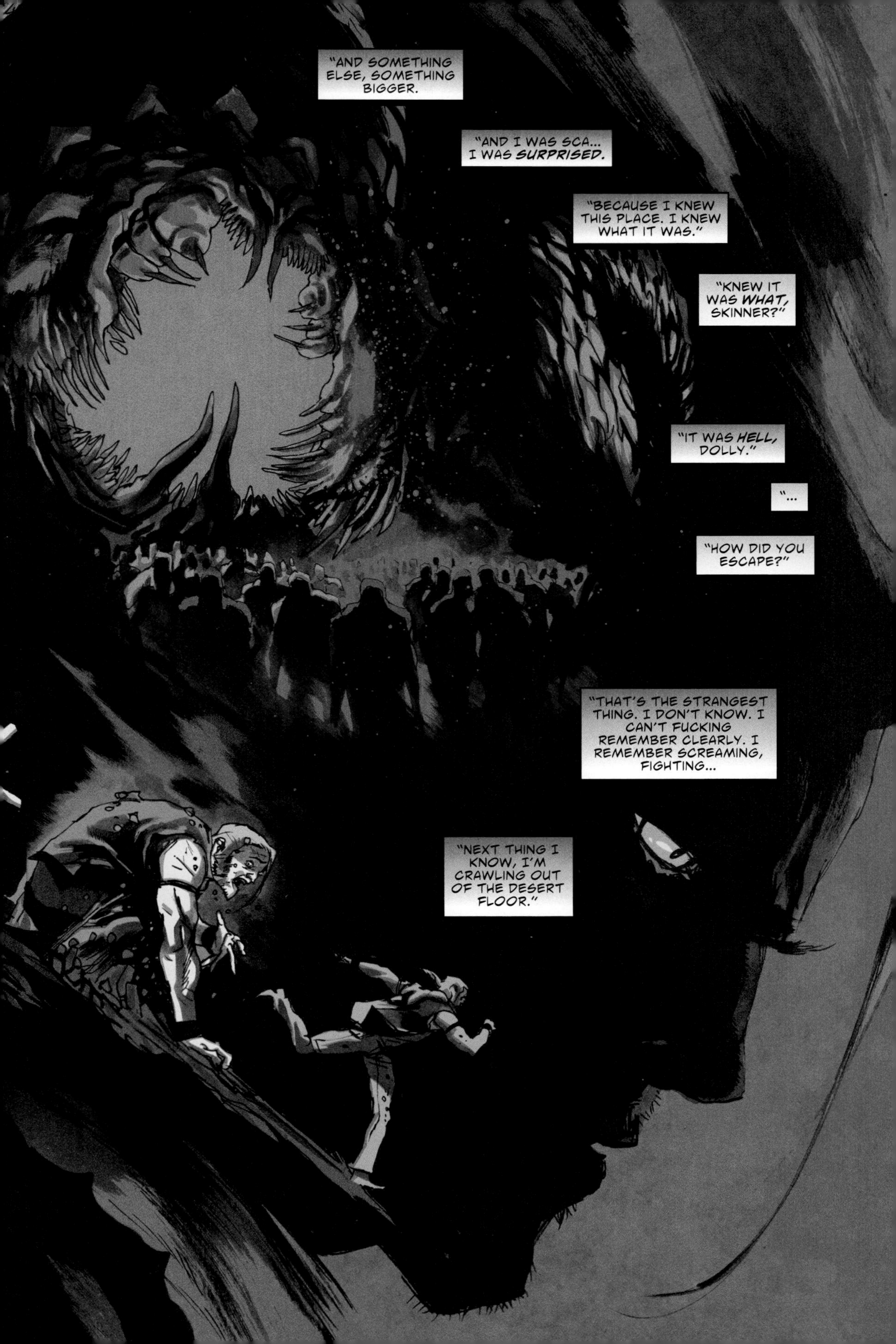
"AND SOMETHING ELSE, SOMETHING BIGGER.
"AND I WAS SCA... I WAS *SURPRISED*.
"BECAUSE I KNEW THIS PLACE. I KNEW WHAT IT WAS."
"KNEW IT WAS *WHAT*, SKINNER?"
"IT WAS *HELL*, DOLLY."
"...
"HOW DID YOU ESCAPE?"
"THAT'S THE STRANGEST THING. I DON'T KNOW. I CAN'T FUCKING REMEMBER CLEARLY. I REMEMBER SCREAMING, FIGHTING...
"NEXT THING I KNOW, I'M CRAWLING OUT OF THE DESERT FLOOR."

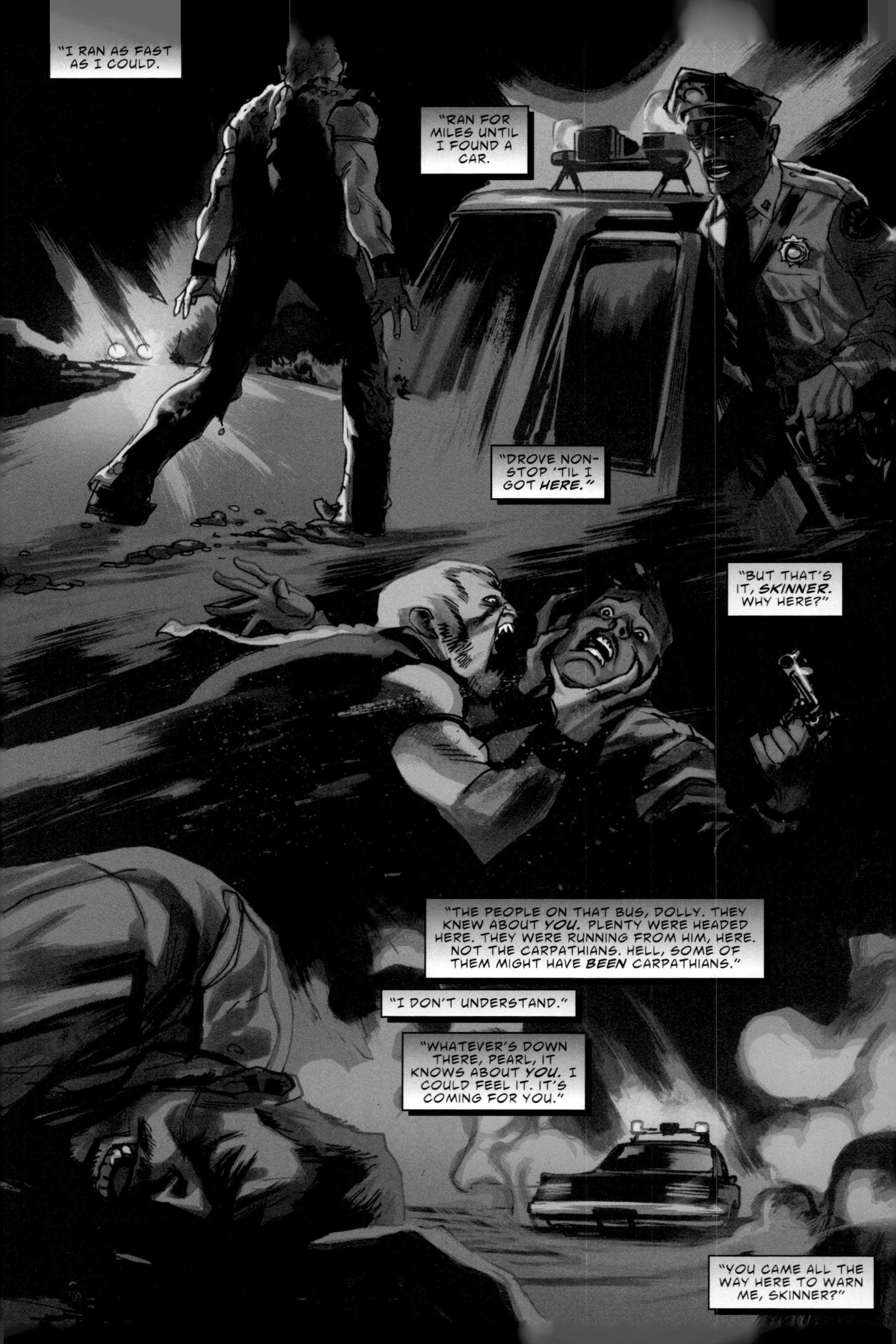
"I RAN AS FAST AS I COULD.
"RAN FOR MILES UNTIL I FOUND A CAR.
"DROVE NON-STOP 'TIL I GOT HERE."
"BUT THAT'S IT, SKINNER. WHY HERE?"
"THE PEOPLE ON THAT BUS, DOLLY. THEY KNEW ABOUT YOU. PLENTY WERE HEADED HERE. THEY WERE RUNNING FROM HIM, HERE. NOT THE CARPATHIANS. HELL, SOME OF THEM MIGHT HAVE BEEN CARPATHIANS."
"I DON'T UNDERSTAND."
"WHATEVER'S DOWN THERE, PEARL, IT KNOWS ABOUT YOU. I COULD FEEL IT. IT'S COMING FOR YOU."
"YOU CAME ALL THE WAY HERE TO WARN ME, SKINNER?"

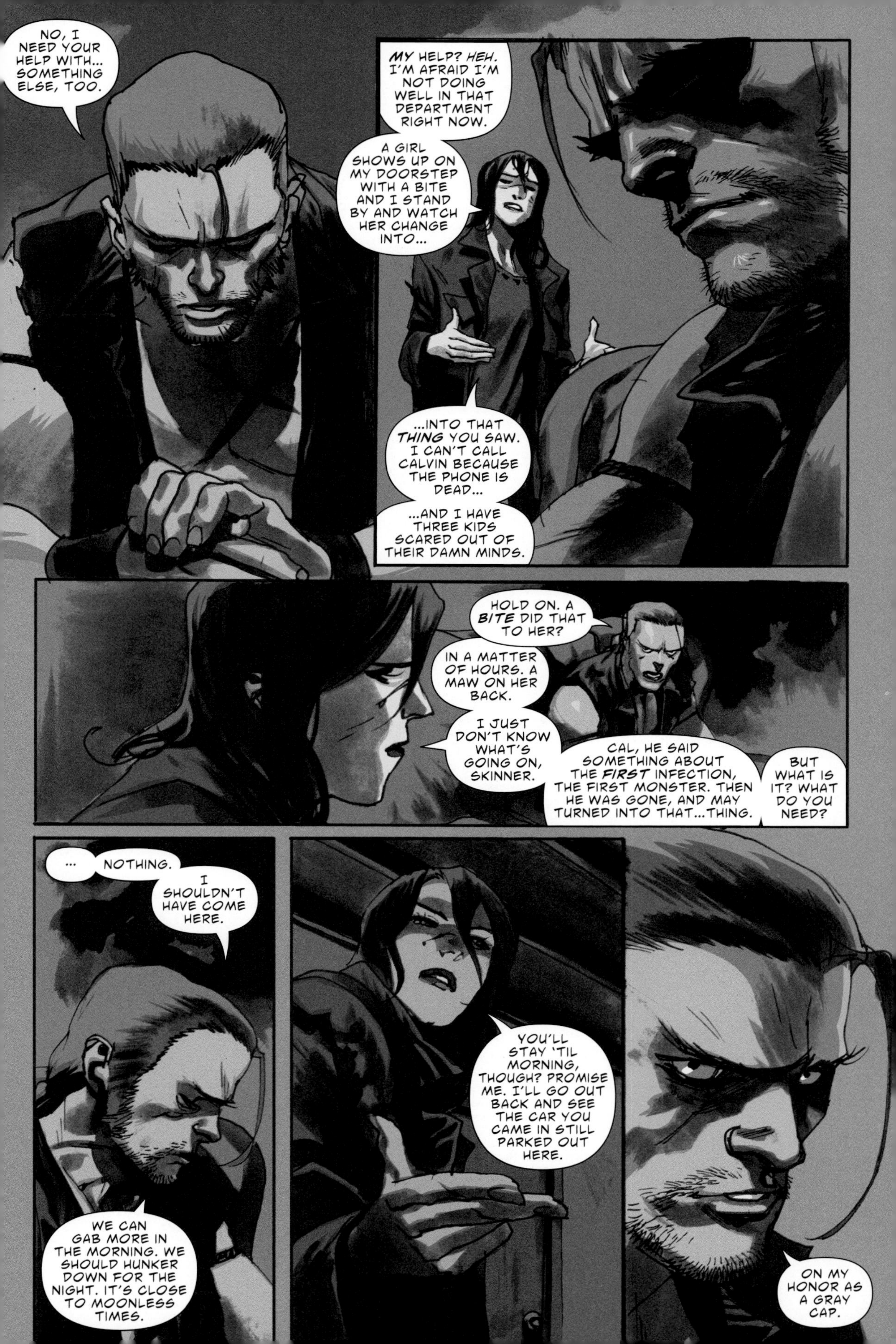
NO, I NEED YOUR HELP WITH... SOMETHING ELSE, TOO.
MY HELP? HEH. I'M AFRAID I'M NOT DOING WELL IN THAT DEPARTMENT RIGHT NOW.
A GIRL SHOWS UP ON MY DOORSTEP WITH A BITE AND I STAND BY AND WATCH HER CHANGE INTO...
...INTO THAT THING YOU SAW. I CAN'T CALL CALVIN BECAUSE THE PHONE IS DEAD...
...AND I HAVE THREE KIDS SCARED OUT OF THEIR DAMN MINDS.
HOLD ON. A BITE DID THAT TO HER?
IN A MATTER OF HOURS. A MAW ON HER BACK.
I JUST DON'T KNOW WHAT'S GOING ON, SKINNER.
CAL, HE SAID SOMETHING ABOUT THE FIRST INFECTION, THE FIRST MONSTER. THEN HE WAS GONE, AND MAY TURNED INTO THAT...THING.
BUT WHAT IS IT? WHAT DO YOU NEED?
...
NOTHING.
I SHOULDN'T HAVE COME HERE.
WE CAN GAB MORE IN THE MORNING. WE SHOULD HUNKER DOWN FOR THE NIGHT. IT'S CLOSE TO MOONLESS TIMES.
YOU'LL STAY 'TIL MORNING, THOUGH? PROMISE ME. I'LL GO OUT BACK AND SEE THE CAR YOU CAME IN STILL PARKED OUT HERE.
ON MY HONOR AS A GRAY CAP.

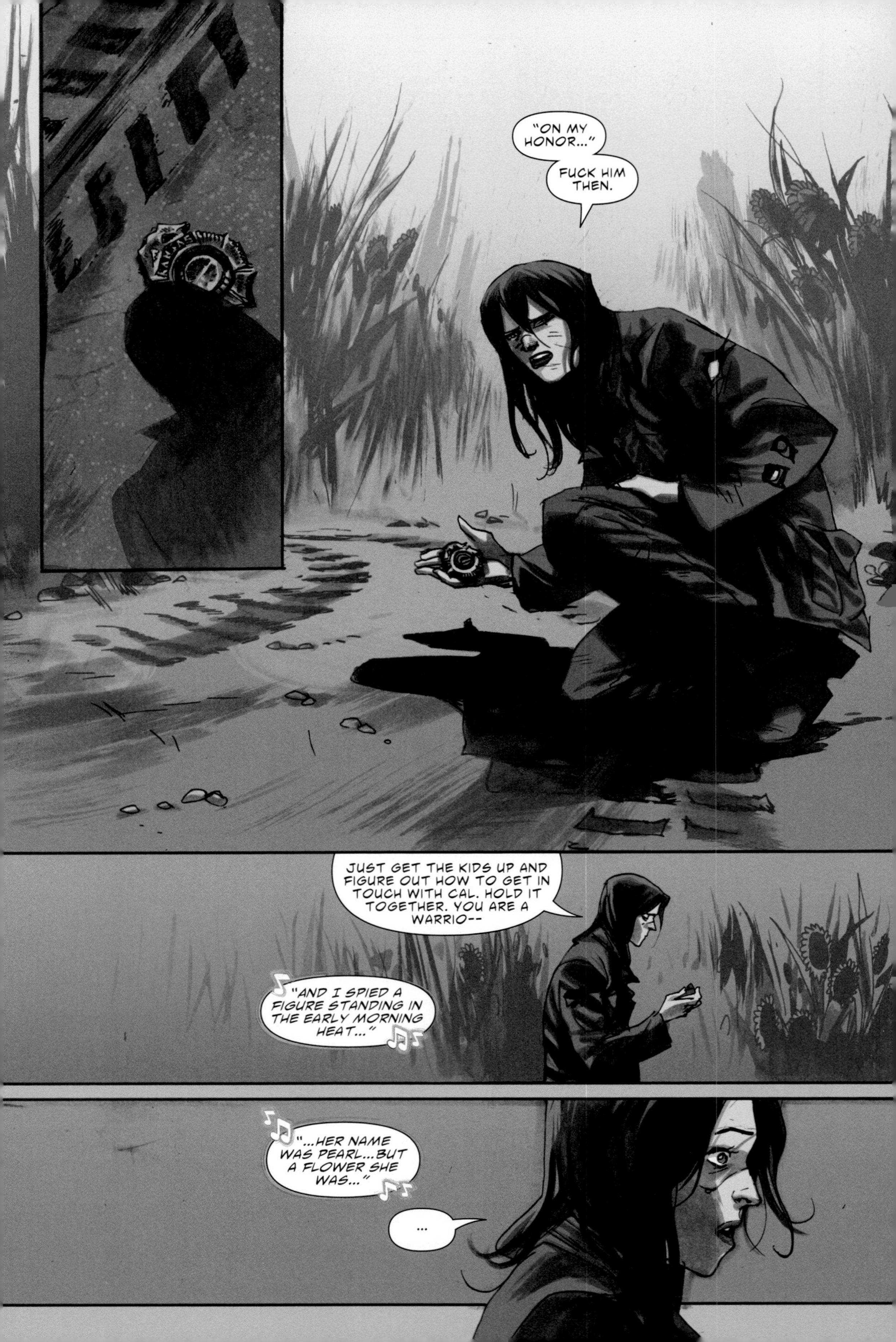
"ON MY HONOR..."
FUCK HIM THEN.
JUST GET THE KIDS UP AND FIGURE OUT HOW TO GET IN TOUCH WITH CAL. HOLD IT TOGETHER. YOU ARE A WARRIO--
"AND I SPIED A FIGURE STANDING IN THE EARLY MORNING HEAT..."
"...HER NAME WAS PEARL...BUT A FLOWER SHE WAS..."
...

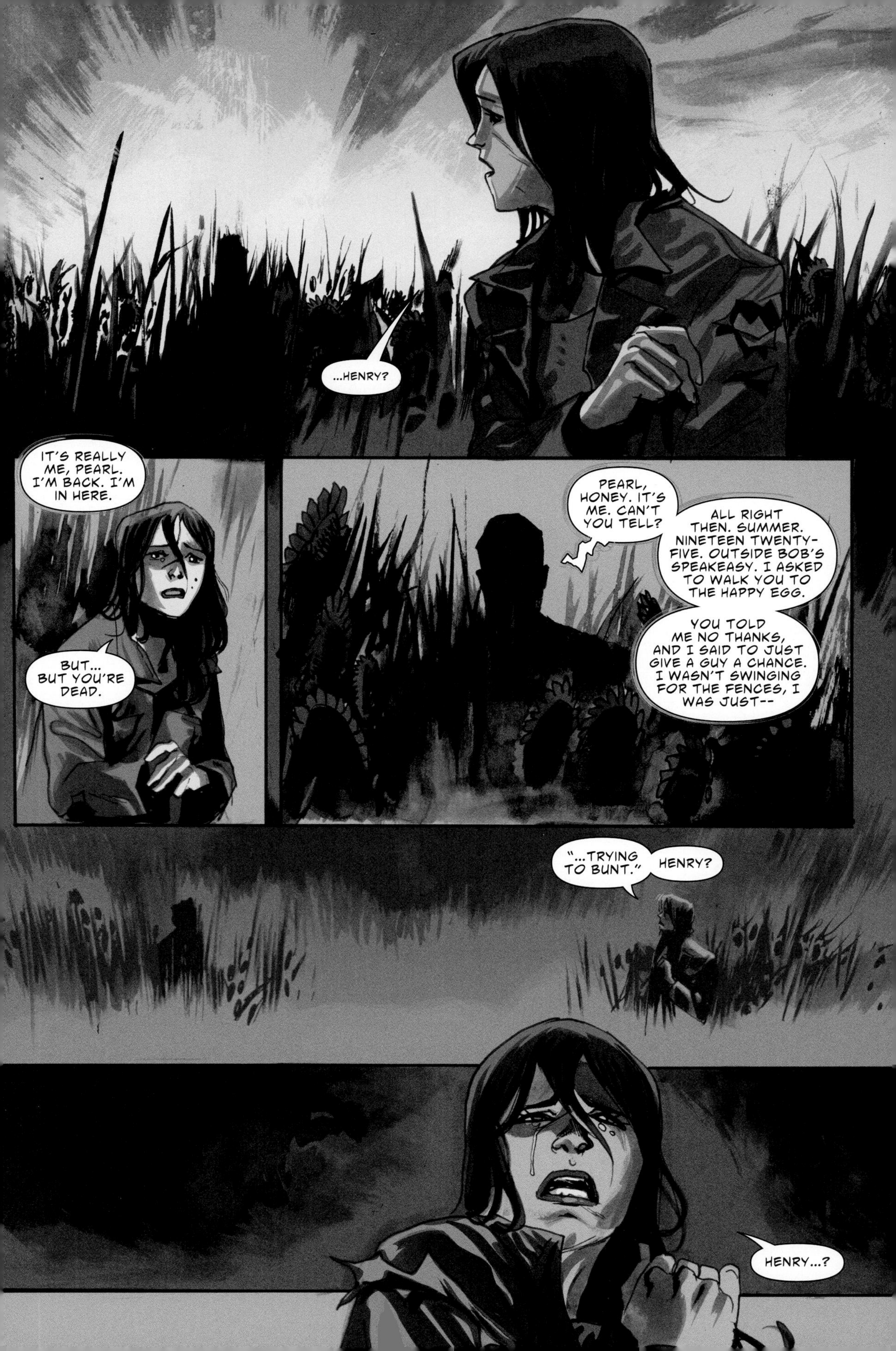
...HENRY?
IT'S REALLY ME, PEARL. I'M BACK. I'M IN HERE.
BUT... BUT YOU'RE DEAD.
PEARL, HONEY. IT'S ME. CAN'T YOU TELL?
ALL RIGHT THEN. SUMMER. NINETEEN TWENTY-FIVE. OUTSIDE BOB'S SPEAKEASY. I ASKED TO WALK YOU TO THE HAPPY EGG.
YOU TOLD ME NO THANKS, AND I SAID TO JUST GIVE A GUY A CHANCE. I WASN'T SWINGING FOR THE FENCES, I WAS JUST--
"...TRYING TO BUNT."
HENRY?
HENRY...?

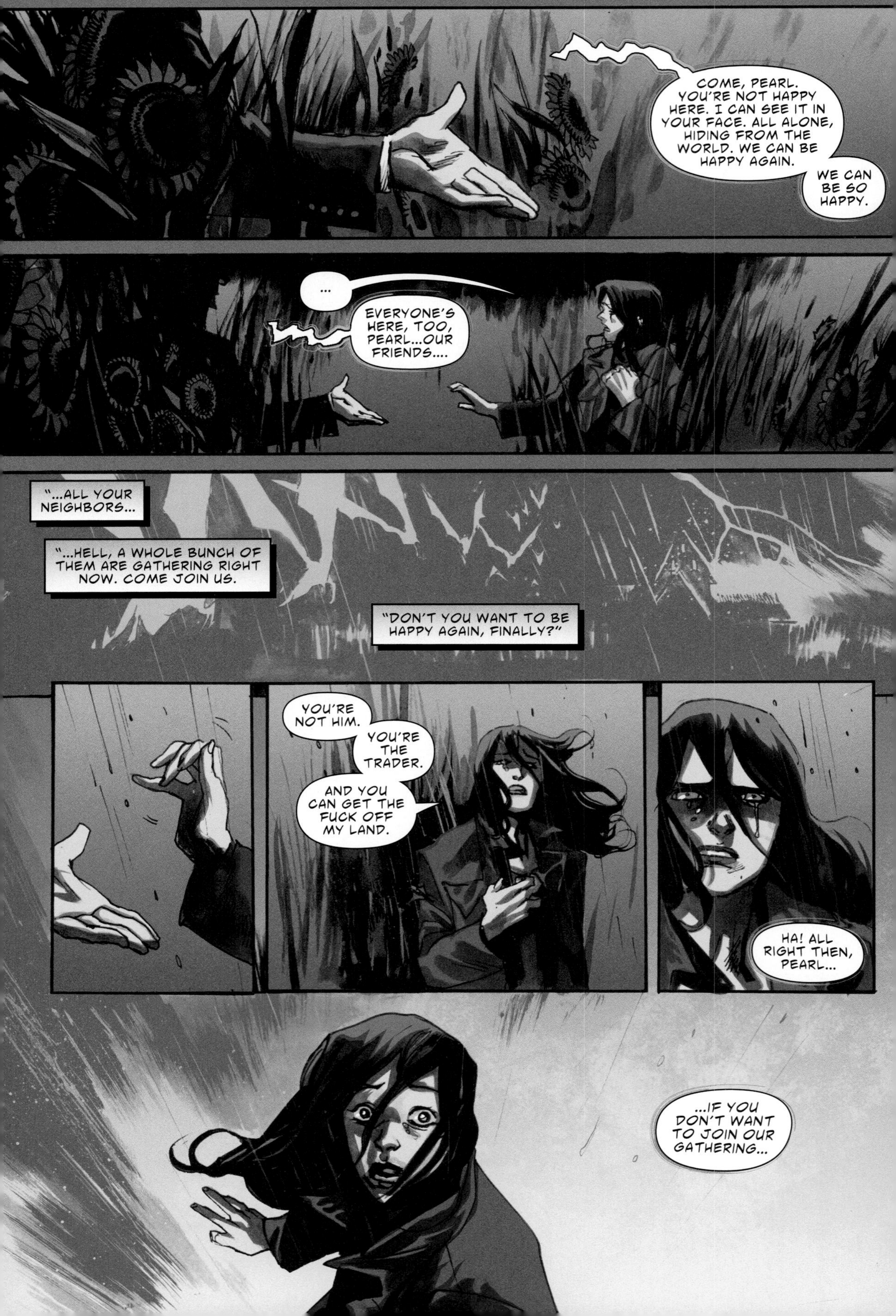
COME, PEARL. YOU'RE NOT HAPPY HERE. I CAN SEE IT IN YOUR FACE. ALL ALONE, HIDING FROM THE WORLD. WE CAN BE HAPPY AGAIN.
WE CAN BE SO HAPPY.
...
EVERYONE'S HERE, TOO, PEARL...OUR FRIENDS....
"...ALL YOUR NEIGHBORS...
"...HELL, A WHOLE BUNCH OF THEM ARE GATHERING RIGHT NOW. COME JOIN US.
"DON'T YOU WANT TO BE HAPPY AGAIN, FINALLY?"
YOU'RE NOT HIM.
YOU'RE THE TRADER.
AND YOU CAN GET THE FUCK OFF MY LAND.
HA! ALL RIGHT THEN, PEARL...
...IF YOU DON'T WANT TO JOIN OUR GATHERING...

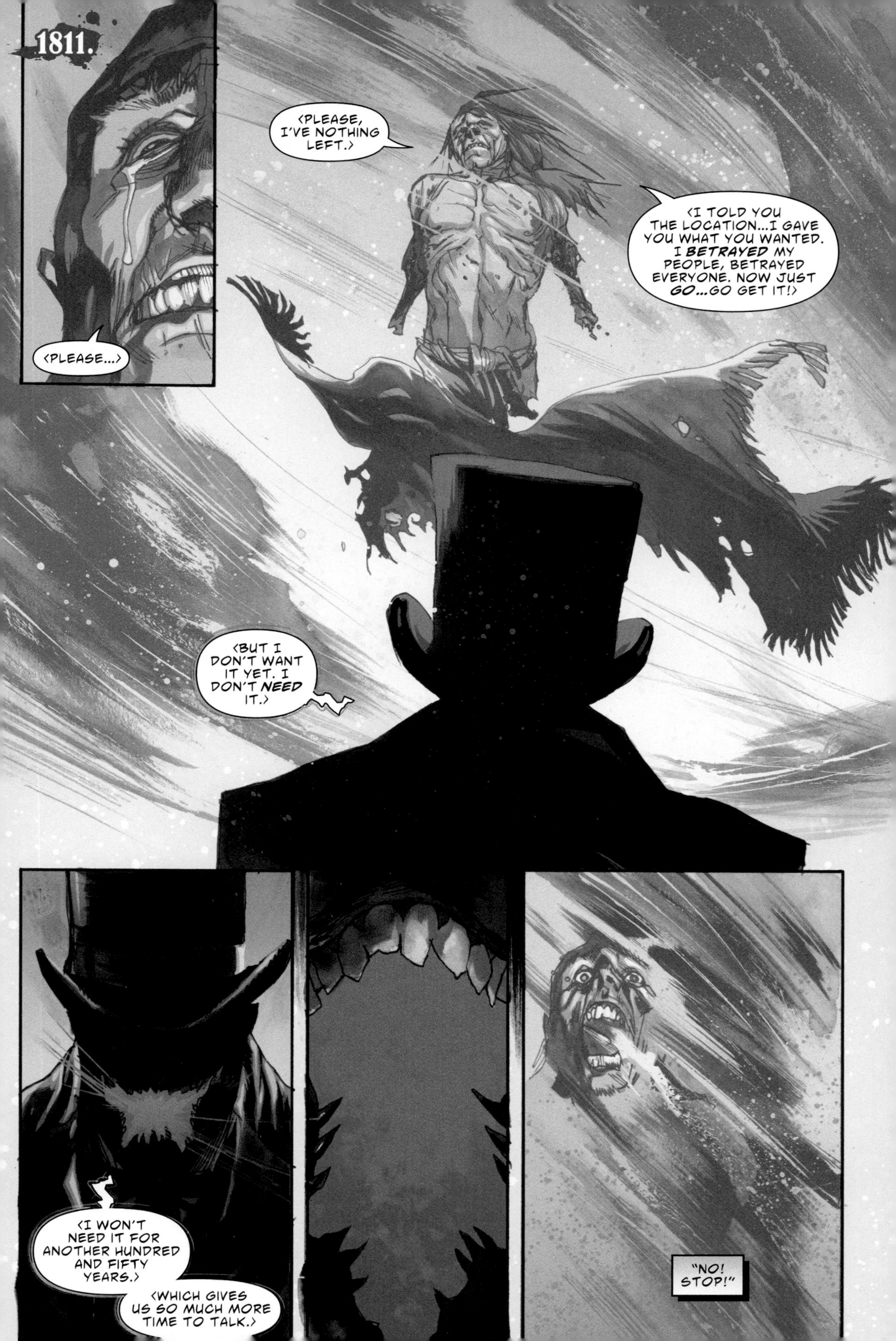
1811.
<PLEASE...>
<PLEASE, I'VE NOTHING LEFT.>
<I TOLD YOU THE LOCATION...I GAVE YOU WHAT YOU WANTED. I BETRAYED MY PEOPLE, BETRAYED EVERYONE. NOW JUST GO...GO GET IT!>
<BUT I DON'T WANT IT YET. I DON'T NEED IT.>
<I WON'T NEED IT FOR ANOTHER HUNDRED AND FIFTY YEARS.>
<WHICH GIVES US SO MUCH MORE TIME TO TALK.>
"NO! STOP!"

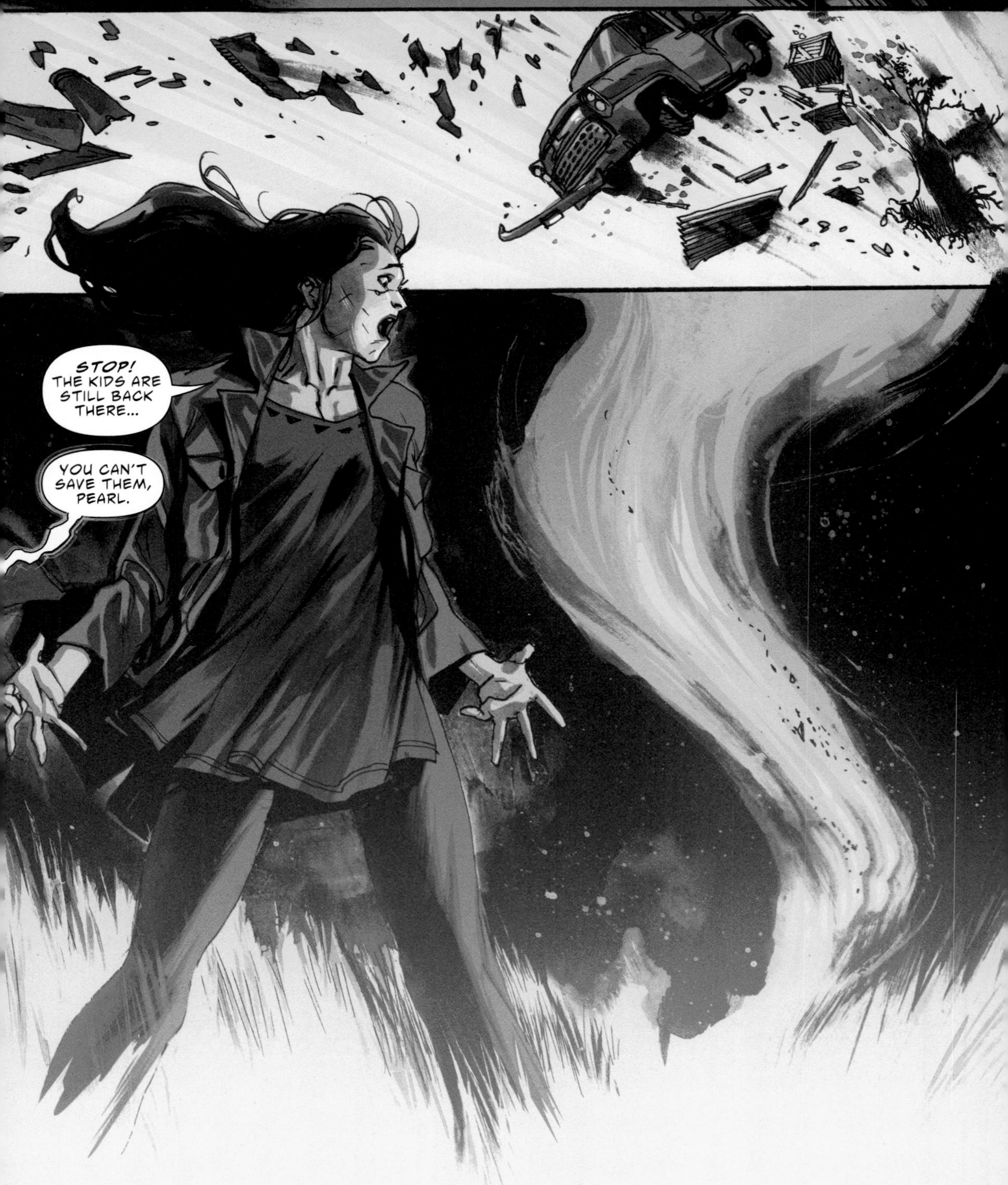
STOP! THE KIDS ARE STILL BACK THERE...
YOU CAN'T SAVE THEM, PEARL.

AMERICAN VAMPIRE SECOND CYCLE **PART FOUR**

WRITER **SCOTT SNYDER** ARTIST **RAFAEL ALBUQUERQUE**
COLORS **DAVE McCAIG** LETTERS **STEVE WANDS**
COVER BY **RAFAEL ALBUQUERQUE**

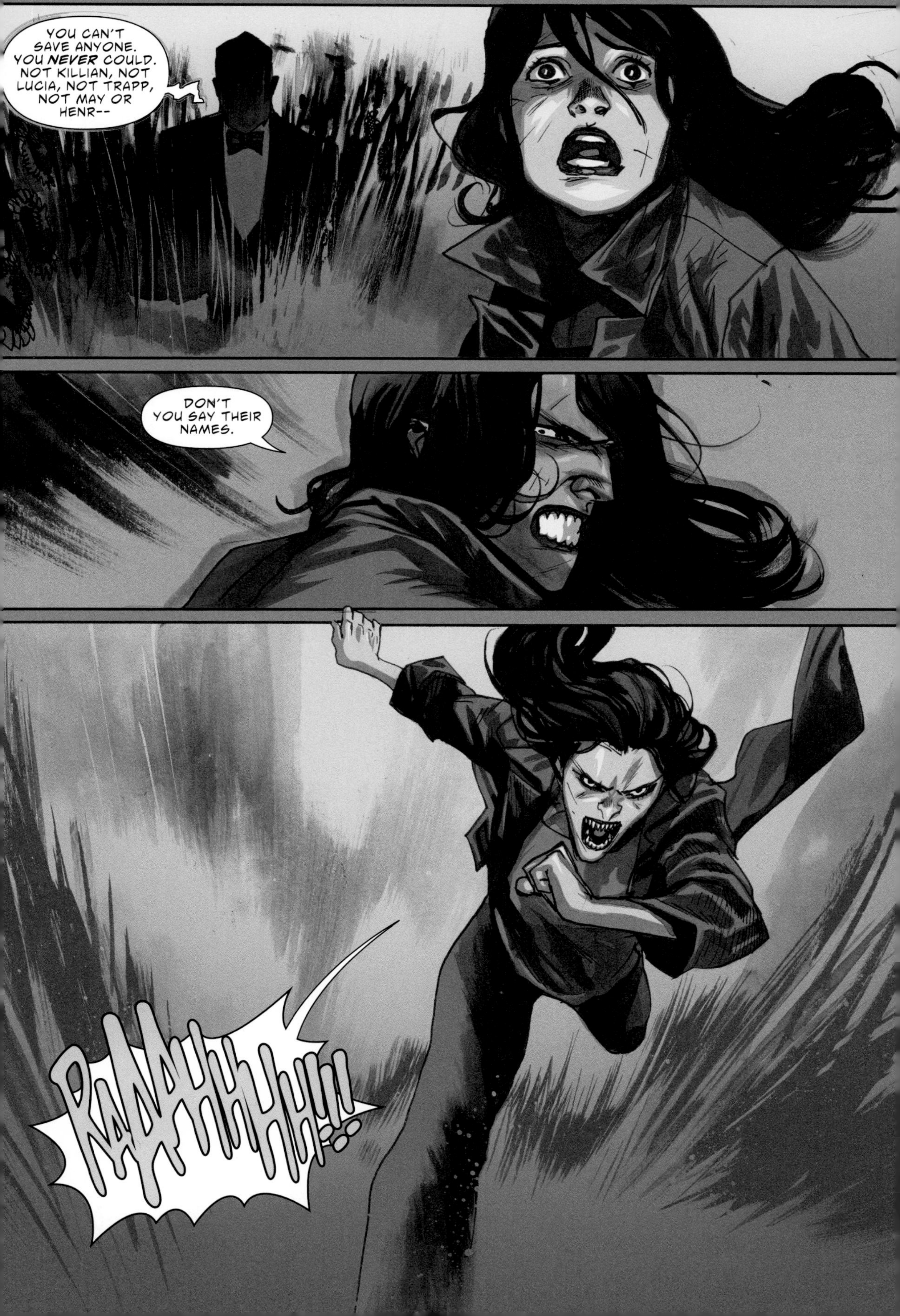

YOU CAN'T SAVE ANYONE. YOU NEVER COULD. NOT KILLIAN, NOT LUCIA, NOT TRAPP, NOT MAY OR HENR--
DON'T YOU SAY THEIR NAMES.
RAAAHHHHH!!!

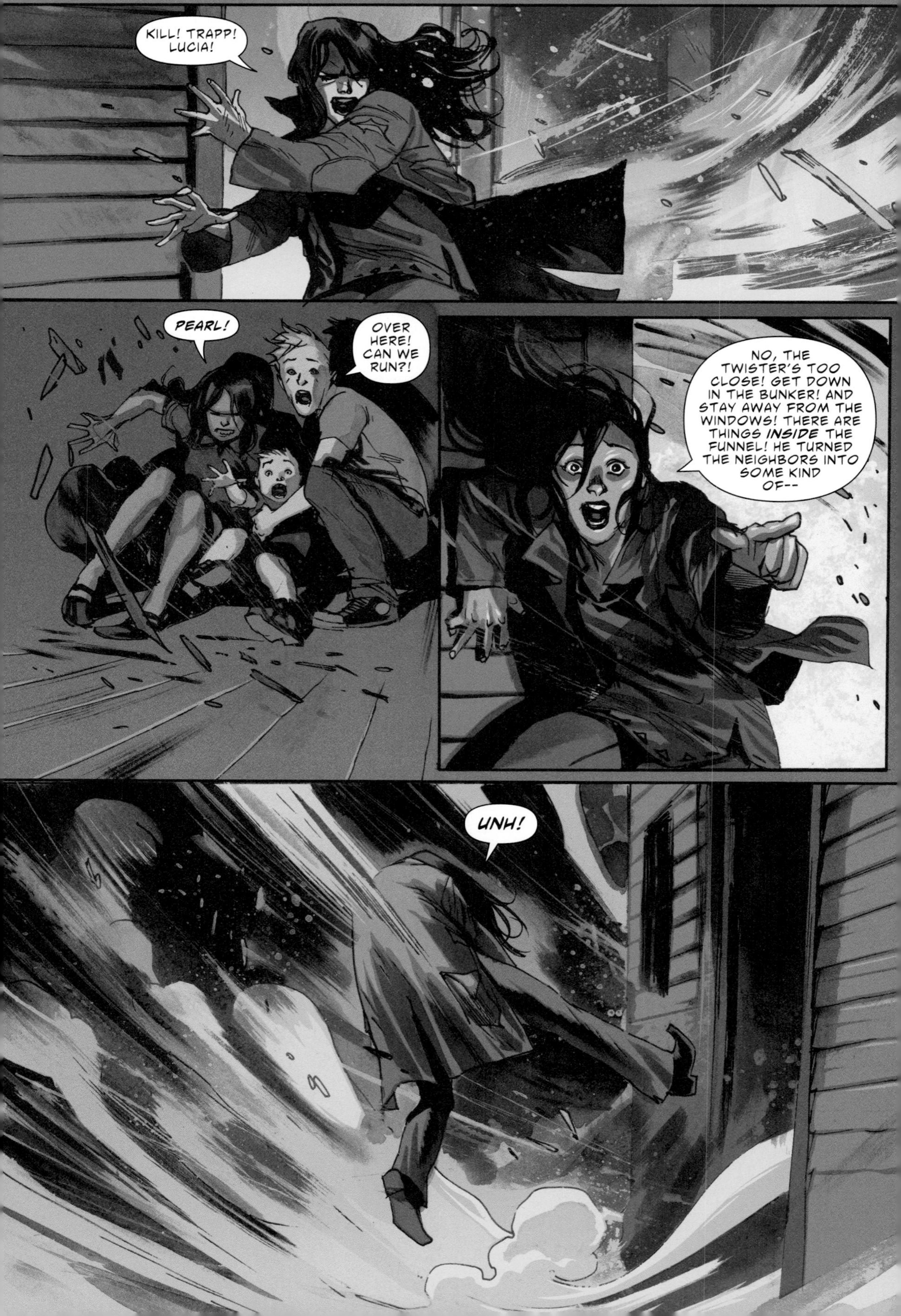
KILL! TRAPP! LUCIA!
PEARL!
OVER HERE! CAN WE RUN?!
NO, THE TWISTER'S TOO CLOSE! GET DOWN IN THE BUNKER! AND STAY AWAY FROM THE WINDOWS! THERE ARE THINGS *INSIDE* THE FUNNEL! HE TURNED THE NEIGHBORS INTO SOME KIND OF--
UNH!

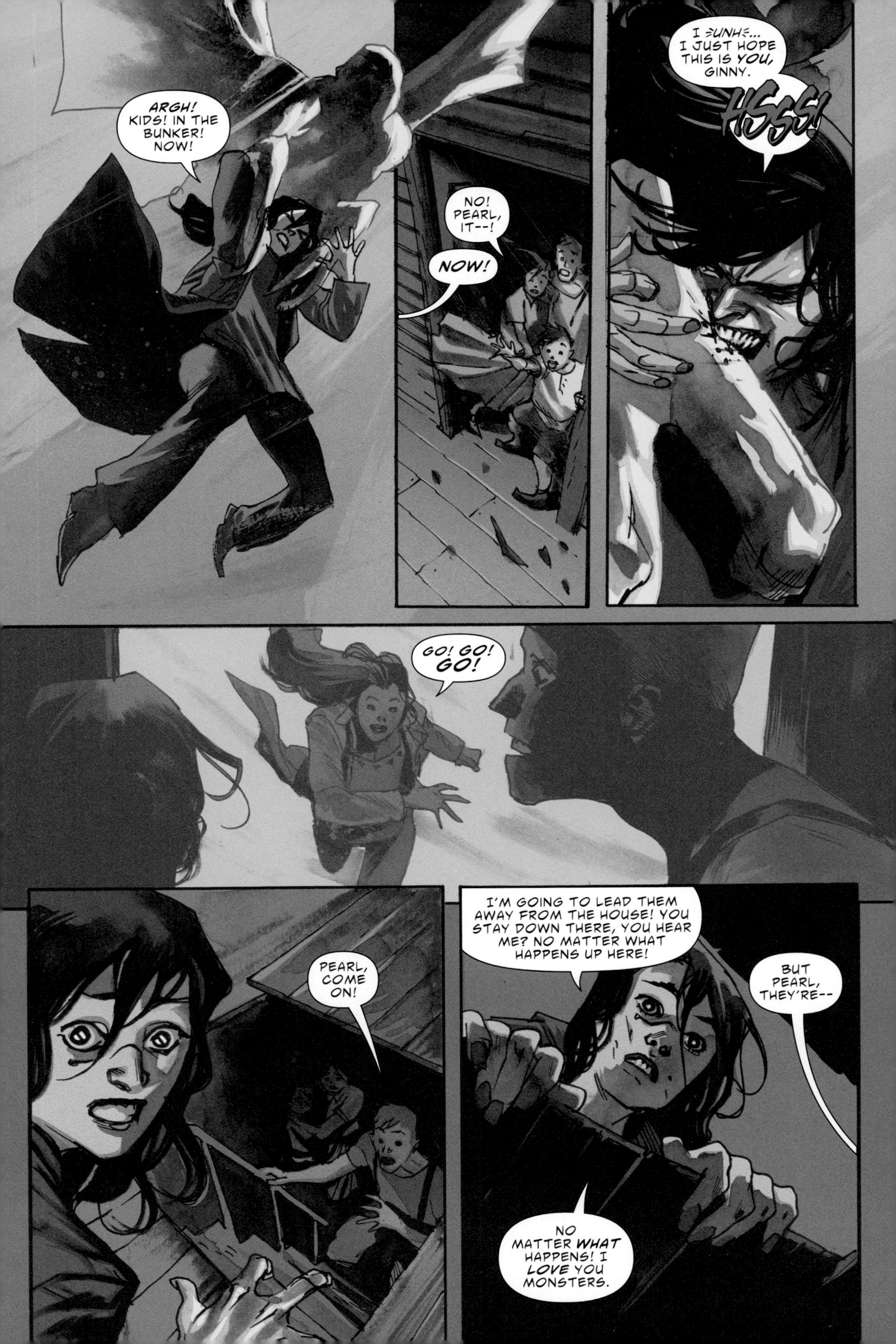
ARGH! KIDS! IN THE BUNKER! NOW!
NO! PEARL, IT--!
NOW!
I -UNH-... I JUST HOPE THIS IS YOU, GINNY.
HSSS!
GO! GO! GO!
PEARL, COME ON!
I'M GOING TO LEAD THEM AWAY FROM THE HOUSE! YOU STAY DOWN THERE, YOU HEAR ME? NO MATTER WHAT HAPPENS UP HERE!
BUT PEARL, THEY'RE--
NO MATTER WHAT HAPPENS! I LOVE YOU MONSTERS.

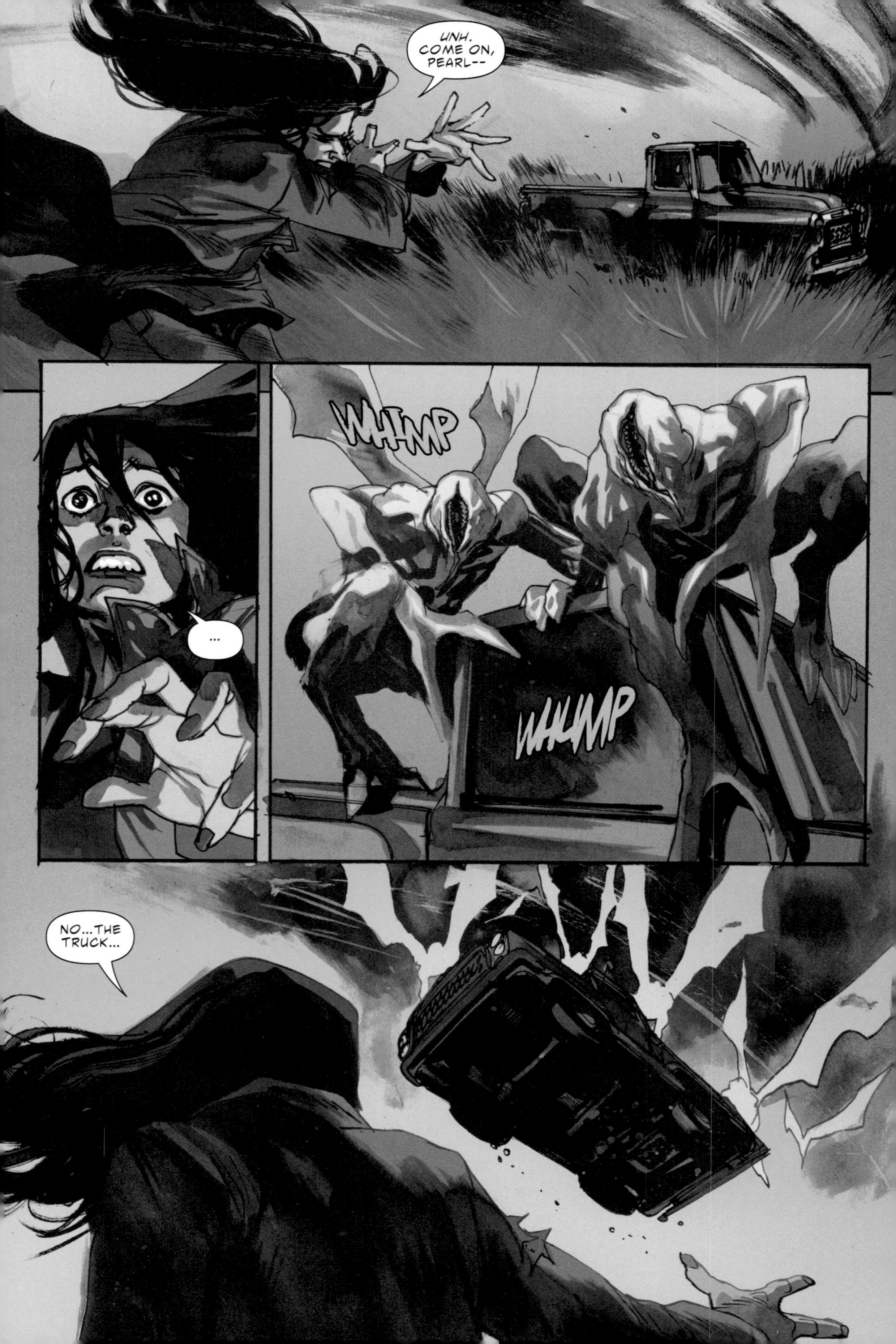
UNH. COME ON, PEARL--
...
WHUMP
WHUMP
NO...THE TRUCK...

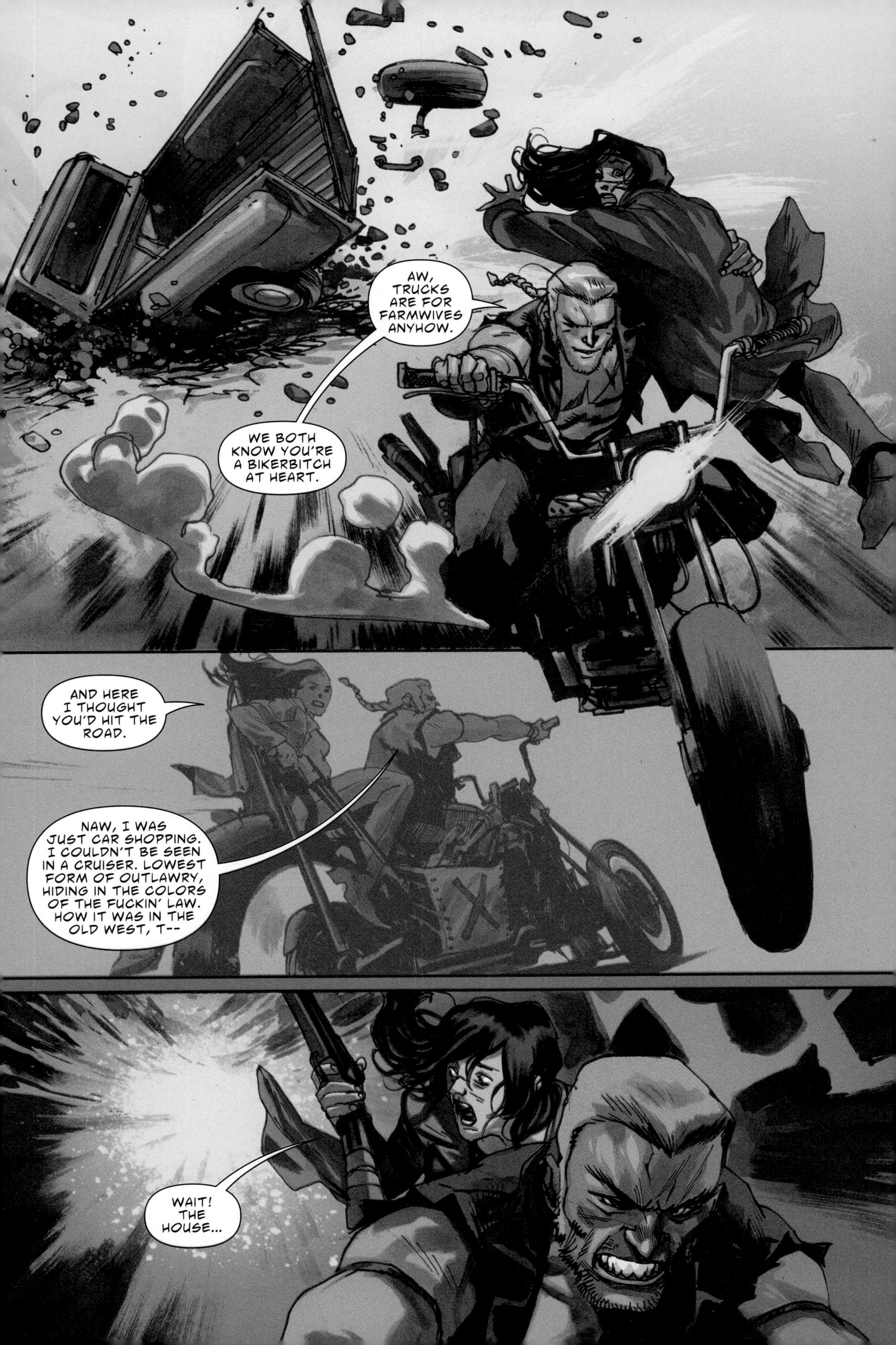
AW, TRUCKS ARE FOR FARMWIVES ANYHOW.
WE BOTH KNOW YOU'RE A BIKERBITCH AT HEART.
AND HERE I THOUGHT YOU'D HIT THE ROAD.
NAW, I WAS JUST CAR SHOPPING. I COULDN'T BE SEEN IN A CRUISER. LOWEST FORM OF OUTLAWRY, HIDING IN THE COLORS OF THE FUCKIN' LAW. HOW IT WAS IN THE OLD WEST, T--
WAIT! THE HOUSE...

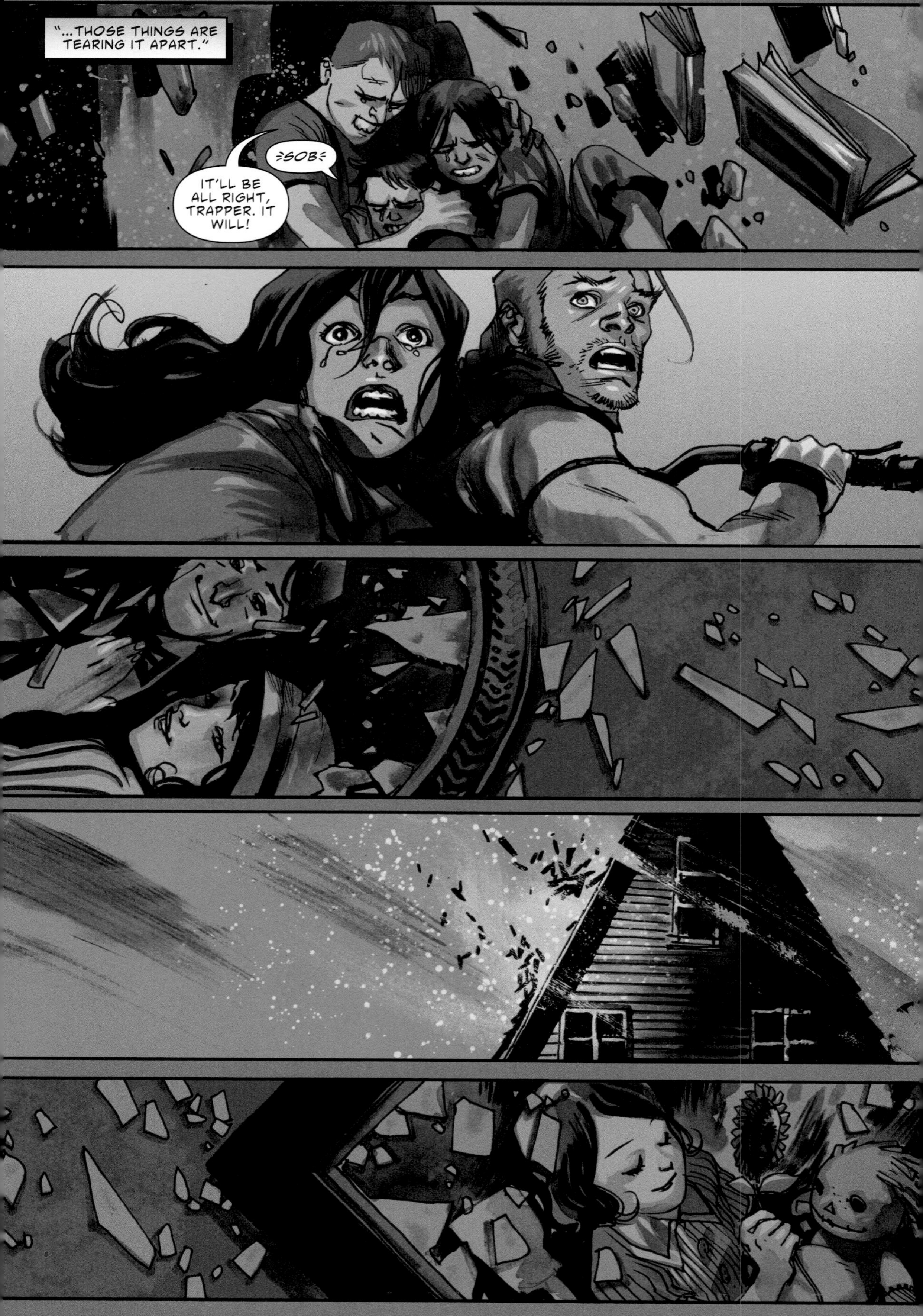
"...THOSE THINGS ARE TEARING IT APART."
SOB
IT'LL BE ALL RIGHT, TRAPPER. IT WILL!

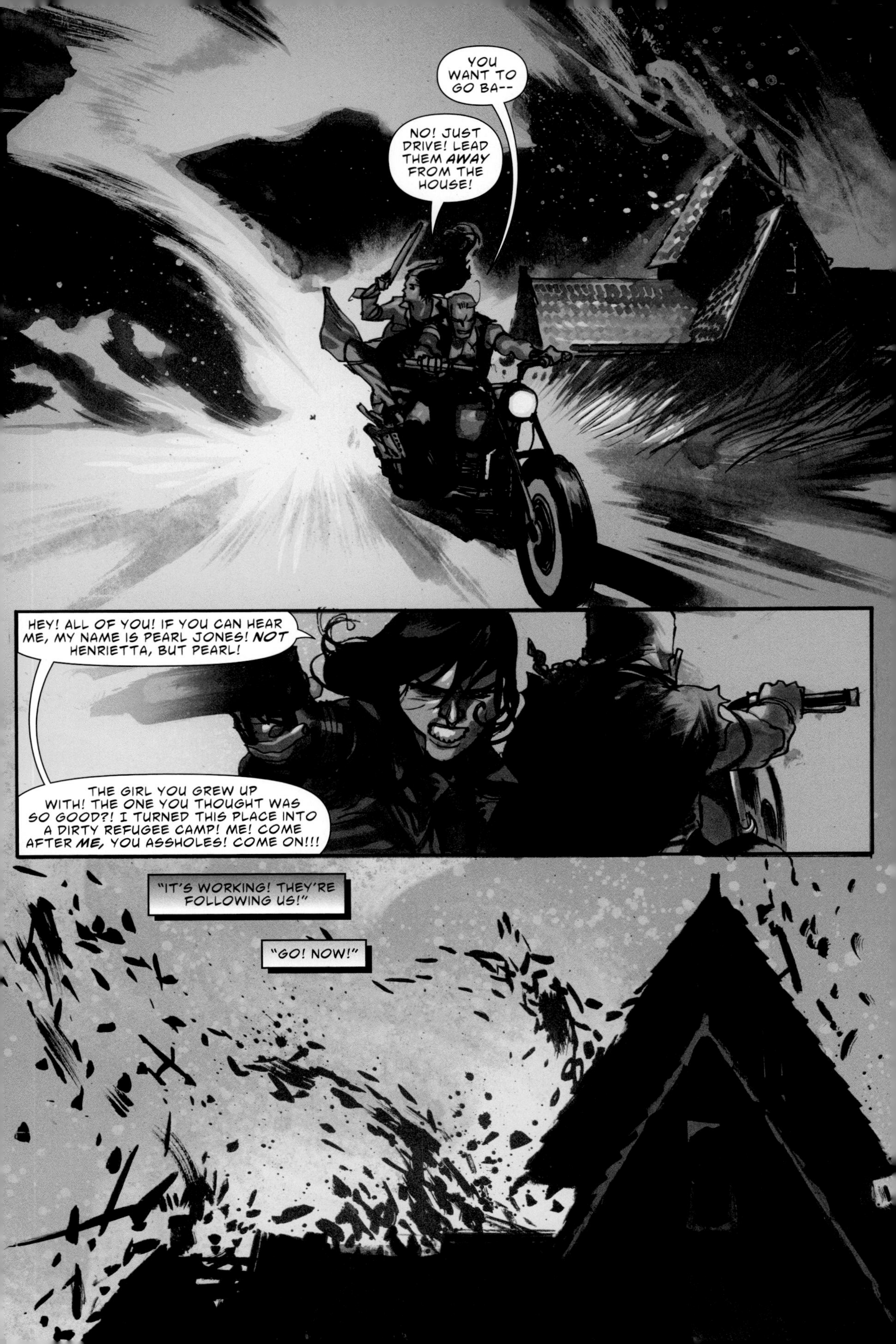
YOU WANT TO GO BA--
NO! JUST DRIVE! LEAD THEM *AWAY* FROM THE HOUSE!
HEY! ALL OF YOU! IF YOU CAN HEAR ME, MY NAME IS PEARL JONES! *NOT* HENRIETTA, BUT PEARL!
THE GIRL YOU GREW UP WITH! THE ONE YOU THOUGHT WAS SO GOOD?! I TURNED THIS PLACE INTO A DIRTY REFUGEE CAMP! ME! COME AFTER *ME,* YOU ASSHOLES! COME ON!!!
"IT'S WORKING! THEY'RE FOLLOWING US!"
"GO! NOW!"

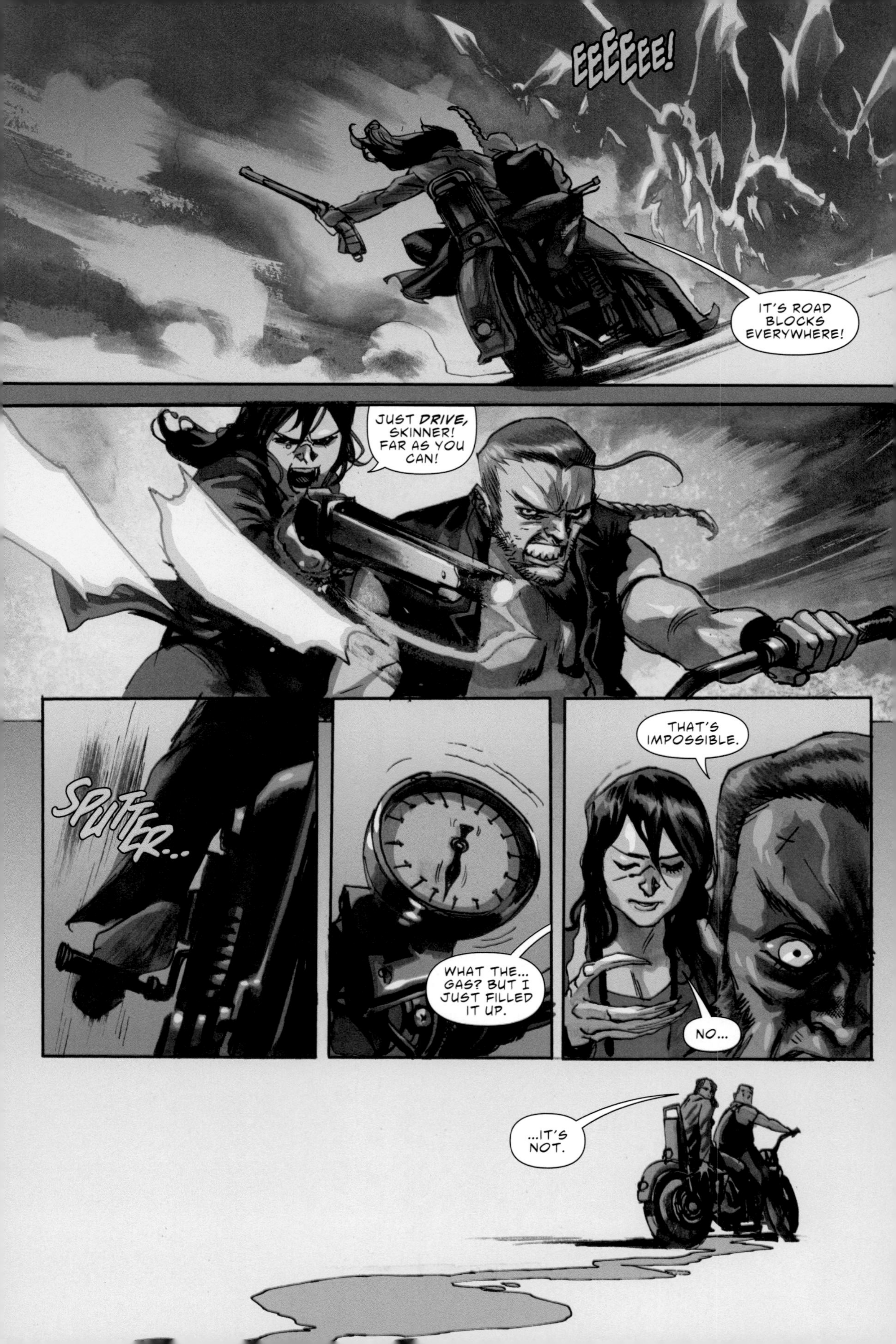
EEEEeee!
IT'S ROAD BLOCKS EVERYWHERE!
JUST DRIVE, SKINNER! FAR AS YOU CAN!
SPUTTER...
WHAT THE... GAS? BUT I JUST FILLED IT UP.
THAT'S IMPOSSIBLE.
NO...
...IT'S NOT.

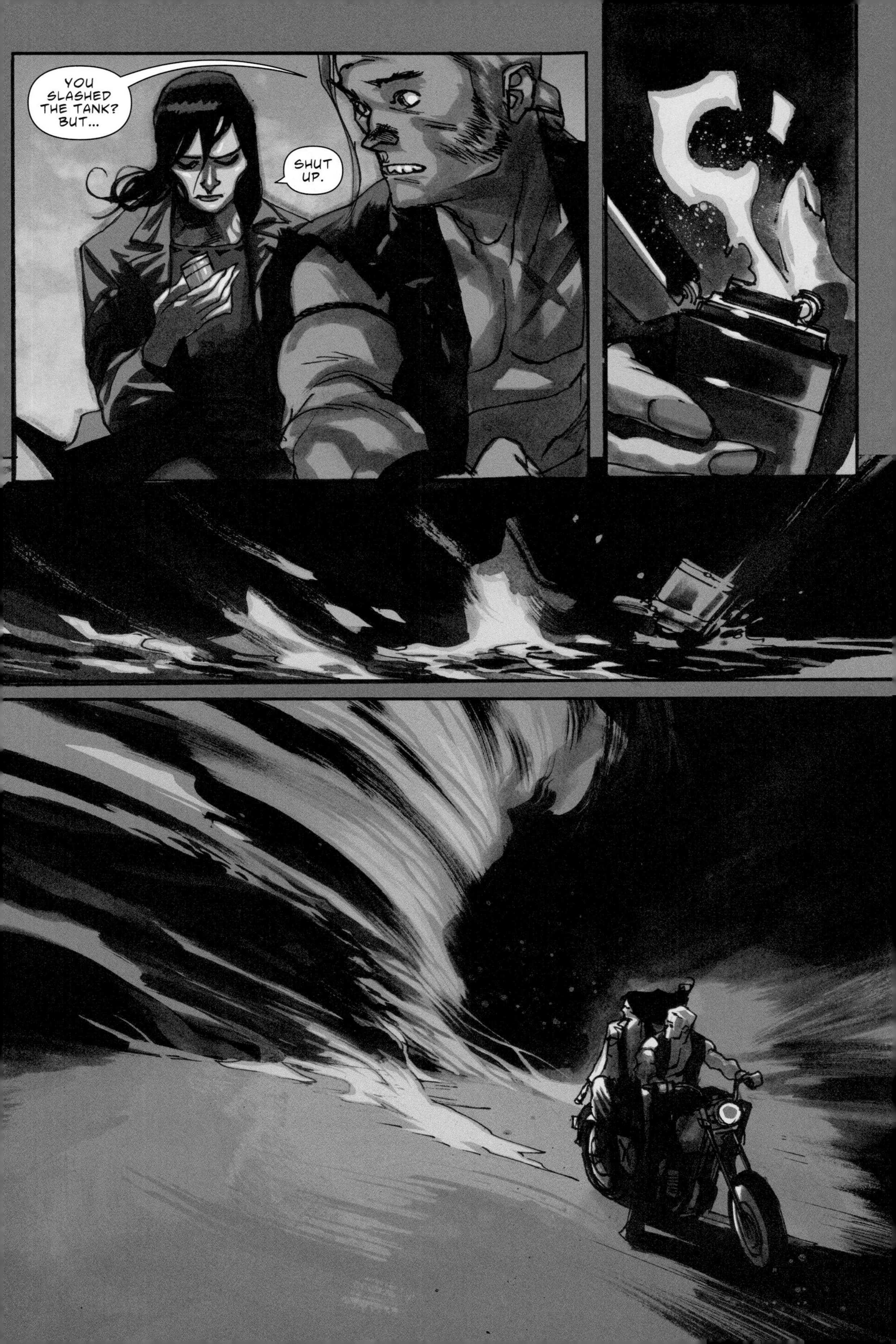
YOU SLASHED THE TANK? BUT...
SHUT UP.

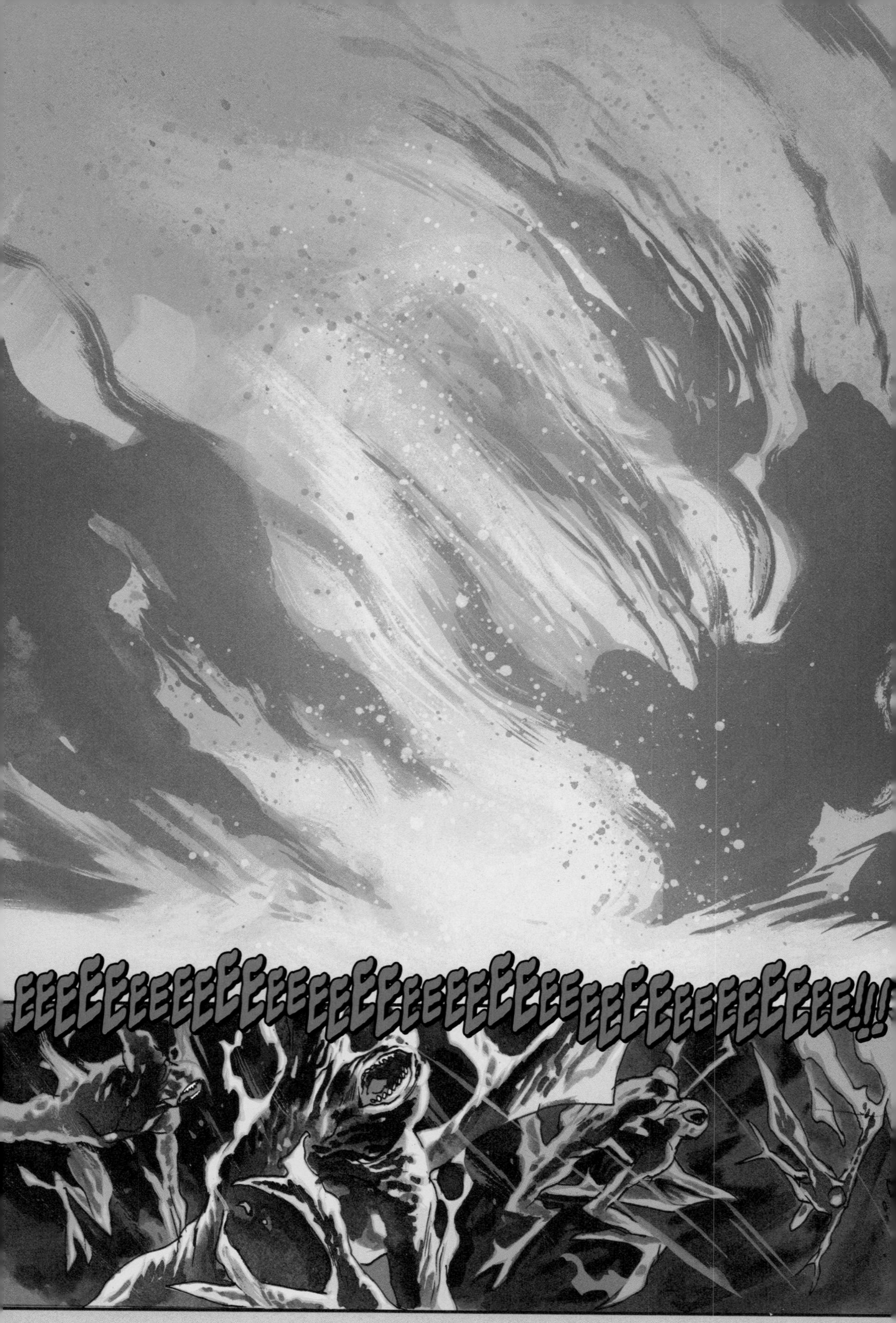

EEEEEEEEEEEEEEEEEEEEEEEEEEEEEEEEEEEEEEEEEE!!!

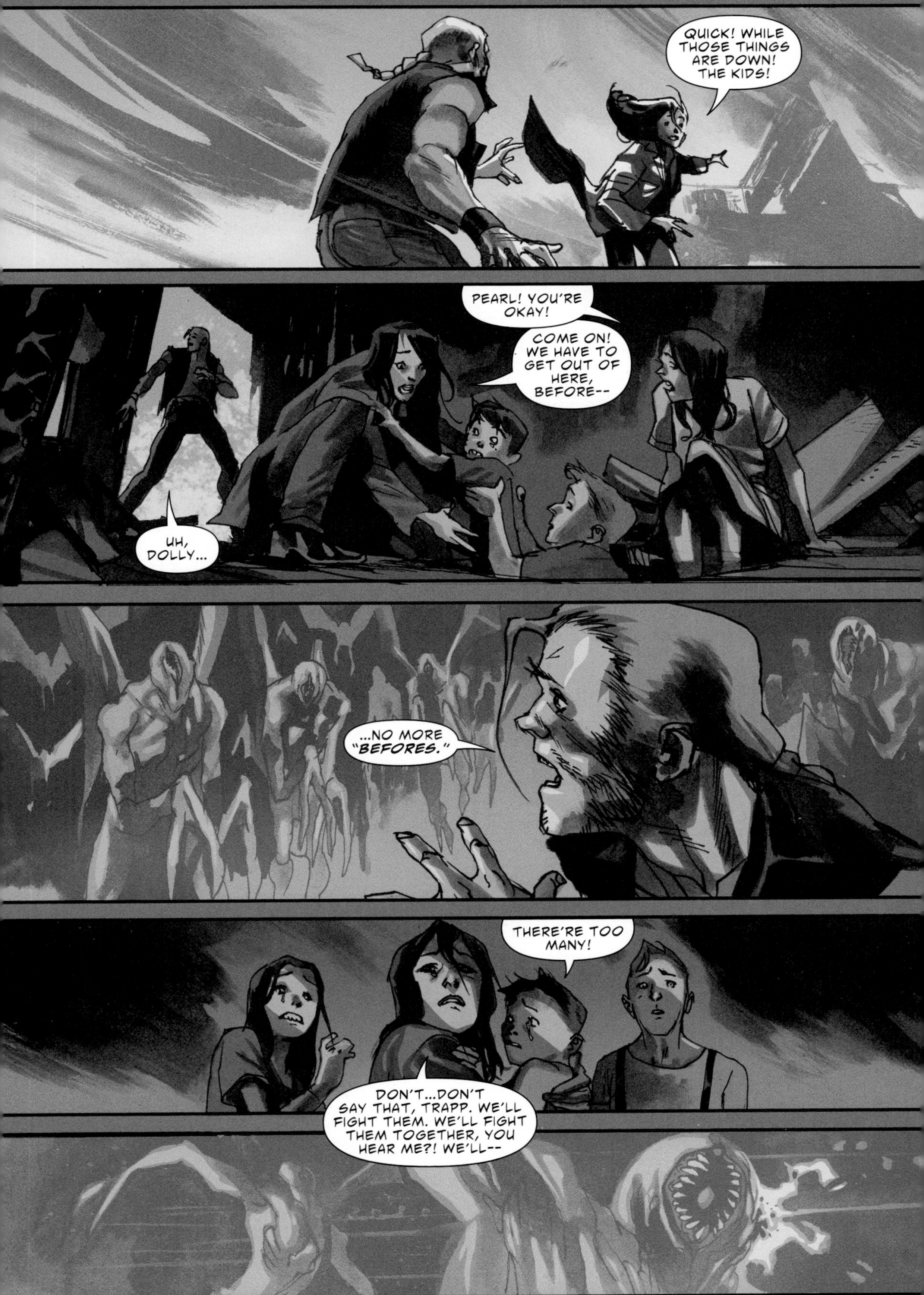
QUICK! WHILE THOSE THINGS ARE DOWN! THE KIDS!
PEARL! YOU'RE OKAY!
COME ON! WE HAVE TO GET OUT OF HERE, BEFORE--
UH, DOLLY...
...NO MORE "BEFORES."
THERE'RE TOO MANY!
DON'T...DON'T SAY THAT, TRAPP. WE'LL FIGHT THEM. WE'LL FIGHT THEM TOGETHER, YOU HEAR ME?! WE'LL--

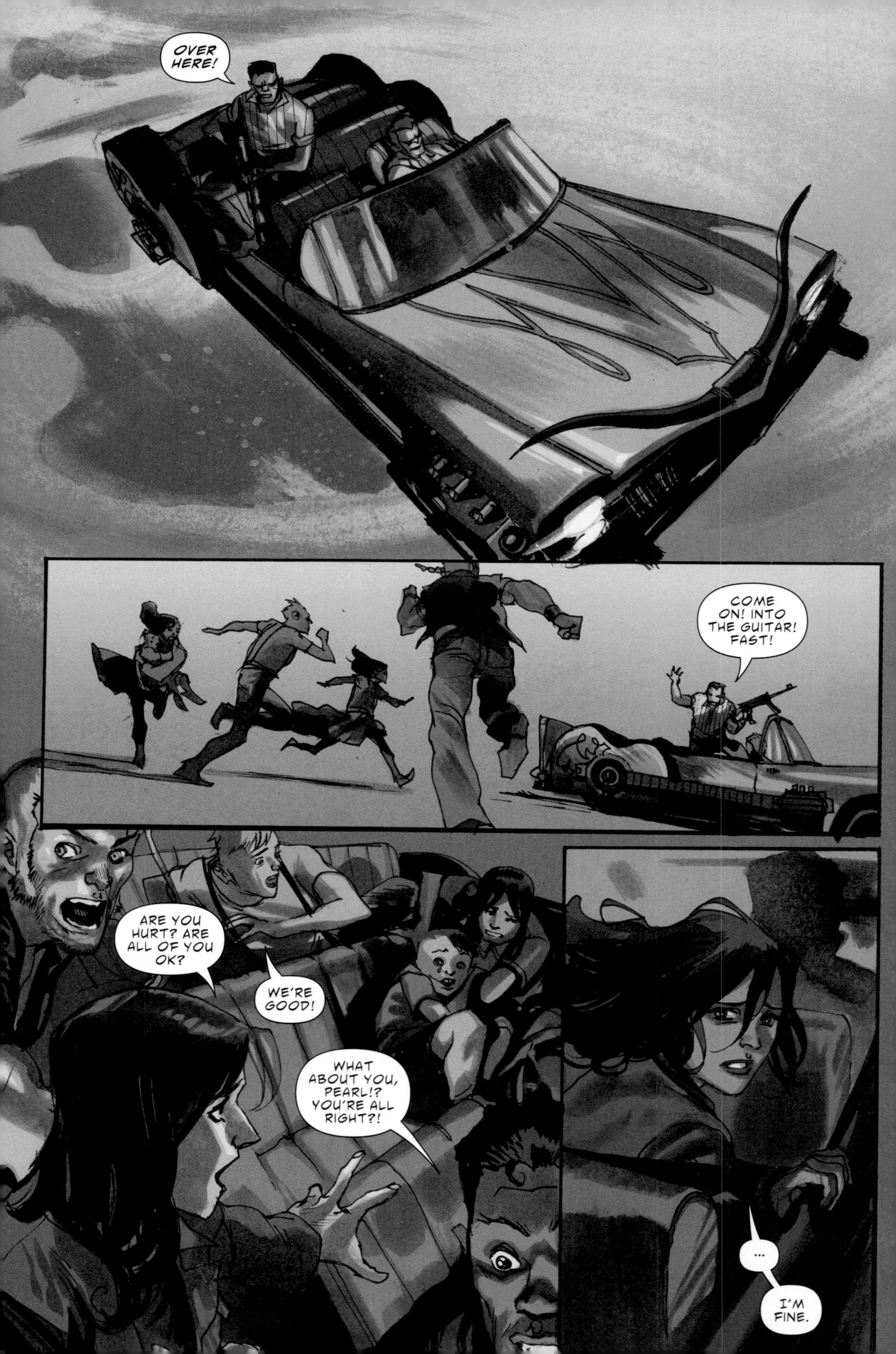
OVER HERE!
COME ON! INTO THE GUITAR! FAST!
ARE YOU HURT? ARE ALL OF YOU OK?
WE'RE GOOD!
WHAT ABOUT YOU, PEARL!? YOU'RE ALL RIGHT?!
...
I'M FINE.

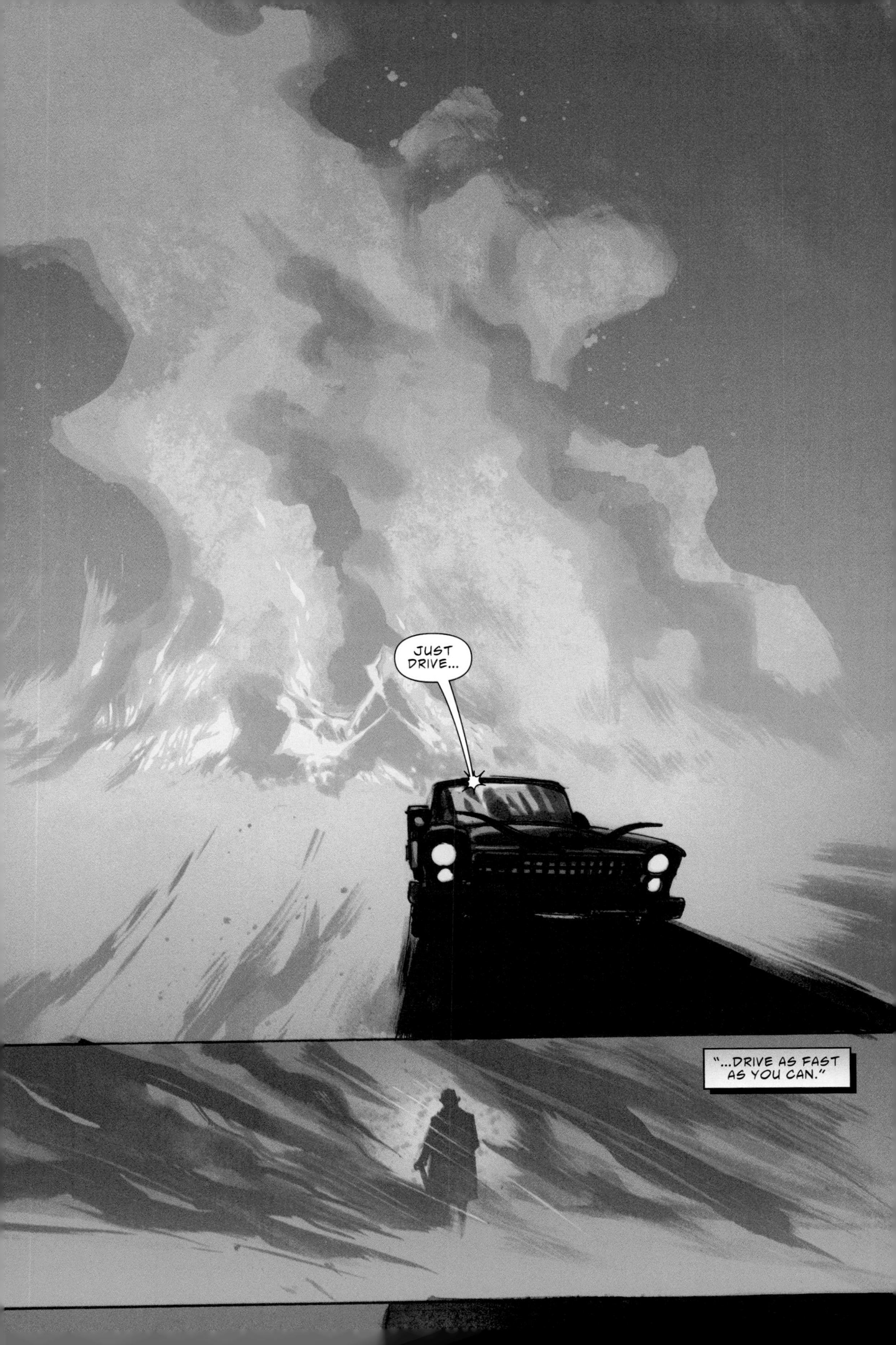
JUST DRIVE...
"...DRIVE AS FAST AS YOU CAN."

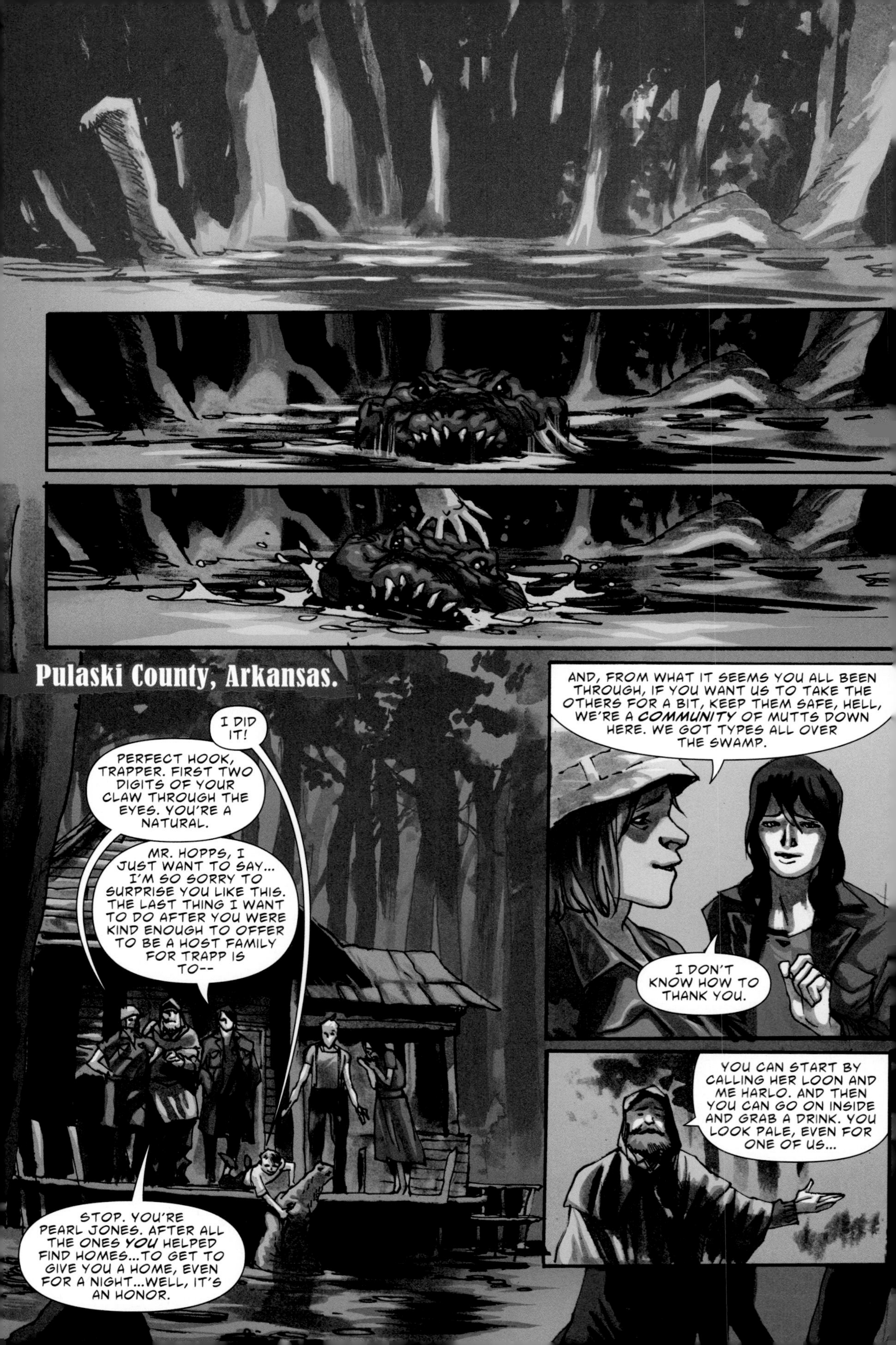
Pulaski County, Arkansas.
I DID IT!
PERFECT HOOK, TRAPPER. FIRST TWO DIGITS OF YOUR CLAW THROUGH THE EYES. YOU'RE A NATURAL.
MR. HOPPS, I JUST WANT TO SAY... I'M SO SORRY TO SURPRISE YOU LIKE THIS. THE LAST THING I WANT TO DO AFTER YOU WERE KIND ENOUGH TO OFFER TO BE A HOST FAMILY FOR TRAPP IS TO--
STOP. YOU'RE PEARL JONES. AFTER ALL THE ONES *YOU* HELPED FIND HOMES...TO GET TO GIVE YOU A HOME, EVEN FOR A NIGHT...WELL, IT'S AN HONOR.
AND, FROM WHAT IT SEEMS YOU ALL BEEN THROUGH, IF YOU WANT US TO TAKE THE OTHERS FOR A BIT, KEEP THEM SAFE, HELL, WE'RE A ***COMMUNITY*** OF MUTTS DOWN HERE. WE GOT TYPES ALL OVER THE SWAMP.
I DON'T KNOW HOW TO THANK YOU.
YOU CAN START BY CALLING HER LOON AND ME HARLO. AND THEN YOU CAN GO ON INSIDE AND GRAB A DRINK. YOU LOOK PALE, EVEN FOR ONE OF US...

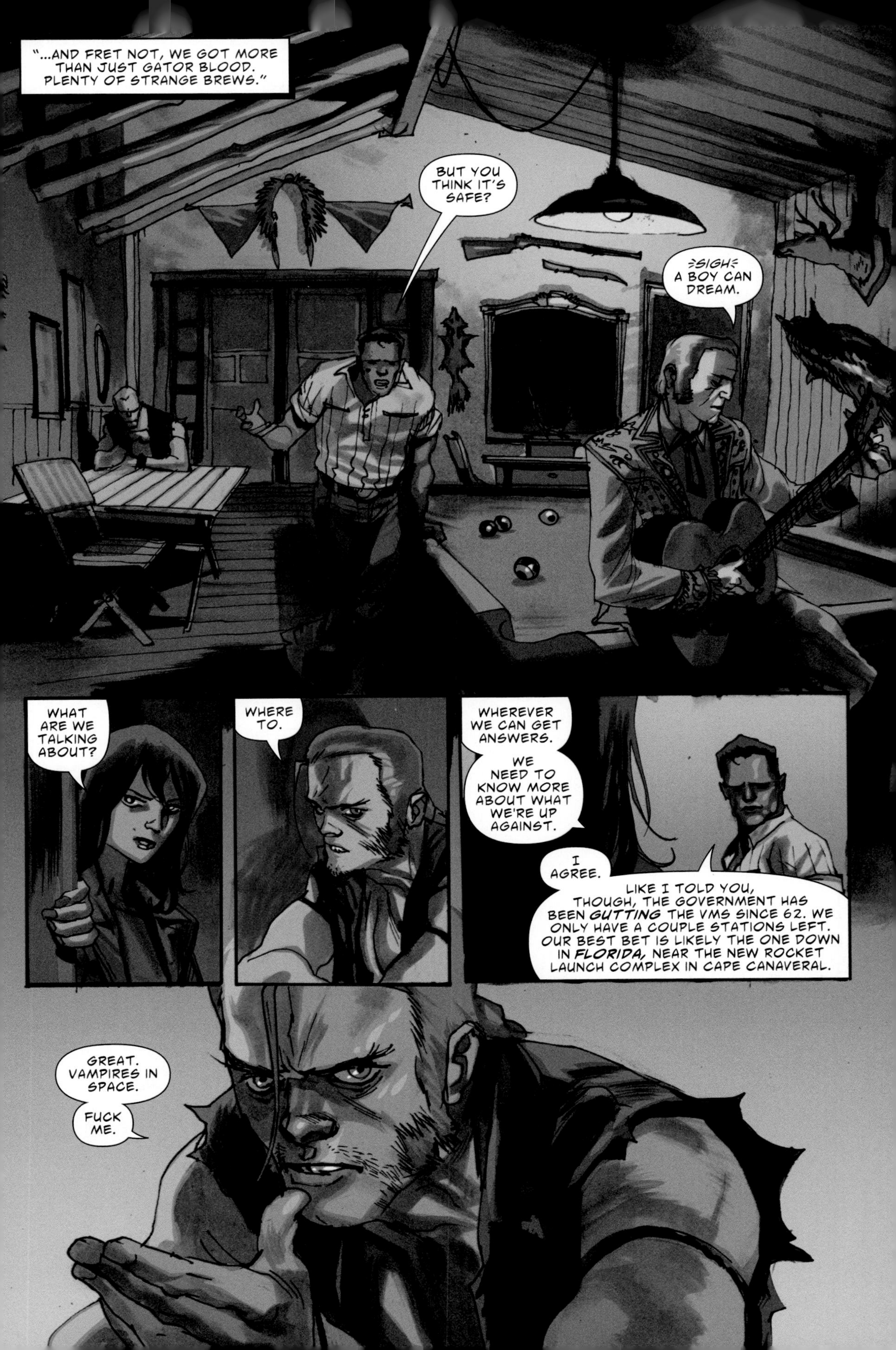
"...AND FRET NOT, WE GOT MORE THAN JUST GATOR BLOOD. PLENTY OF STRANGE BREWS."
BUT YOU THINK IT'S SAFE?
=SIGH= A BOY CAN DREAM.
WHAT ARE WE TALKING ABOUT?
WHERE TO.
WHEREVER WE CAN GET ANSWERS.
WE NEED TO KNOW MORE ABOUT WHAT WE'RE UP AGAINST.
I AGREE.
LIKE I TOLD YOU, THOUGH, THE GOVERNMENT HAS BEEN GUTTING THE VMS SINCE 62. WE ONLY HAVE A COUPLE STATIONS LEFT. OUR BEST BET IS LIKELY THE ONE DOWN IN FLORIDA, NEAR THE NEW ROCKET LAUNCH COMPLEX IN CAPE CANAVERAL.
GREAT. VAMPIRES IN SPACE.
FUCK ME.

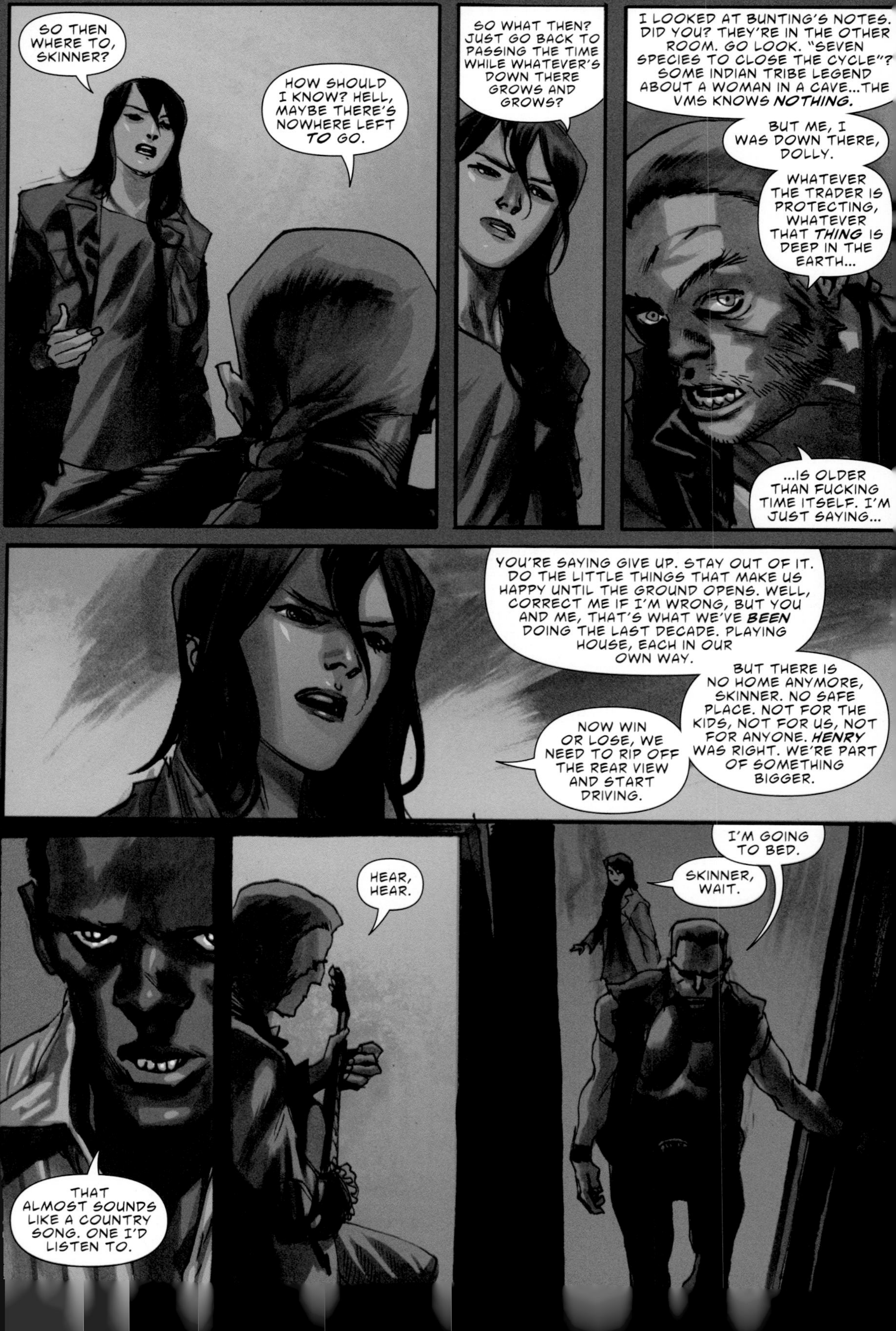
SO THEN WHERE TO, SKINNER?
HOW SHOULD I KNOW? HELL, MAYBE THERE'S NOWHERE LEFT TO GO.
SO WHAT THEN? JUST GO BACK TO PASSING THE TIME WHILE WHATEVER'S DOWN THERE GROWS AND GROWS?
I LOOKED AT BUNTING'S NOTES. DID YOU? THEY'RE IN THE OTHER ROOM. GO LOOK. "SEVEN SPECIES TO CLOSE THE CYCLE"? SOME INDIAN TRIBE LEGEND ABOUT A WOMAN IN A CAVE...THE VMS KNOWS NOTHING.
BUT ME, I WAS DOWN THERE, DOLLY.
WHATEVER THE TRADER IS PROTECTING, WHATEVER THAT THING IS DEEP IN THE EARTH...
...IS OLDER THAN FUCKING TIME ITSELF. I'M JUST SAYING...
YOU'RE SAYING GIVE UP. STAY OUT OF IT. DO THE LITTLE THINGS THAT MAKE US HAPPY UNTIL THE GROUND OPENS. WELL, CORRECT ME IF I'M WRONG, BUT YOU AND ME, THAT'S WHAT WE'VE BEEN DOING THE LAST DECADE. PLAYING HOUSE, EACH IN OUR OWN WAY.
BUT THERE IS NO HOME ANYMORE, SKINNER. NO SAFE PLACE. NOT FOR THE KIDS, NOT FOR US, NOT FOR ANYONE. HENRY WAS RIGHT. WE'RE PART OF SOMETHING BIGGER.
NOW WIN OR LOSE, WE NEED TO RIP OFF THE REAR VIEW AND START DRIVING.
THAT ALMOST SOUNDS LIKE A COUNTRY SONG. ONE I'D LISTEN TO.
HEAR, HEAR.
I'M GOING TO BED.
SKINNER, WAIT.

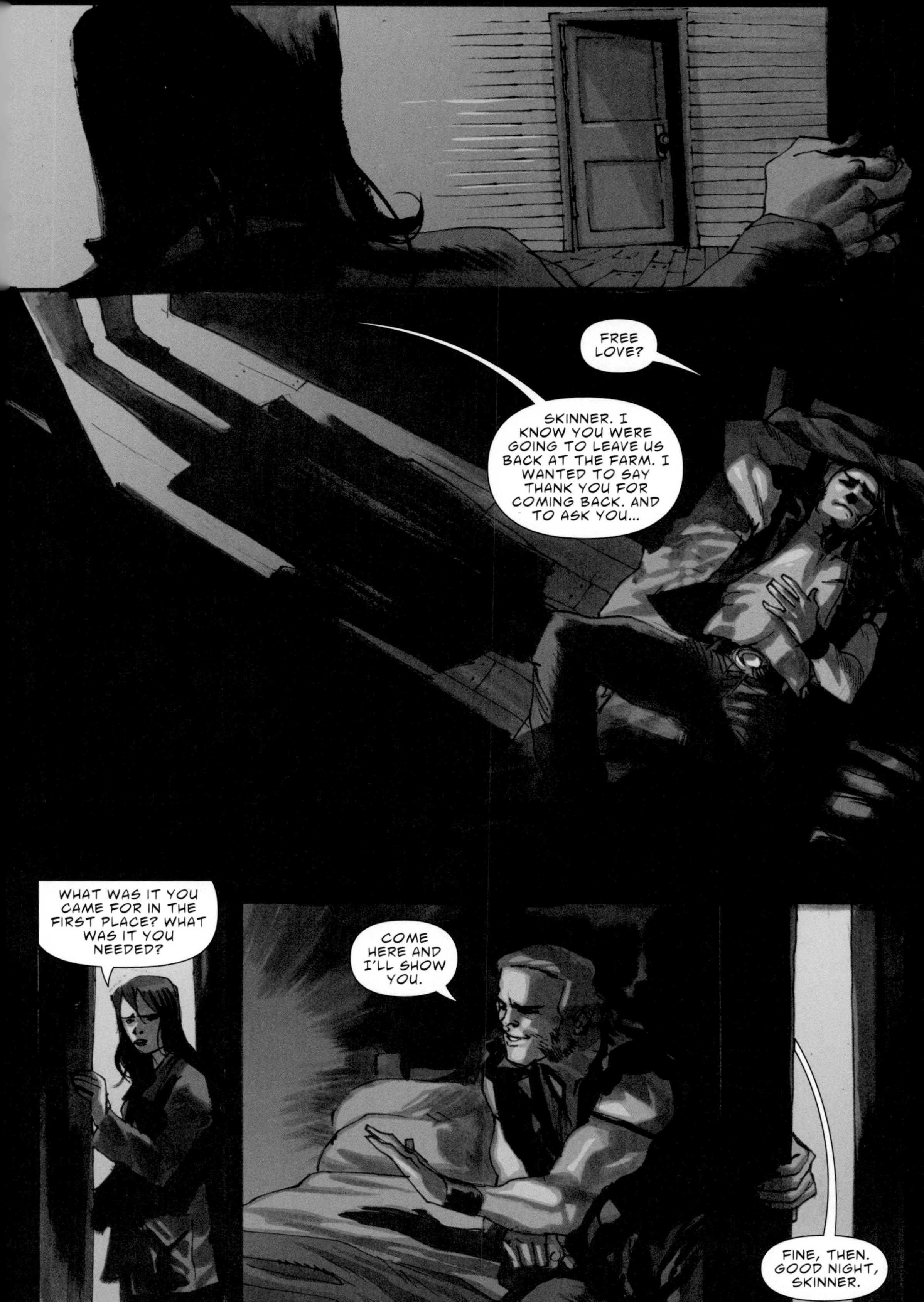
FREE LOVE?
SKINNER. I KNOW YOU WERE GOING TO LEAVE US BACK AT THE FARM. I WANTED TO SAY THANK YOU FOR COMING BACK. AND TO ASK YOU...
WHAT WAS IT YOU CAME FOR IN THE FIRST PLACE? WHAT WAS IT YOU NEEDED?
COME HERE AND I'LL SHOW YOU.
FINE, THEN. GOOD NIGHT, SKINNER.

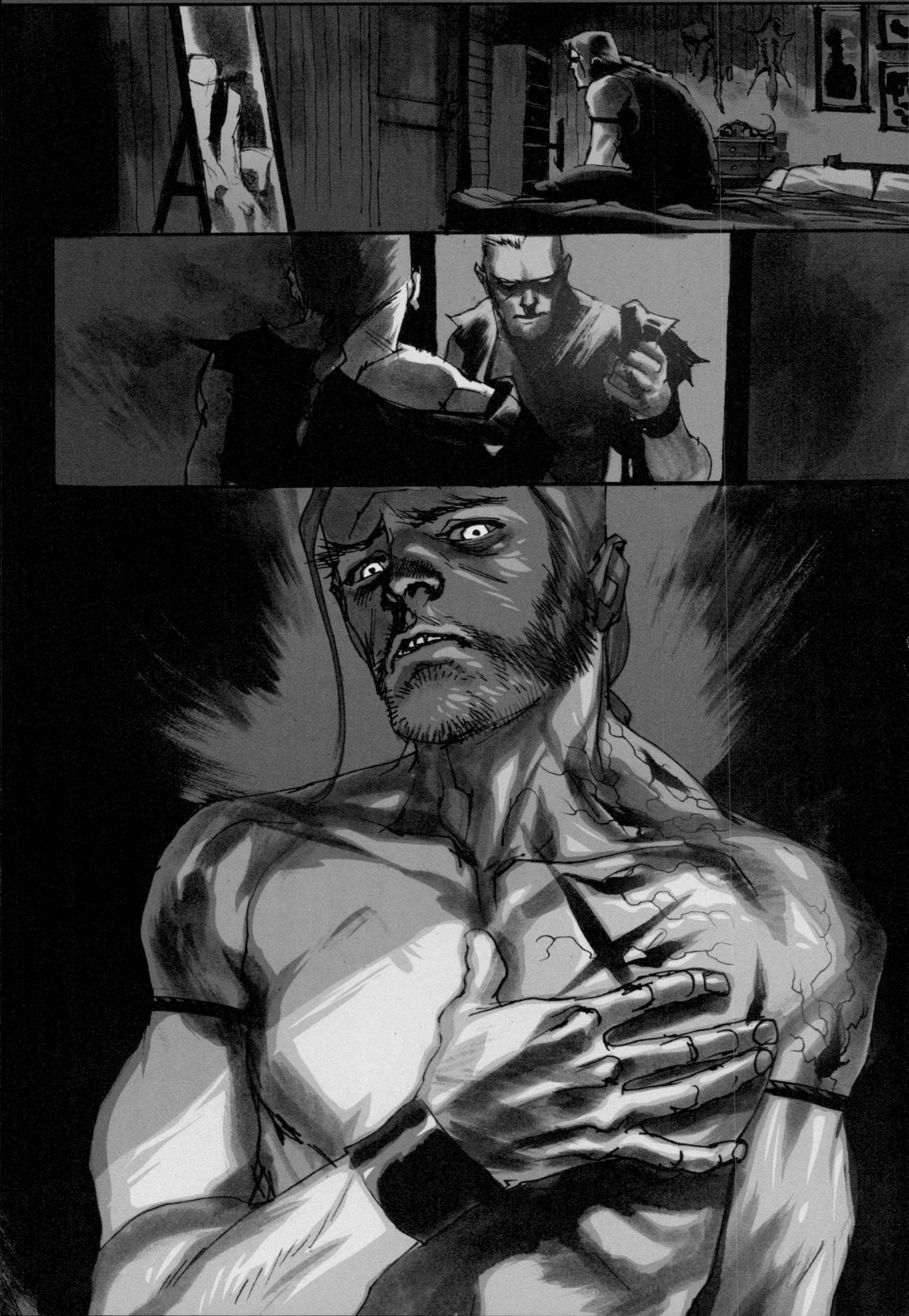

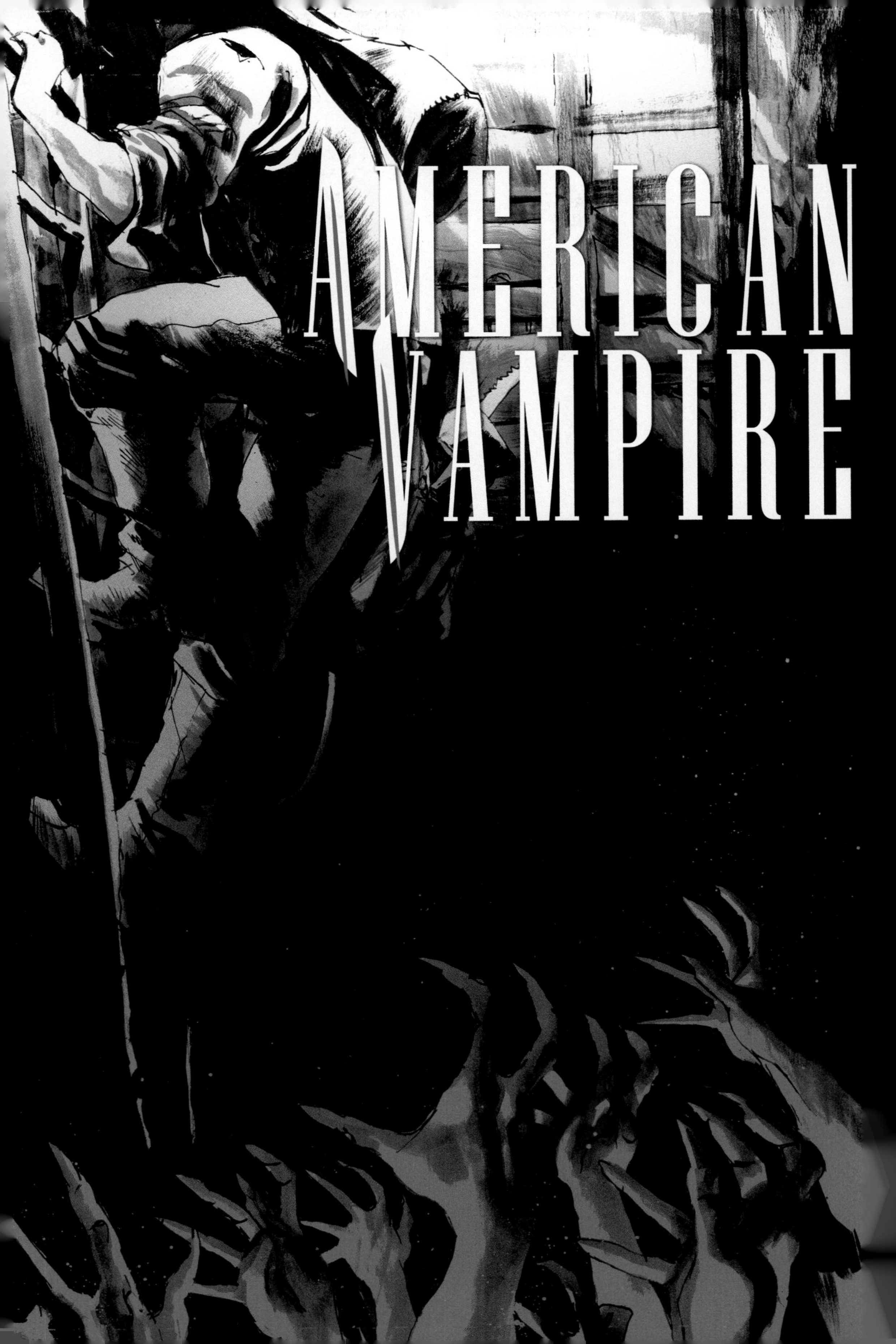
AMERICAN
VAMPIRE

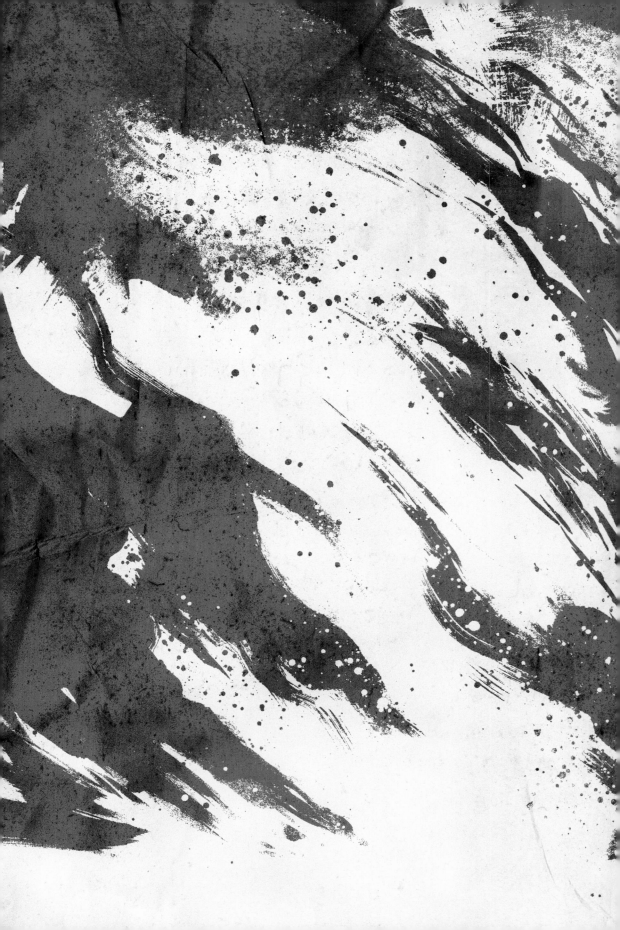

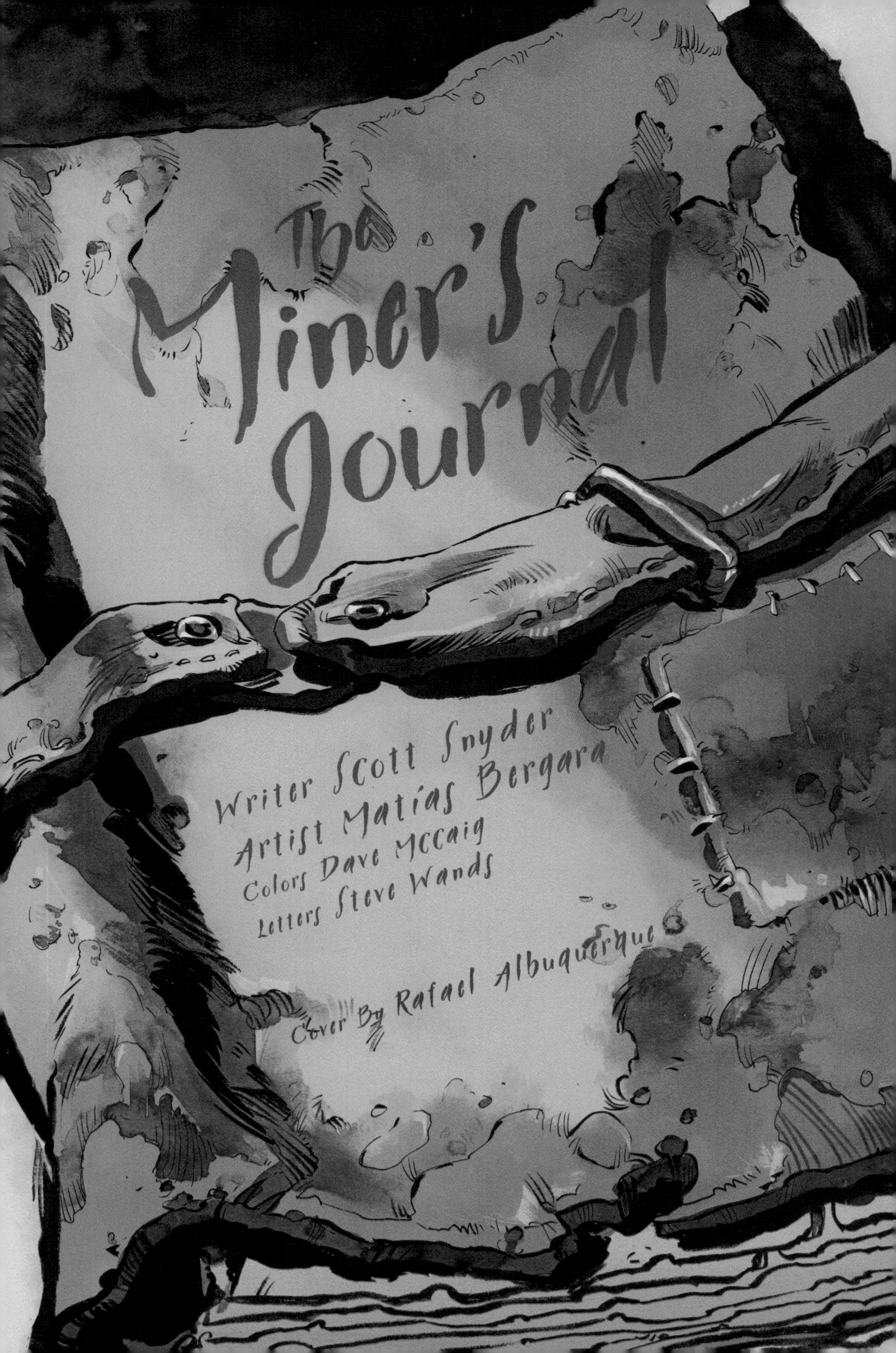
The Miner's Journal
Writer Scott Snyder
Artist Matías Bergara
Colors Dave McCaig
Letters Steve Wands
Cover By Rafael Albuquerque

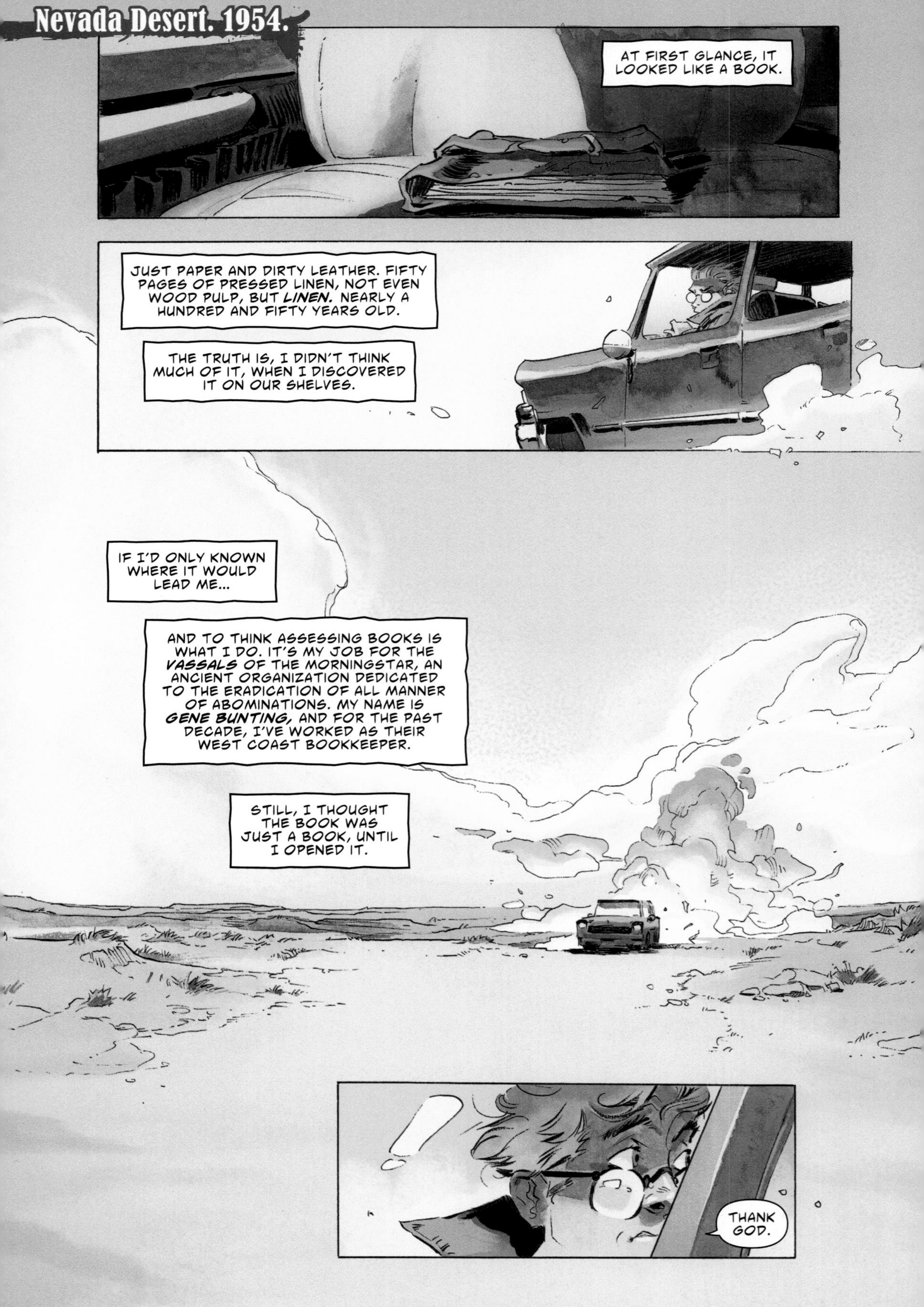
Nevada Desert. 1954.
AT FIRST GLANCE, IT LOOKED LIKE A BOOK.
JUST PAPER AND DIRTY LEATHER. FIFTY PAGES OF PRESSED LINEN, NOT EVEN WOOD PULP, BUT LINEN. NEARLY A HUNDRED AND FIFTY YEARS OLD.
THE TRUTH IS, I DIDN'T THINK MUCH OF IT, WHEN I DISCOVERED IT ON OUR SHELVES.
IF I'D ONLY KNOWN WHERE IT WOULD LEAD ME...
AND TO THINK ASSESSING BOOKS IS WHAT I DO. IT'S MY JOB FOR THE VASSALS OF THE MORNINGSTAR, AN ANCIENT ORGANIZATION DEDICATED TO THE ERADICATION OF ALL MANNER OF ABOMINATIONS. MY NAME IS GENE BUNTING, AND FOR THE PAST DECADE, I'VE WORKED AS THEIR WEST COAST BOOKKEEPER.
STILL, I THOUGHT THE BOOK WAS JUST A BOOK, UNTIL I OPENED IT.
THANK GOD.

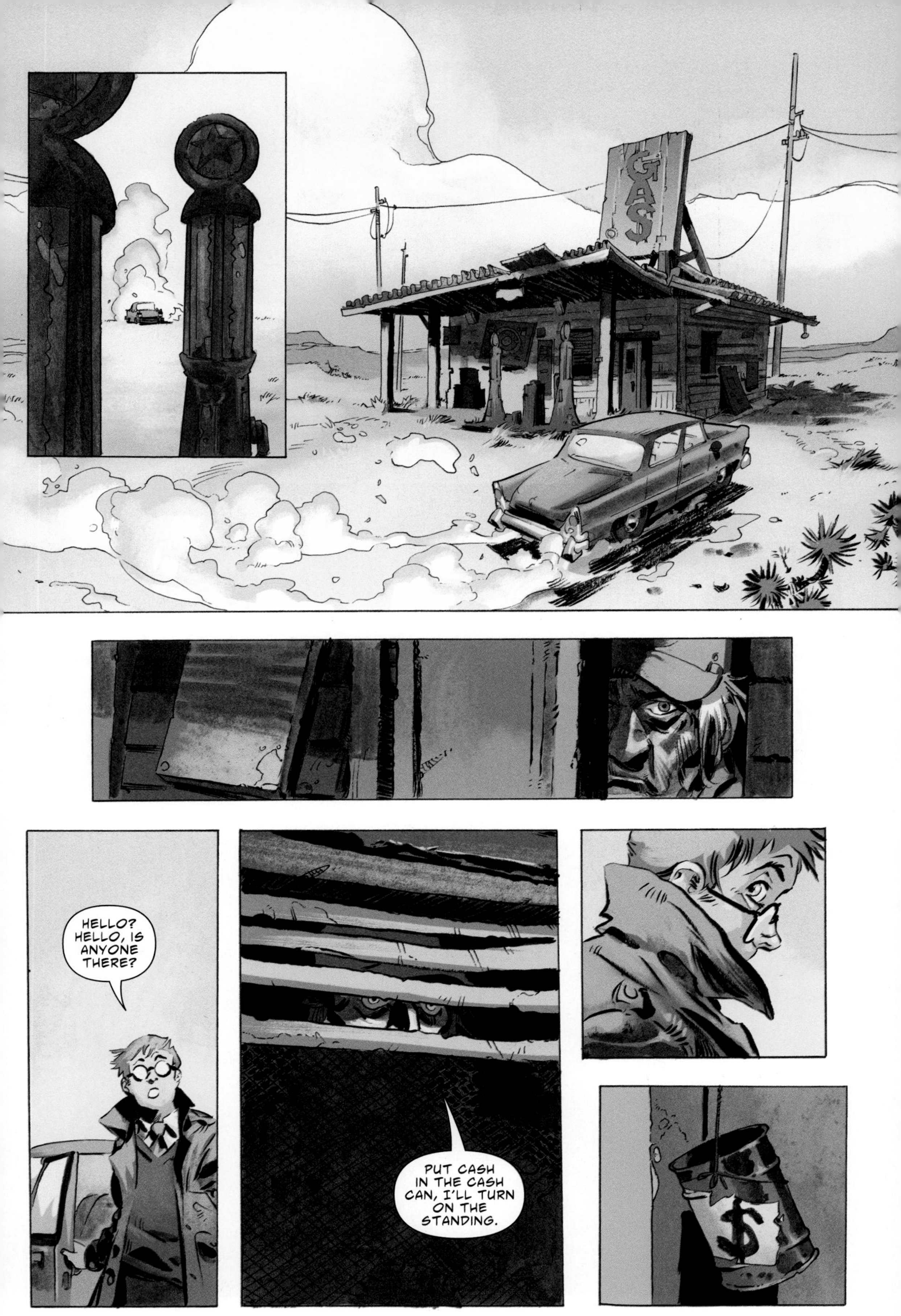
GAS
HELLO? HELLO, IS ANYONE THERE?
PUT CASH IN THE CASH CAN, I'LL TURN ON THE STANDING.

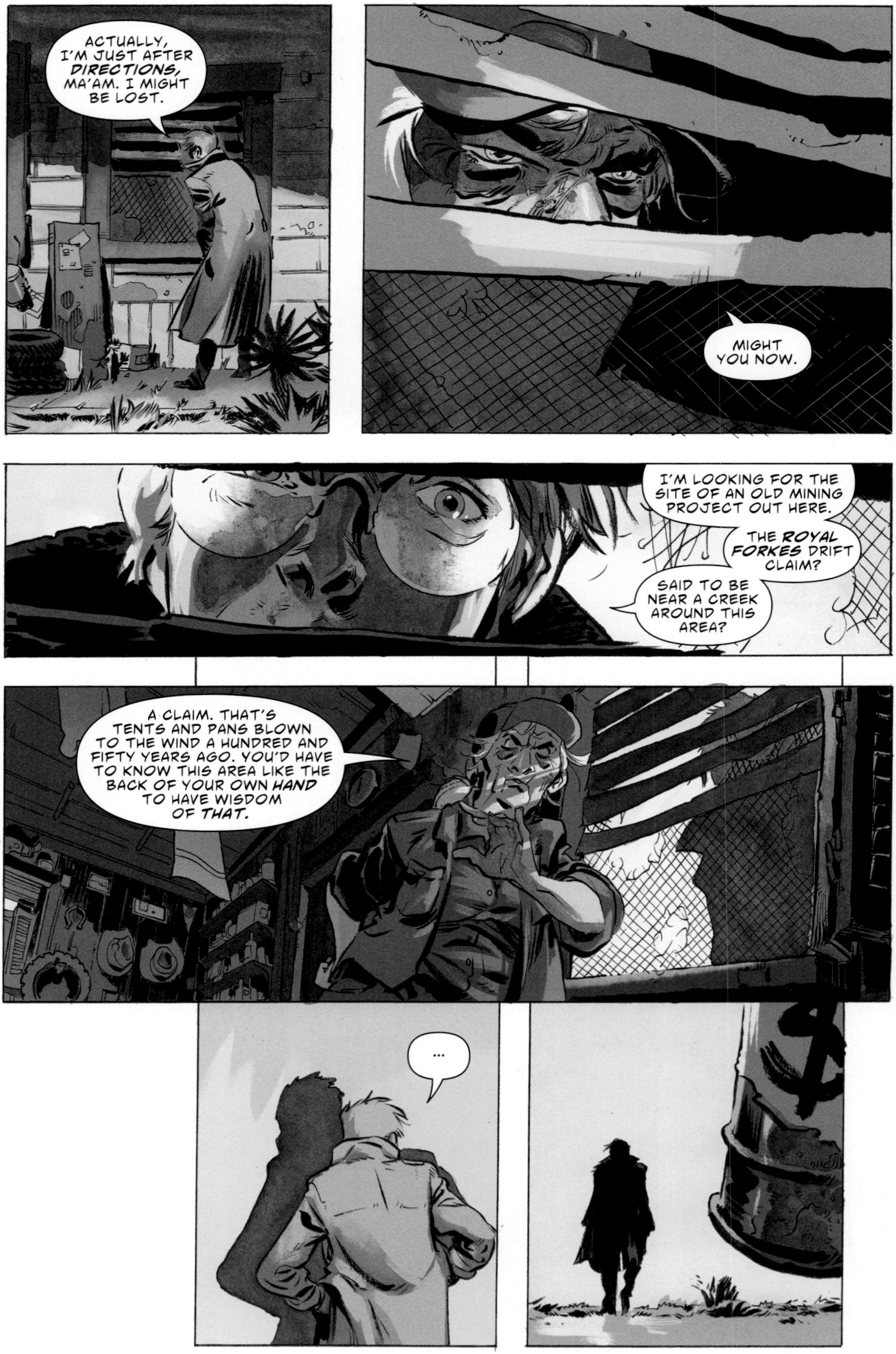
ACTUALLY, I'M JUST AFTER DIRECTIONS, MA'AM. I MIGHT BE LOST.
MIGHT YOU NOW.
I'M LOOKING FOR THE SITE OF AN OLD MINING PROJECT OUT HERE.
THE ROYAL FORKES DRIFT CLAIM?
SAID TO BE NEAR A CREEK AROUND THIS AREA?
A CLAIM. THAT'S TENTS AND PANS BLOWN TO THE WIND A HUNDRED AND FIFTY YEARS AGO. YOU'D HAVE TO KNOW THIS AREA LIKE THE BACK OF YOUR OWN HAND TO HAVE WISDOM OF THAT.
...

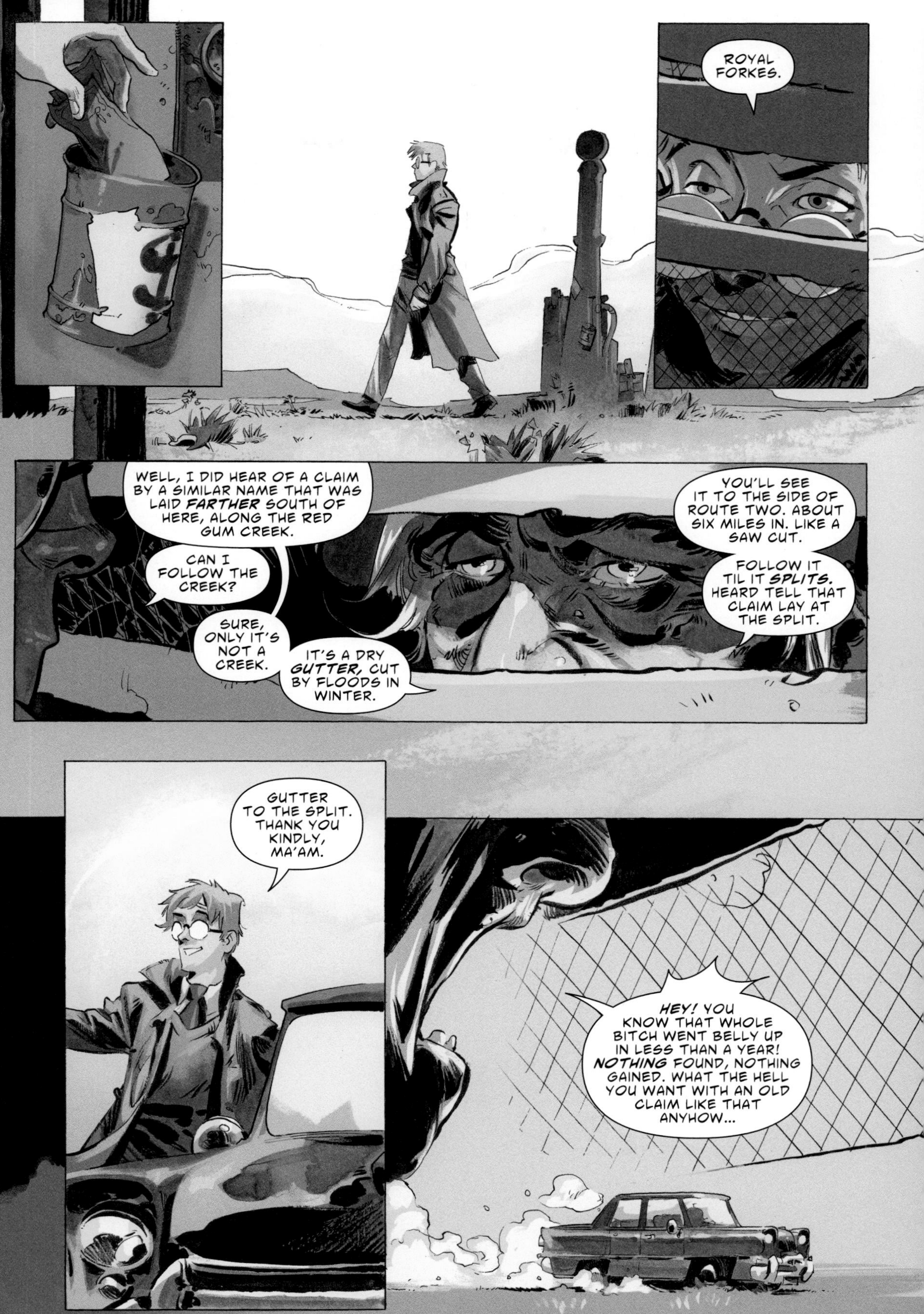
ROYAL FORKES.
WELL, I DID HEAR OF A CLAIM BY A SIMILAR NAME THAT WAS LAID FARTHER SOUTH OF HERE, ALONG THE RED GUM CREEK.
CAN I FOLLOW THE CREEK?
SURE, ONLY IT'S NOT A CREEK.
IT'S A DRY GUTTER, CUT BY FLOODS IN WINTER.
YOU'LL SEE IT TO THE SIDE OF ROUTE TWO. ABOUT SIX MILES IN. LIKE A SAW CUT.
FOLLOW IT TIL IT SPLITS. HEARD TELL THAT CLAIM LAY AT THE SPLIT.
GUTTER TO THE SPLIT. THANK YOU KINDLY, MA'AM.
HEY! YOU KNOW THAT WHOLE BITCH WENT BELLY UP IN LESS THAN A YEAR! NOTHING FOUND, NOTHING GAINED. WHAT THE HELL YOU WANT WITH AN OLD CLAIM LIKE THAT ANYHOW...

"WHAT ARE YOU LOOKING FOR?"

May 19th, 1850

CALIFORNIA
WEALTH TO BE HA
Gentlemen of fortitude, a n
endeavor is being undertak
by the Royal Forkes Mini
Enterprise! One of the olde
mining companies in the wor
the proprietors of Royal Fork
are confident the area alo
Red Gum Creek in southe
Nevada to be rich in miner
wealth! We are looking for
few intrepid men, scientif
capitalists, to aid us in th
extraction of precious meta
Men of God, we will pay a dolla
a week!

I was looking for quartz when Seb hurried over with a page torn out the newspaper, It was an advertisement and he was pushing it at me, panting, flushed with excitement.

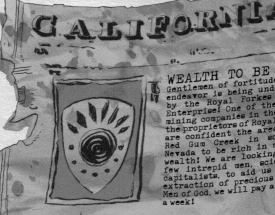

"Take a look," he said, handing me the page, wet from his hand. I was hot and tired from wet panning all day. There was no shade along the Sacremento, but here was Seb, pushing a page of the Californian at me.

"Take a look at what?" I said. The company was called Royal Forkes and I'd never heard of it. It had an insignia like hair standing on end.

I saw nothing special in it and I told Seb so.

my pal Seb

"What are you, sun blind?" he said. He pointed to a spot on the advertisement I could barely read, as the sweat from his thumb had corrupted it. I looked closely and saw that it was the promise of a dollar a week pay.

I held the page out to him. "No one pays that," I said. "It's a trick."

"It's British coal, Dodger," he said. Dodgerman was my surname. Sebberton his. "British coal treats their people right. My father told me, if I ever got a chance to try British, I should. I'm telling you."

"Your father never mined a day in his life," I said. Seb took the advertisement back. "Look," he said. "We need to throw in with this, Hell, there's nothing for us here anyway."

I looked at the empty pan in my hands and then at Seb. He was my oldest friend. We'd met in a schoolhouse in ST. Louis at nine years old, nearly ten years ago. He wanted to be a writer for the papers. Me, I wanted to be an illustrator. Our fathers were both tannery men and wanted us with them. Demanded it. But instead we'd set off together when the boom had begun, Two young men defying their fathers, off to find our fortune. Now here we were, in the mountains of California, no money, no prospects...

And so today we are on our way south to Nevada. We've spent every last cent on a coach down. The wheels are missing spokes and the fellow driving us looks like he will kill us in our sleep, but Seb is smiling from ear to ear.

Looking at him, I cannot help but be optimistic about what we might find.

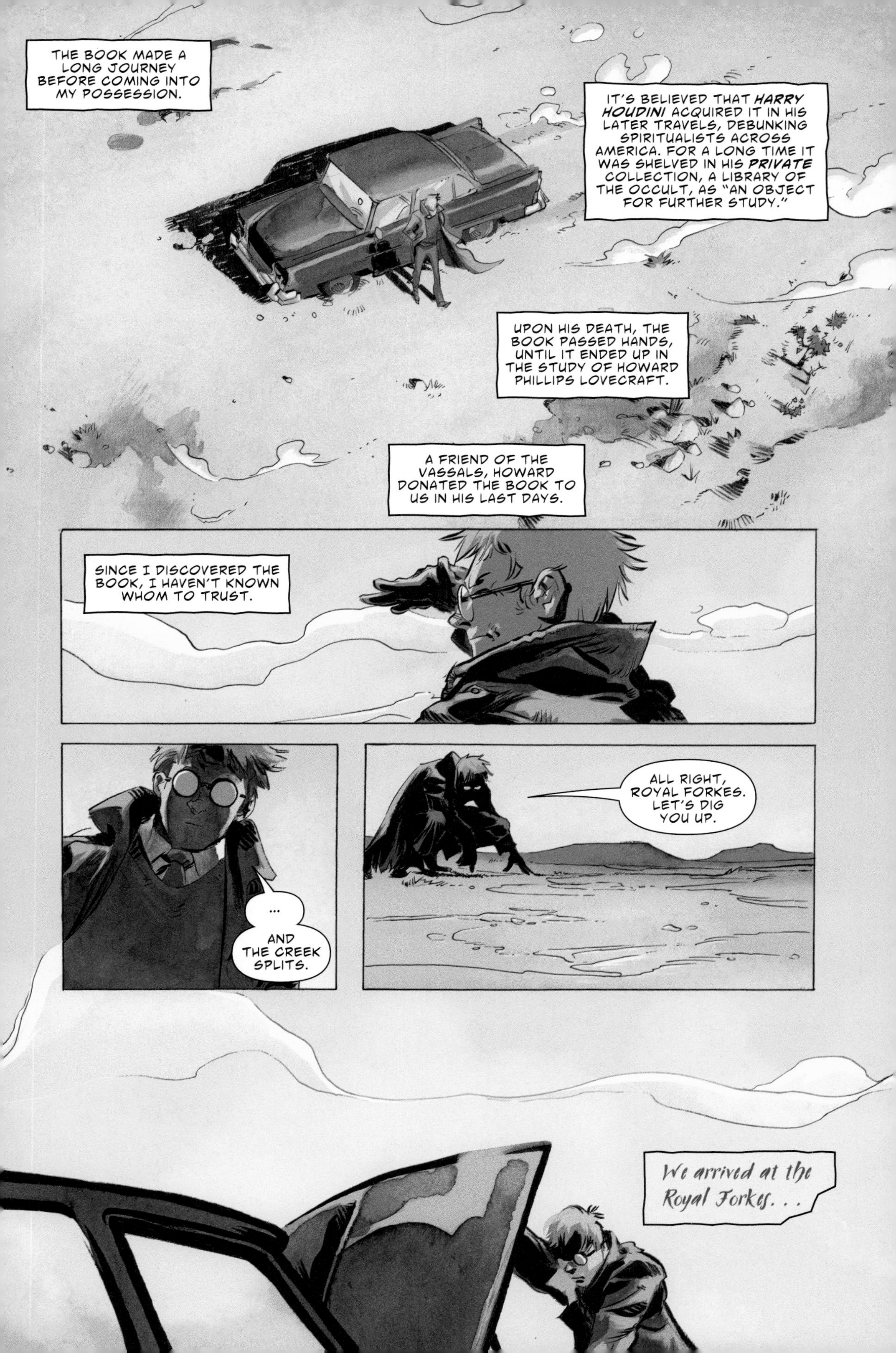
THE BOOK MADE A LONG JOURNEY BEFORE COMING INTO MY POSSESSION.
IT'S BELIEVED THAT HARRY HOUDINI ACQUIRED IT IN HIS LATER TRAVELS, DEBUNKING SPIRITUALISTS ACROSS AMERICA. FOR A LONG TIME IT WAS SHELVED IN HIS PRIVATE COLLECTION, A LIBRARY OF THE OCCULT, AS "AN OBJECT FOR FURTHER STUDY."
UPON HIS DEATH, THE BOOK PASSED HANDS, UNTIL IT ENDED UP IN THE STUDY OF HOWARD PHILLIPS LOVECRAFT.
A FRIEND OF THE VASSALS, HOWARD DONATED THE BOOK TO US IN HIS LAST DAYS.
SINCE I DISCOVERED THE BOOK, I HAVEN'T KNOWN WHOM TO TRUST.
...
AND THE CREEK SPLITS.
ALL RIGHT, ROYAL FORKES. LET'S DIG YOU UP.
We arrived at the Royal Forkes. . .

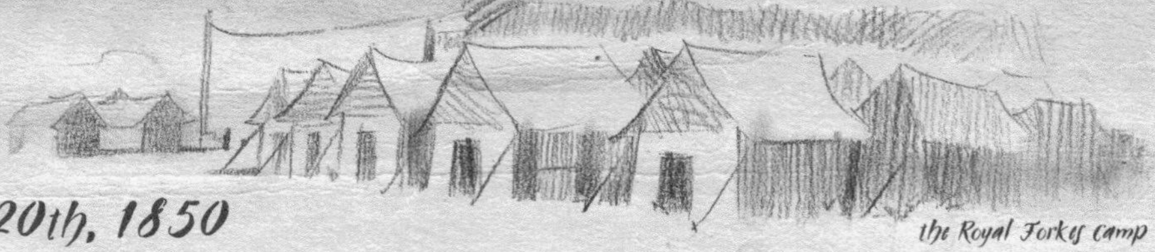

June 20th, 1850

the Royal Forkes camp

We arrived at the Royal Forkes camp today, and I will say that the site is not what I expected.

It was early morning when we approached the camp. The odd thing was, after traveling nearly five hundred miles with us, our horses gave out not five miles from the camp. It was peculiar to be sure.

We were traveling lightly across the cracked, bright dirt, so close to camp we could almost see it, and suddenly the animals simply stopped. Mine halted first. It happened so abruptly I nearly fell. The beast froze, and, for a moment, touched its knees to the dirt, as though in protest. Seb's animal planted its feet as well.

After such a long journey, Seb and I were so glad to be near the site that we found the whole incident wildly humorous. Our horses giving out here, so close to our destination. We gave them water and tried to coax them, but they would not move. We were laughing, pulling on them, when we heard a voice behind us.

"Sirs," said the voice.

We turned to find a man standing along the creek. He was dressed as a gentleman, in vests, and he was strikingly handsome. He could not have looked more out of place in the Nevada desert.

His accent was evident. British, and Seb elbowed me in the ribs at the sound of it. "British coal"... he mouthed.

"My name is Joseph Pell," said the man, touching his own vest. "And as the assistant foreman of the Royal Forkes site, it's my honor and pleasure to welcome you both to camp. The site is just this way. Can I take anything for you?"

Seb and I exchanged a glance. What a voice. Like something forged from silver by the queen's metallurgist. He was a gentleman in the desert, asking to carry our bags.

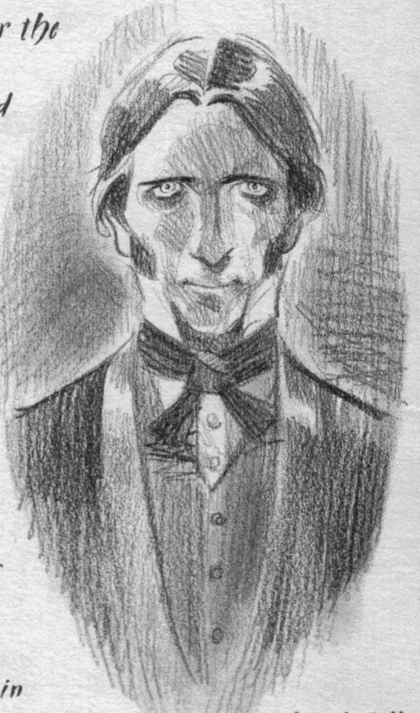

Joseph Pell

"So kind of you," said Seb. And before I could protest, Seb had handed this man - Pell - his satchel. It was cumbersome, but Pell took it without so much as flinching.

He turned to me. "And yours, sir?" he said.

I wanted to keep it, but his hand was there, waiting, and I surrendered it.

"Let me thank you both for coming, on behalf of our foreman," he said, our bags hanging from his slender shoulders, heavy with equipment. He seemed unbothered. "If you'll follow me. I assure you we'll compensate you for the animals, if they've expired. Set them free, and don't trouble yourselves."

He turned and began walking away. Again Seb and I looked at each other. We had to restrain ourselves from laughing. What an oddity, this man, this desert, this situation...

But we followed him, our horses staying behind, watching us go.

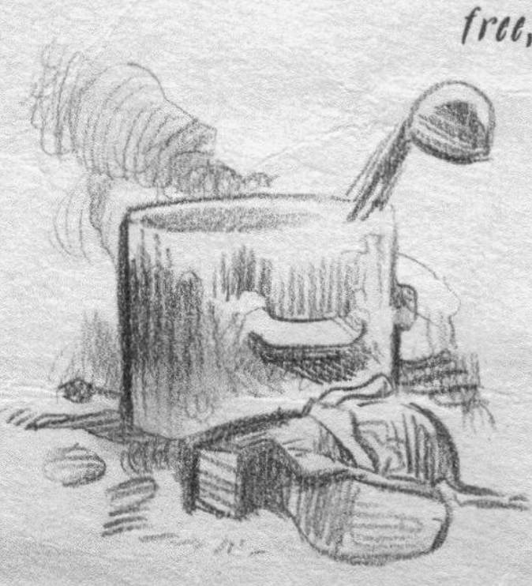

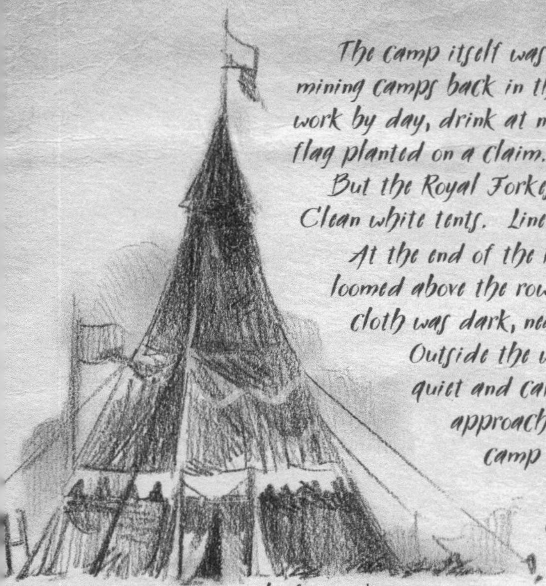

the foreman's tent

The camp itself was a surprise for both Seb and myself. We had tried three mining camps back in the Sierras and all were raucous, filthy places. Men would work by day, drink at night, fight, curse, sing, fornicate, kill. . . Every tent its own flag planted on a claim. Little ragged countries, all at war with one another.

But the Royal Forkes site it. . . was like nothing either of us had encountered. Clean white tents. Lined up in a row. . . Like polished shoes.

At the end of the line of tents was a larger tent, exceedingly large in fact. It loomed above the row, its peak like a steeple poking high above the others. Its cloth was dark, nearly black.

Outside the white row of tents were miners, men like us. Except they were quiet and calm, sitting or standing by the flaps. Each watched our approach in silence, with a kind smile and a nod. I wondered if the camp had religion.

Pell showed us to our tent, which was clean and spacious as the others. Better than anything either of us could have hoped for. After placing our bags inside, Pell reached inside his vest and produced two shiny objects.

The disks sat in his palm, catching the light from outside. "In advance of your good work," he said.

Seb took his right away but it took me a moment to understand what it was I was looking at. It was bright and gleaming. A dollar coin. I looked at Pell. He was smiling at me and I was struck again by his handsomeness. "We believe in treating our workers right," he said. "That's what the foreman believes, I should say."

And just then I felt a sudden wave of gratitude rise in me. Towards Seb, for bringing me the advertisement, for this gentleman carrying our bags. I could draw you a sketch of my own heart, swollen. "Please tell the foreman back in jolly old England how much we appreciate it," I said. "If we could take back the revolution, we would." He smiled even more broadly. His eyes were a cloudy blue, nearly white. Pools of water in a desert. "You can thank him yourself sometime," said Pell. "He's staying here. His tent is at the end of the row, see?" I looked through the flaps of our tent at that large black structure in the distance, the top rising above the rest, dark against the sky.

"He's with his wife," said Pell. "She's with child. Not easy out here, as you can imagine. He's a devoted man." I thanked the foreman silently. Pell bid us goodbye and told us to explore the camp, sleep, whatever we wanted to do. I wanted to rest but it was early, and Seb encouraged me to explore the camp with him. We couldn't stop smiling, glancing at each other as we walked the rows of perfect tents. . . Oddly, all the other miners were gone now, presumably having gone inside their tents to rest. It was like Seb and I were the only men around, the whole camp built for us.

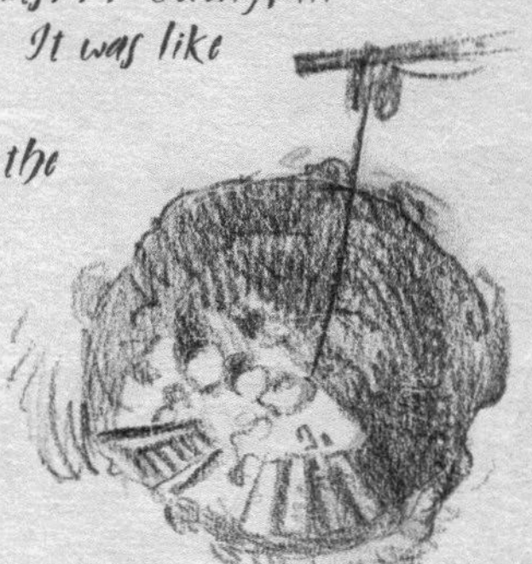

We walked past the tents, past the well, the creek, out into the desert, where the beginnings of the shaft itself had been sunk. The others hadn't gotten very far, but even so, the mouth was wide and deep. An impressive start. We were just about to walk back to our tent when Seb took my arm.

"It is a bit strange," he said.

"If it's a dream, don't wake me," I said.

"No," he said, "there's no material for extraction. All this," he said, gesturing to the rigging, the narrow elevator, "it's for digging a hole. Not pulling anything out of that hole."

"Like I said, don't wake me." I tapped his head with my coin. "If they want us to dig a hole, so be it. We can do it, then we'll be gone with our pay, never to be seen again!"

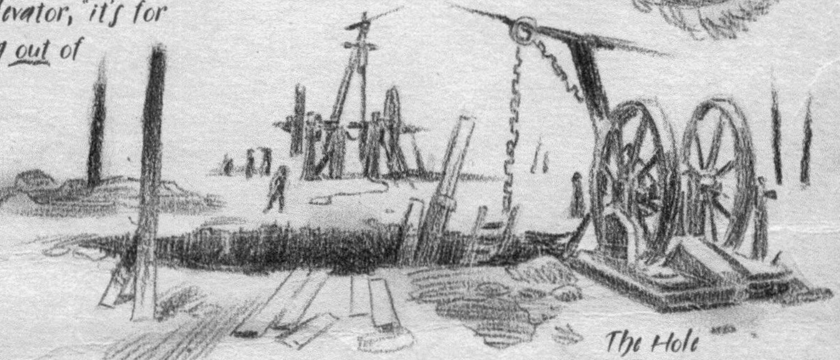

The Hole

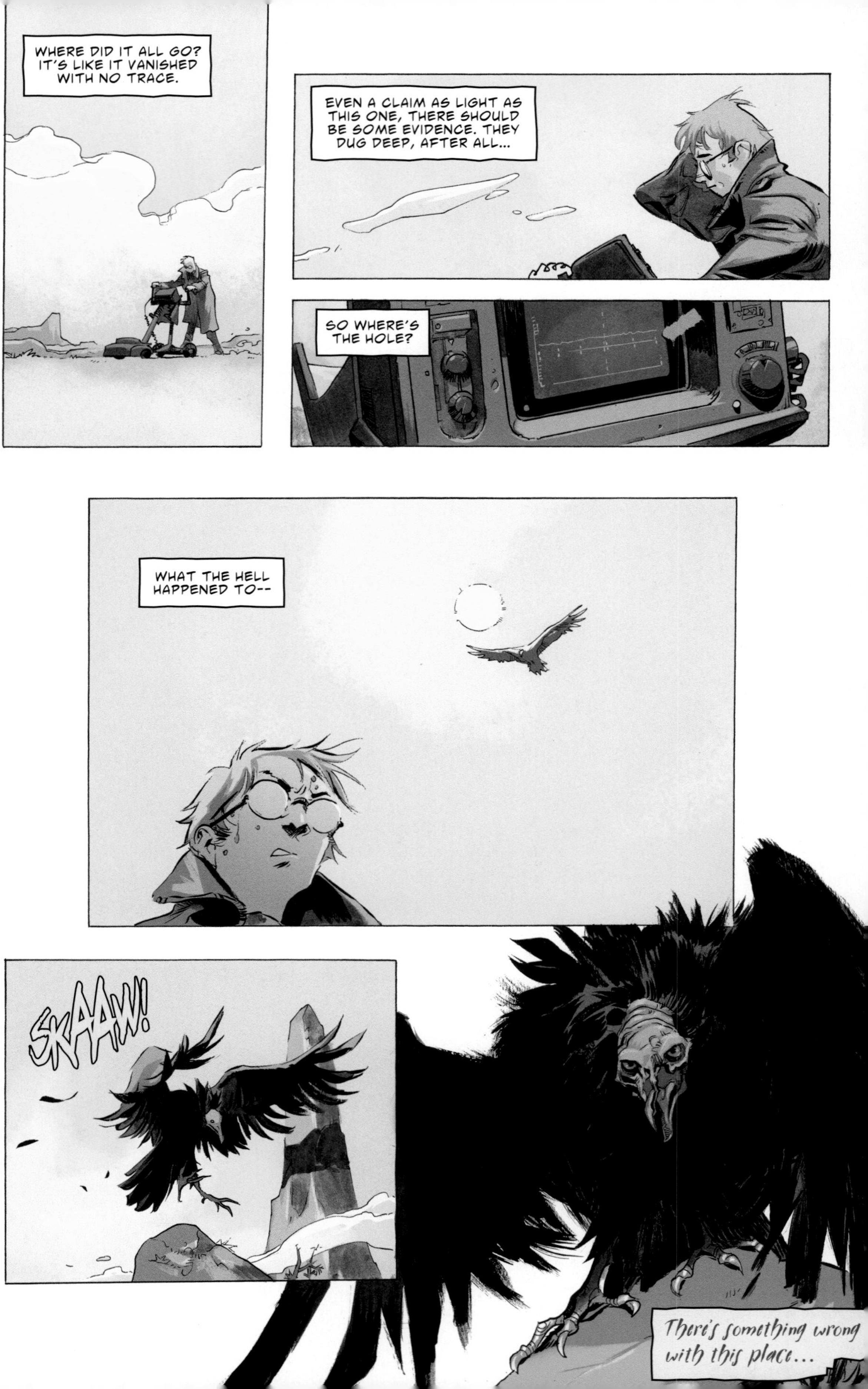
WHERE DID IT ALL GO? IT'S LIKE IT VANISHED WITH NO TRACE.
EVEN A CLAIM AS LIGHT AS THIS ONE, THERE SHOULD BE SOME EVIDENCE. THEY DUG DEEP, AFTER ALL...
SO WHERE'S THE HOLE?
WHAT THE HELL HAPPENED TO--
SKAAW!
There's something wrong with this place...

July 5th, 1850

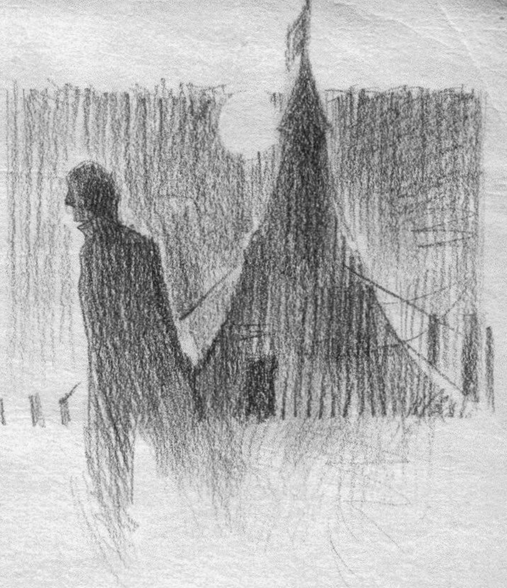

There's something wrong with this place. . . That's what Seb believes. He's become increasingly fearful these past days. As I said, he has been suspicious from the very first day. Lately, though, the things he's imagining. . . At night he spends hours peeking through the flaps at the foreman's black tent at the end of the row, hoping to catch a glimpse. He was always the more excitable of the two of us, though. Full of wild humors, his father liked to say. I love Seb for it, but his father used to give him soda waters to calm him down.

Still, I admit, there is strangeness here. Seb's initial observation about the site was correct. Royal Forkes does seem more interested in digging a hole than extracting anything from it. We dig straight down, pressurizing the water, blasting away what we can, then chopping, chopping. We blast now and then. No diagonal shafts, nothing to buttress this one. No exploring. Just straight down. We're getting deep, fast. There are sorts of damps in the air already. Black damp. . . A skunk damp.

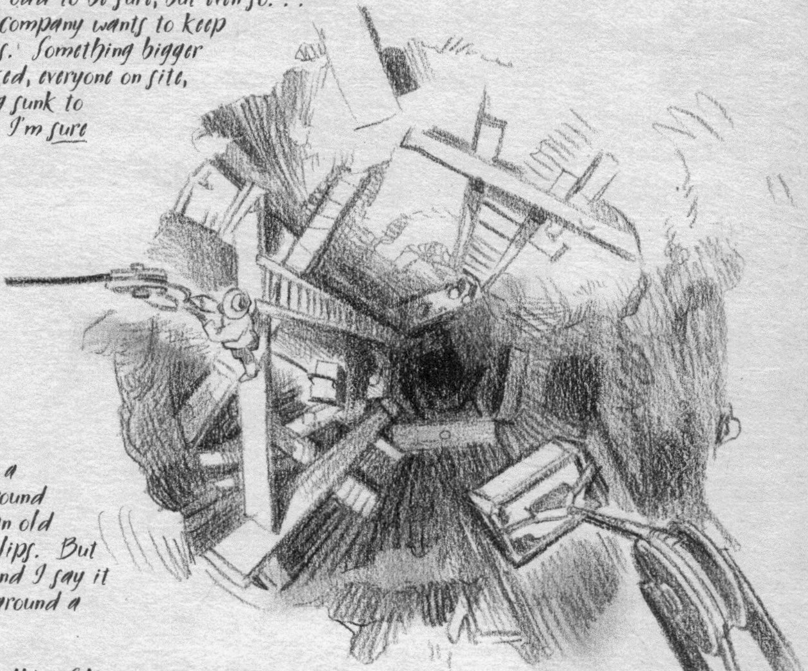

And yes, a single hole, directly down is odd to be sure, but even so. . . perhaps there's some other purpose the company wants to keep private. A geological survey is my guess. Something bigger than just mining for wealth. When asked, everyone on site, including Pell, claims the shaft is being sunk to extract precious metal, but I saw what I'm sure was silver the other day, and we kept sinking the hole, right past it. No one seemed to care when I made mention of it.

"We'll examine all we've got when we get deep enough, good sir," said Pell. Then he put a hand on my shoulder. It was oddly heavy. "I hear you're an artist. I'd love to see your illustrations some time. You keep them in that book of yours?"

The other day Pell asked them to pour a kind of red dust - like brick dust - around the edge of the hole. He said it was an old trick to add moisture and harden the lips. But it's a trick of which I've never heard, and I say it does look strange, like a ring of blood around a gaping black mouth...

All of this, though, I truly believe it's all of Seb's nonsense poisoning my thoughts. The full truth is, he has come to see all sorts of paranoid nonsense around us. He says the other miners are watching us. He believes something has been done to them so he has stopped eating anything but bread. "I can see the makings of bread," he says. I see him stare at the mining company symbol sometimes as though he detects evil in it. I keep telling myself it's only a few more weeks, though. At the rate we're digging, the hole will be insupportably deep in a matter of days. And the money. . . We've made more in a few weeks than we would in a year.

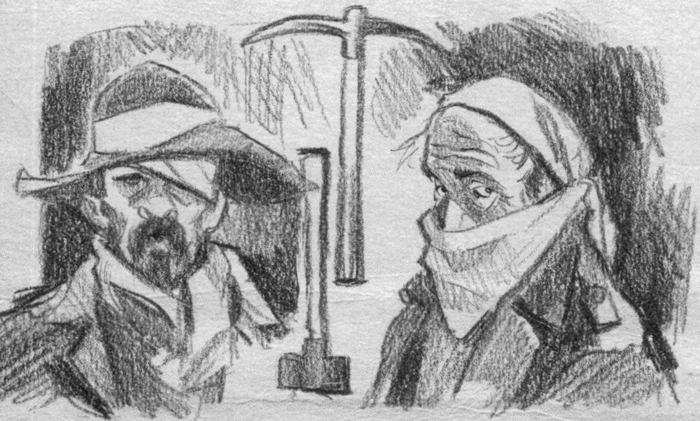

I have the coins stacked next to this journal right now. It's nearly midnight, and their shine in the pale moonlight coming in the flaps. . . the flaps letting in light because Seb is peeking out again. Staring at the black tent at the end of the row. He is whispering something to himself. I cannot hear what.

I'd lay a hand on him if I didn't think he'd jump.

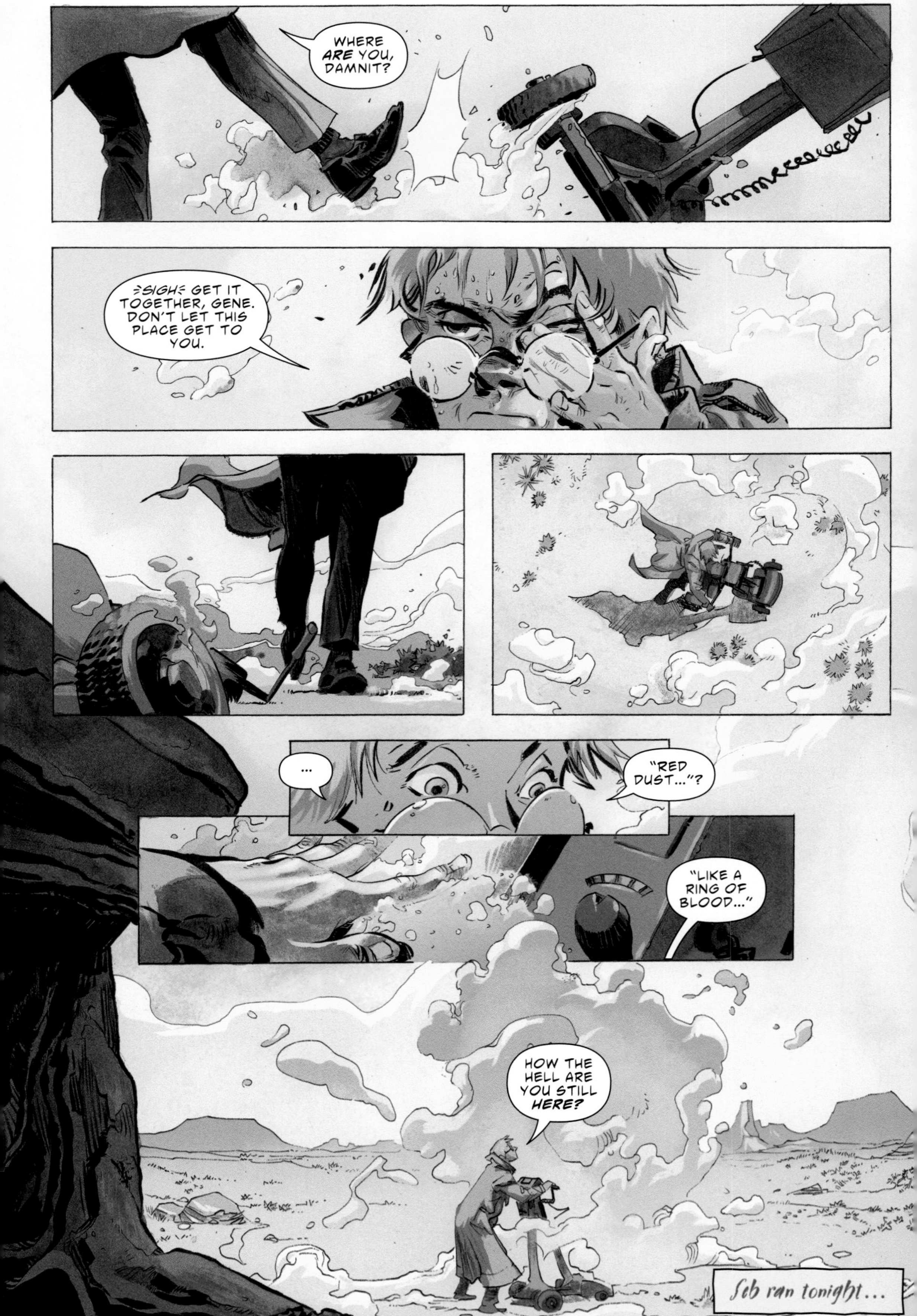
WHERE ARE YOU, DAMNIT?
=SIGH= GET IT TOGETHER, GENE. DON'T LET THIS PLACE GET TO YOU.
...
"RED DUST..."?
"LIKE A RING OF BLOOD..."
HOW THE HELL ARE YOU STILL HERE?
Seb ran tonight...

July 19th, 1850

Seb ran tonight. He just fled, all at once. I tried to dissuade him, but there was no reasoning with him. He was like a man possessed.

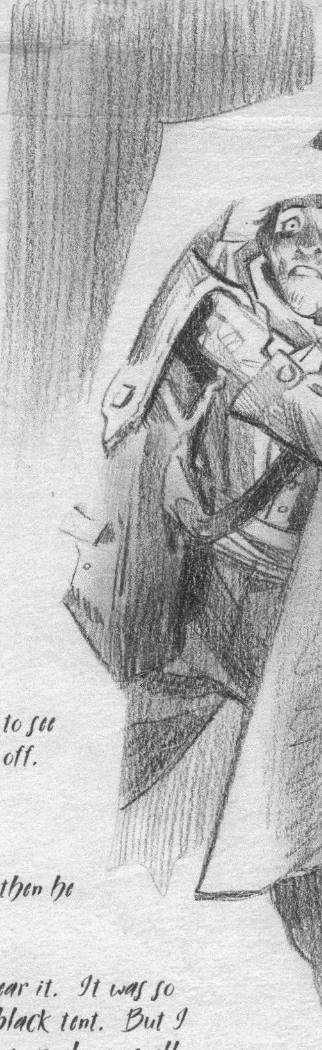

His decision to flee was apparently prompted by something he saw moments ago. Over the course of the past few nights, there've been screams from the foreman's tent. His wife, screaming in pain. Of course, we all assumed it was the start of her labor. But the screams went on all night. In the morning, they stopped, only to start again when the sun was down. Yesterday morning, again they halted abruptly. And last night, at almost the instant the sun sank below the horizon, they began again. Shrieks, blood-curdling. Every few minutes, one spiraling up into the sky, the pitch growing higher and higher as the night wore on, growing impossibly high, inhumanly so. Like the scream of a sheep, or a goat being torn apart.

Seb and I lay awake, listening. I was about to talk to him, to see how he was holding up, when he stood, angrily, and stormed off.

"Where are you going?" I said.

"To meet our foreman and his wife, of course" he said, and then he was through the flaps before I could stop him.

"Seb!" I called after him. "Seb, wait!" But he wouldn't hear it. It was so dark that night I lost sight of him before he neared the black tent. But I could see the tent itself, blacker than the night sky, peeking up above us all.

I started out of the tent, but then something seized in me and I stayed put. Why didn't I follow my friend? Was I afraid? I don't know, but I didn't follow him, and moments later, Seb returned and began to pack - frantically.

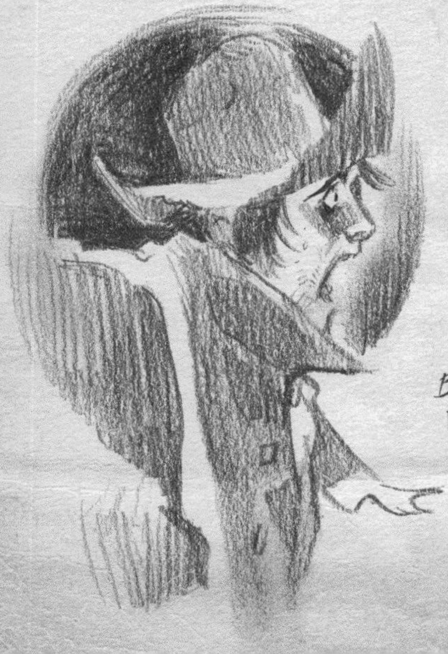

I asked him what he'd seen but he wouldn't say. He was shaking, his face pale. He seemed to see nothing but his belongings. He'd barely filled his bag when he slung it over his shoulder.

He looked at me.

"I saw him," he said. "The foreman. And the. . . the wife. We need to leave. Now."

I told him to stop, to talk this through a moment.

But then, before I could say anything more, he was gone. My friend. Vanished into the night. It was only later I noticed he hadn't even taken his coins. He'd left them all in the tent. A small fortune.

I only pray he makes it where he wants to go. I worry he was right. I worry I should run too, before it's too late. I worry one of these times. . .

...I'll go down in that hole, and won't come back up.

JUST A LITTLE FARTHER, GENE...

...YOU'RE *ALMOST* THERE.

ALL YOUR SUSPICIONS, ALL THE RESEARCH THESE PAST WEEKS... HIDDEN FROM THE OTHERS. ROYAL FORKES. THE *INSIGNIA,* HOW IT CONTAINS THE OLDER AKKADIAN MARK. THE SEVEN TONGUES. OR "TONGS." THE *PITCHFORK,* THE SPECIES THE THING MAKES BEFORE EMERGING...

IT WAS PUT DOWN *HERE,* YOU KNOW IT. BY THE ROYAL FORKES, JUST LIKE IT SAYS IN THE BOOK.

IT'S ALL TRUE.

A LITTLE FARTHER AND YOU'LL PRO
IT. YOU'LL HAVE ENOUGH TO SHOW
AGENT BOOK, ASSUMING YOU CAN
TRUST HER. YOU CAN, GENE. YOU CA
YOU KNOW HER. SHE'S A FRIEND.

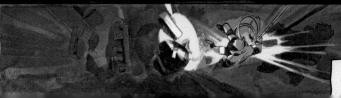

Seb came bac
night *ago*

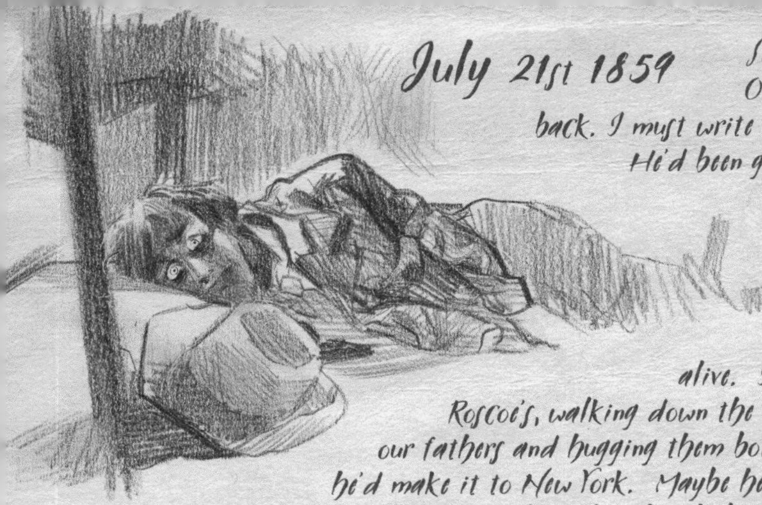

July 21st 1859

Seb came back two nights ago... Or rather, whatever replaced him came back. I must write faster, as I don't have much time. He'd been gone for two nights when it happened. I'd actually become hopeful that he'd made it, escaped from camp. I'd taken to imagining him arriving back in St. Louis, tired and dirty, but alive. I imagined him going straight into Roscoe's, walking down the barrel drains and tanners and finding our fathers and hugging them both. Or maybe he'd make it, maybe he'd make it to New York. Maybe he'd write about me, and I'd live on in his stories. I was thinking these thoughts, half asleep, when he came back. Or when I noticed he was simply there.

I heard a stirring, a rustling sound like dirt scraping, and when I looked, he was lying there in his bed. Like he'd never gone anywhere. His eyes were open, and he was staring at me. He looked filthy, but his expression was calm and peaceful.

"Seb?" I said. "Seb, what happened?"

"Nothing at all, Dodger," he said. He lay there, staring at me, unblinking.

The woman's screams from the tent started again just then. EEEEEEEEEeeeeeeee!!!!!!!

This thing says it's Seb but it's not. It watches me at night.

This morning the Seb thing pissed and shat itself and didn't even move. It just smiled.

July 24th 1859

I know this will likely be my last entry.

This morning the Seb thing, moments ago, without warning, it got up and walked out of the tent. I was shocked. Why had it left? I noticed then that the foreman's wife - her screams sounded louder, closer than usual. They'd become commonplace, like the howling of the wind. I peeked out of the tent and what I saw. . .

She was not with child, but with something else, stretched to bursting. . .

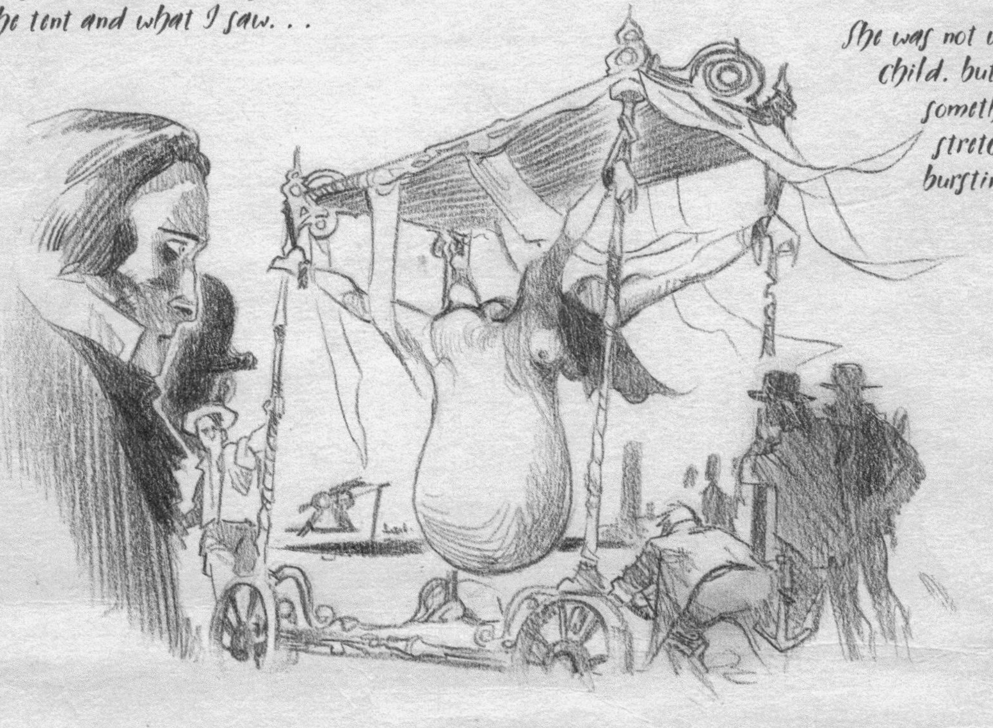

She hung from a bed built upside down. Her cries were terrible, ecstatic, shrieks of glee for what was coming. I wanted to scream, to run, but I stood frozen to the spot. That's when I saw him. The foreman himself. . .

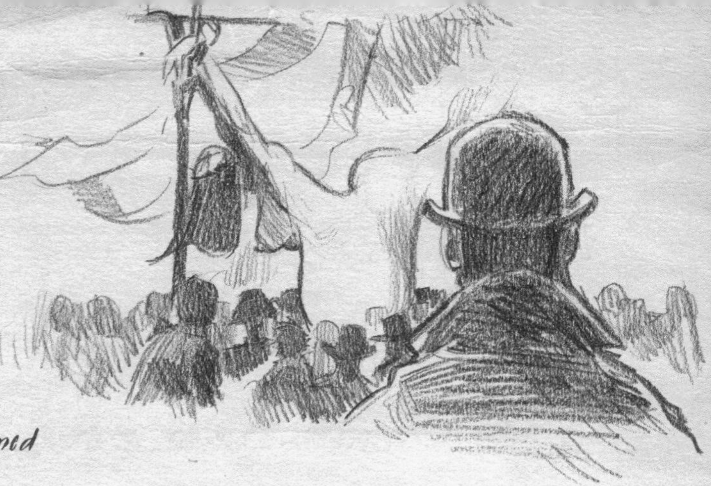

He had his back to me, but I knew it was him. He stood taller than the other men, looming like his tent had loomed over the others.

I had a sense that he was very old. Older than this place. Older than the dirt.

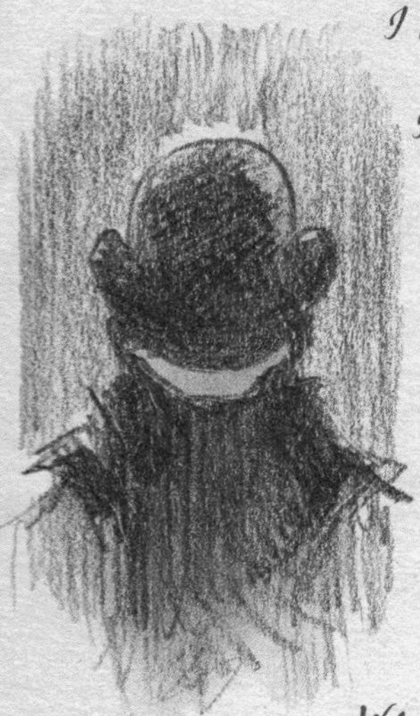

I had a sense of something timeless and evil and then he turned to me. . .

I could feel my pulse in my hands, throbbing.

He smiled. A slow smile that stretched too widely across his face. His whole face seemed a mouth.

And then it was as though the spell was broken and I rushed inside the tent.

I write this knowing I will not escape.

I will die here.

We have dug a pit.

A Nest for something. I have no heart left. No spirit.

Supplies come in every week, and I will try to hide this journal in the rigging. It will likely be found and burned. But even so. I will try. And above all. . .

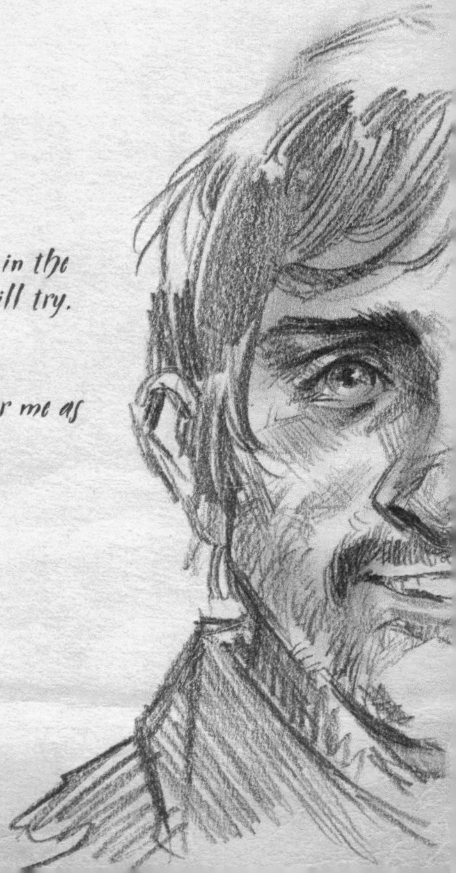

. . . I beg whoever finds it never to come here. And to remember me as I was, not as I am now, a wasted, haunted shell of myself.

My name was William Dodgeman of Chicago.

This was my face.

This was my face.

This was my face...

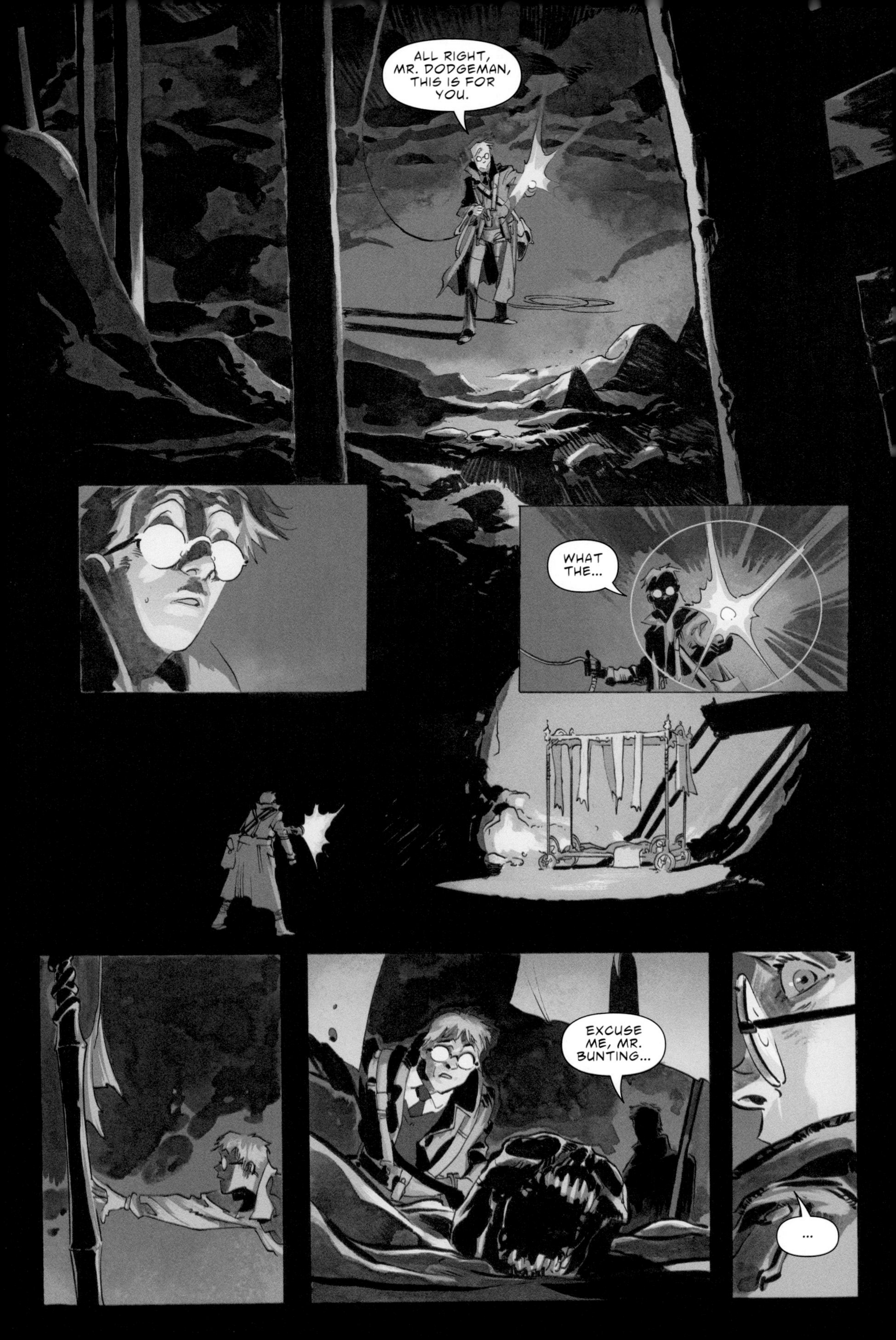
ALL RIGHT, MR. DODGEMAN, THIS IS FOR YOU.
WHAT THE...
EXCUSE ME, MR. BUNTING...
...

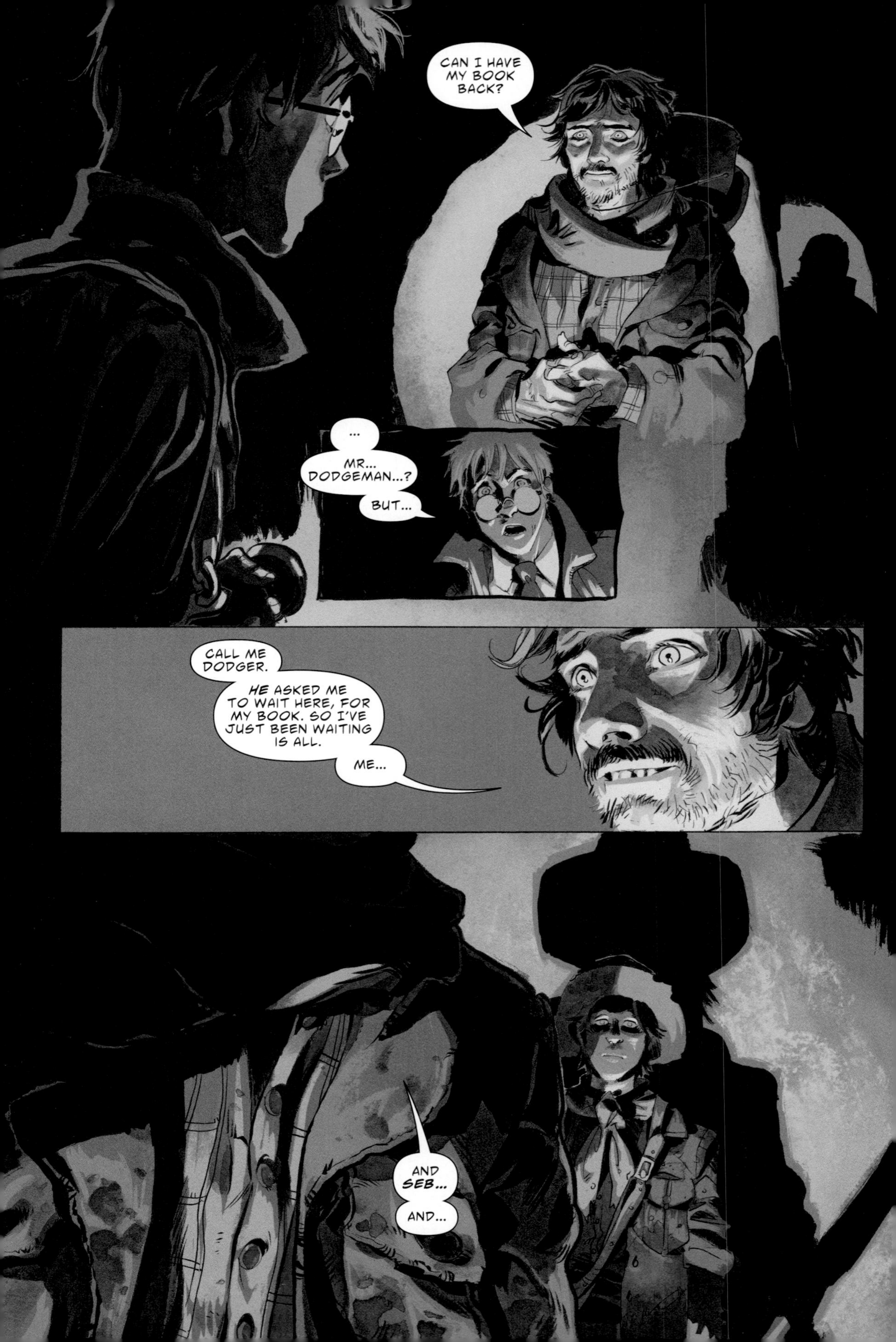
CAN I HAVE MY BOOK BACK?
...
MR... DODGEMAN...?
BUT...
CALL ME DODGER.
HE ASKED ME TO WAIT HERE, FOR MY BOOK. SO I'VE JUST BEEN WAITING IS ALL.
ME...
AND SEB...
AND...

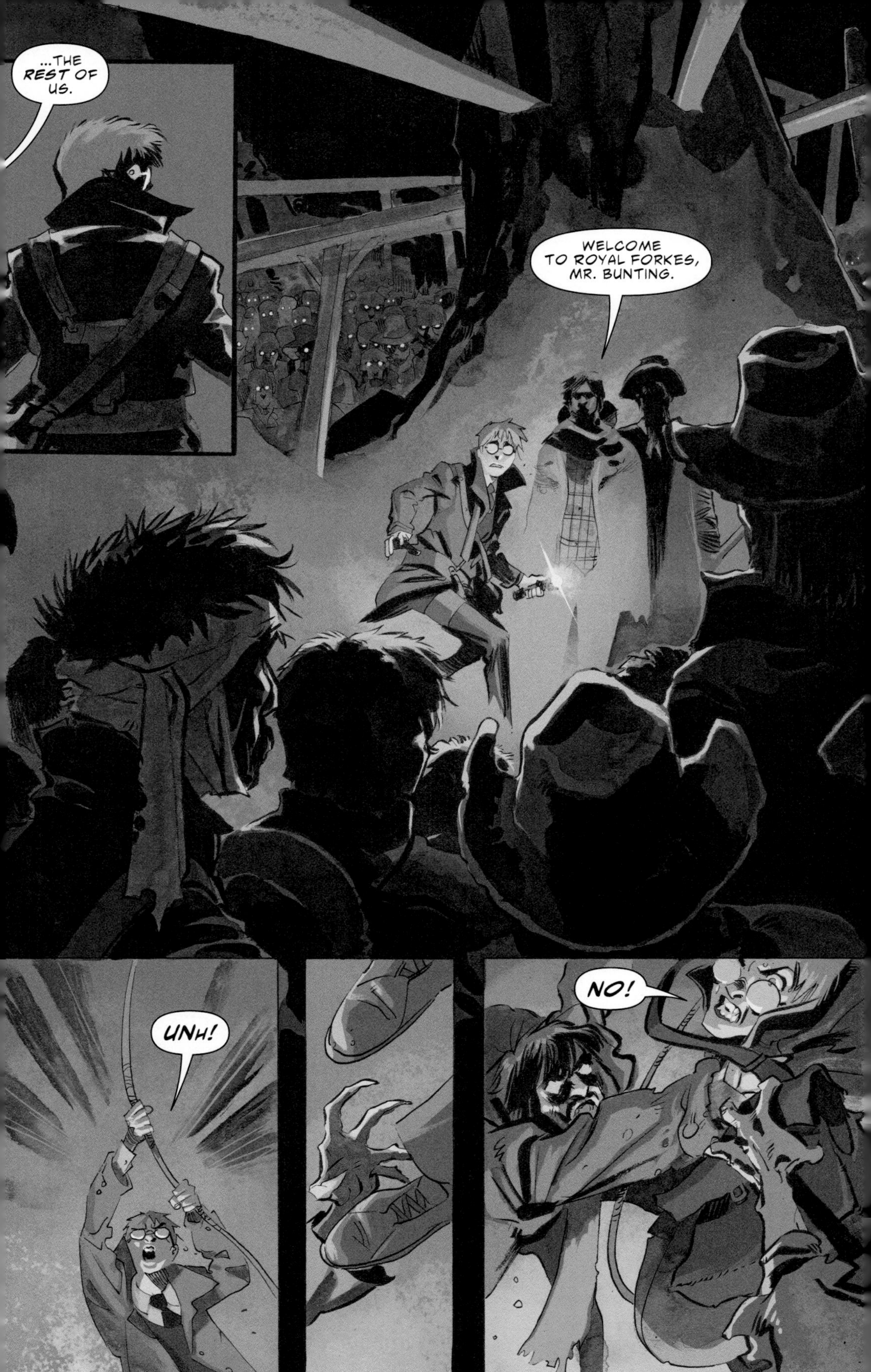
...THE REST OF US.
WELCOME TO ROYAL FORKES, MR. BUNTING.
UNH!
NO!

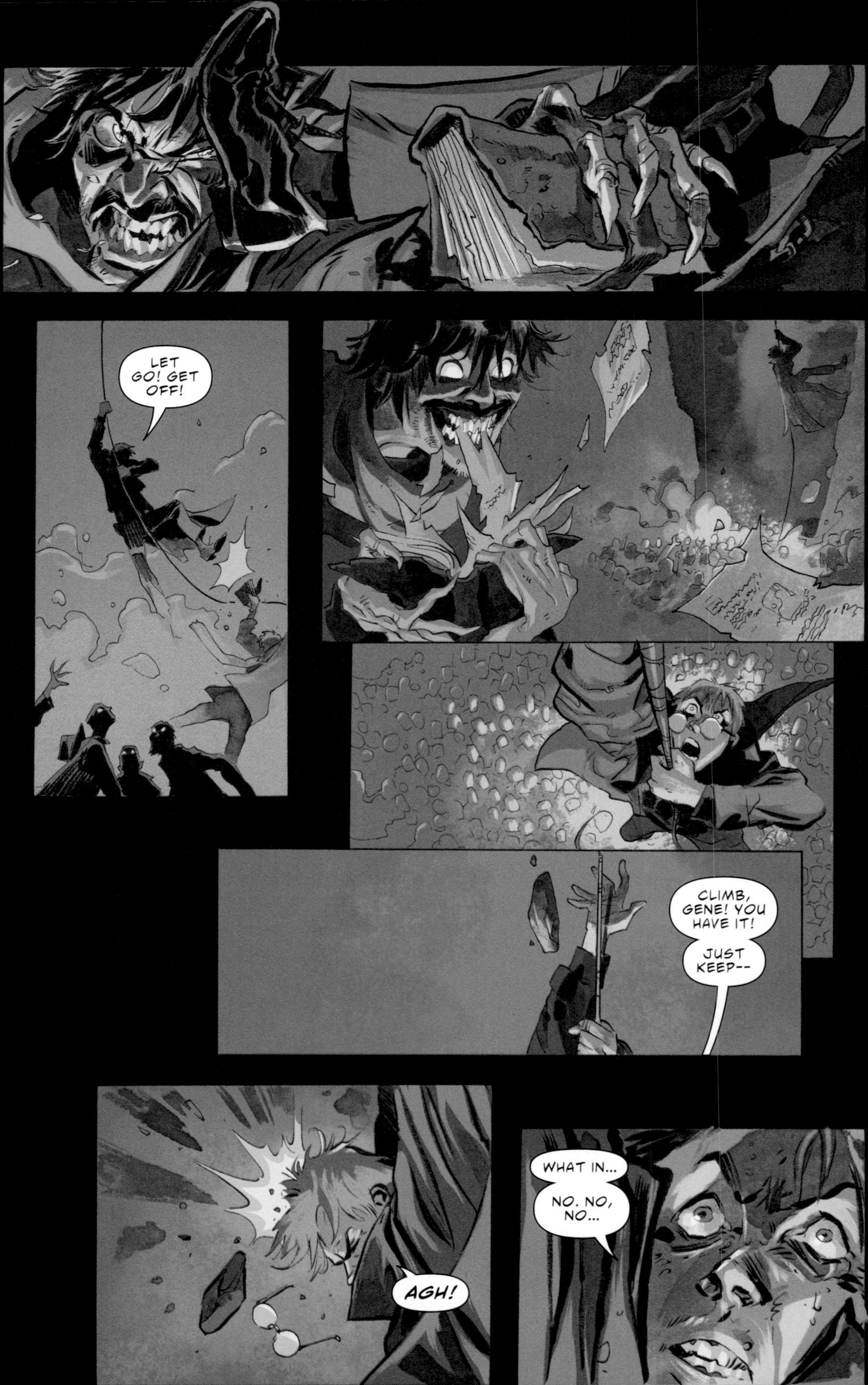

LET GO! GET OFF!
CLIMB, GENE! YOU HAVE IT!
JUST KEEP--
AGH!
WHAT IN...
NO. NO, NO...

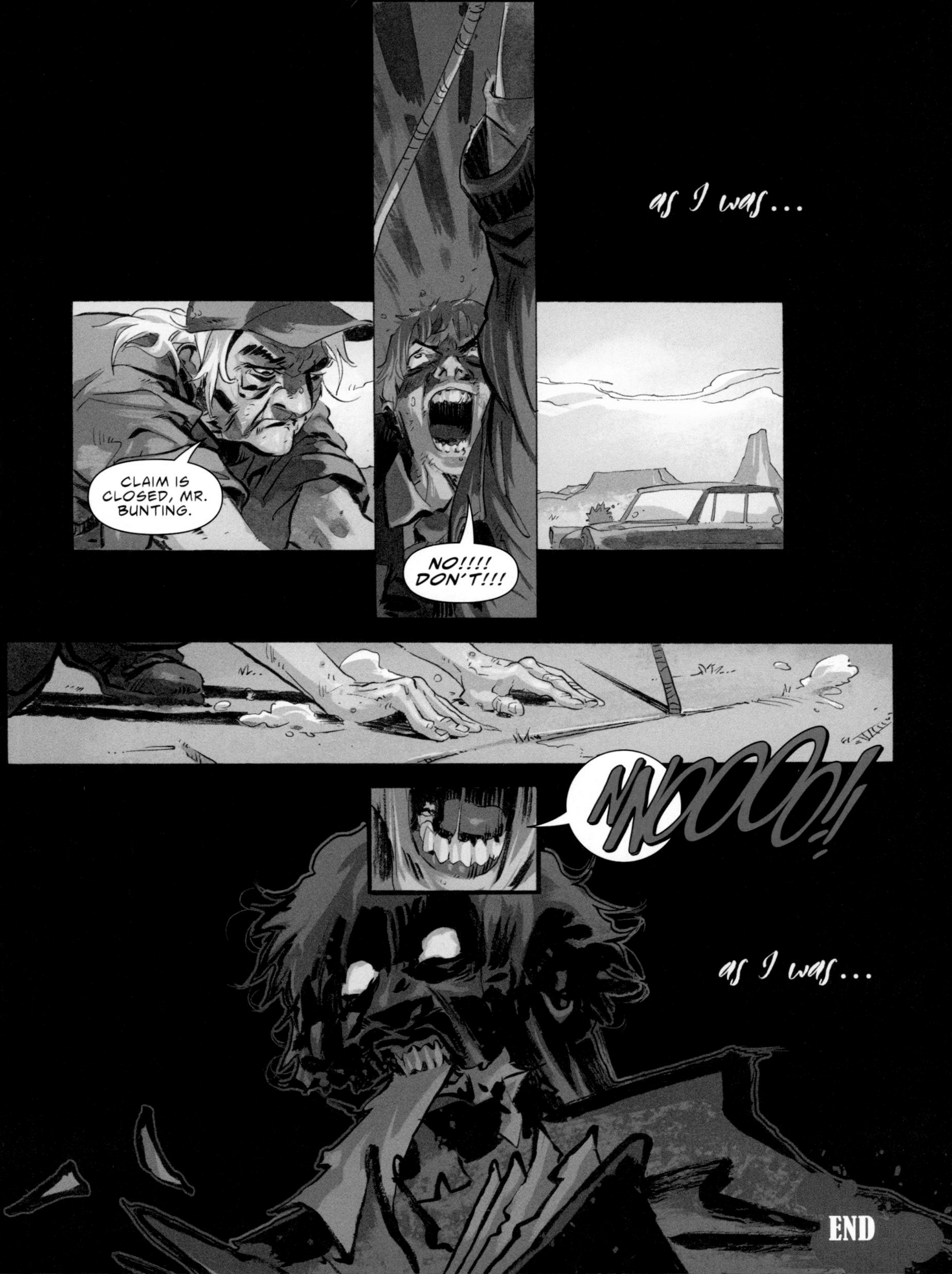
as I was...
CLAIM IS CLOSED, MR. BUNTING.
NO!!!! DON'T!!!
NNOOOO!!
as I was...
END

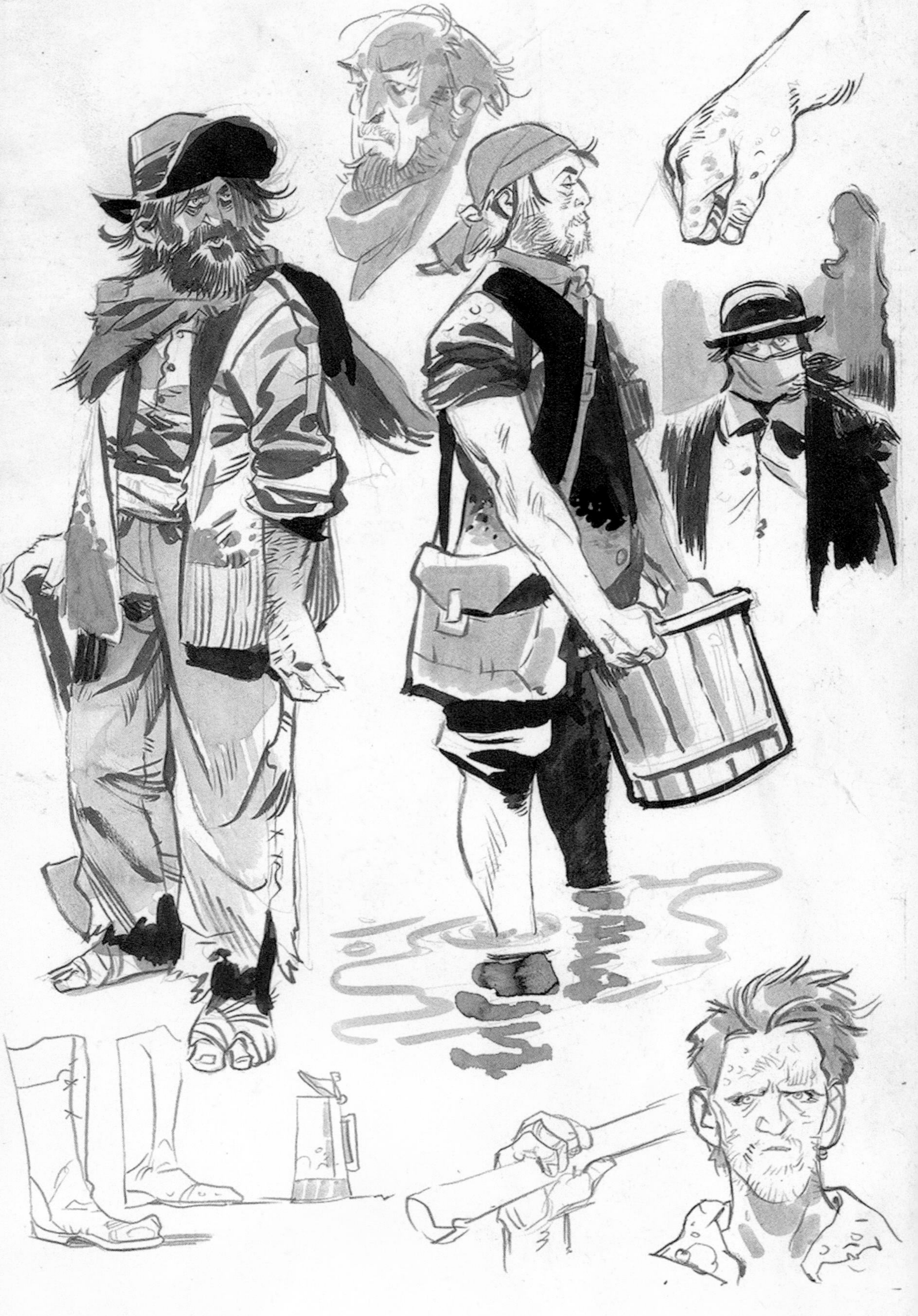

Character sketches by Matías Bergara

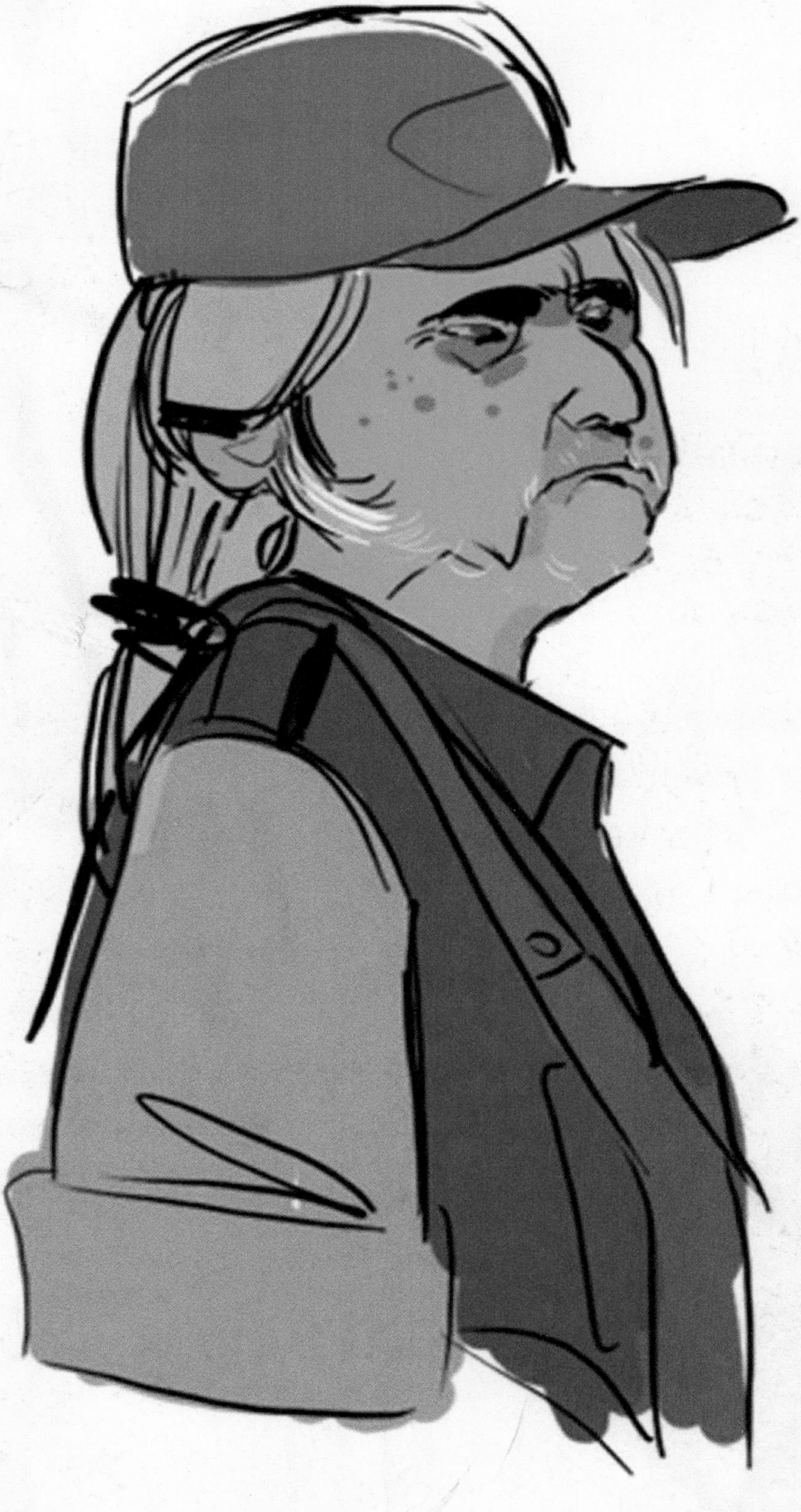

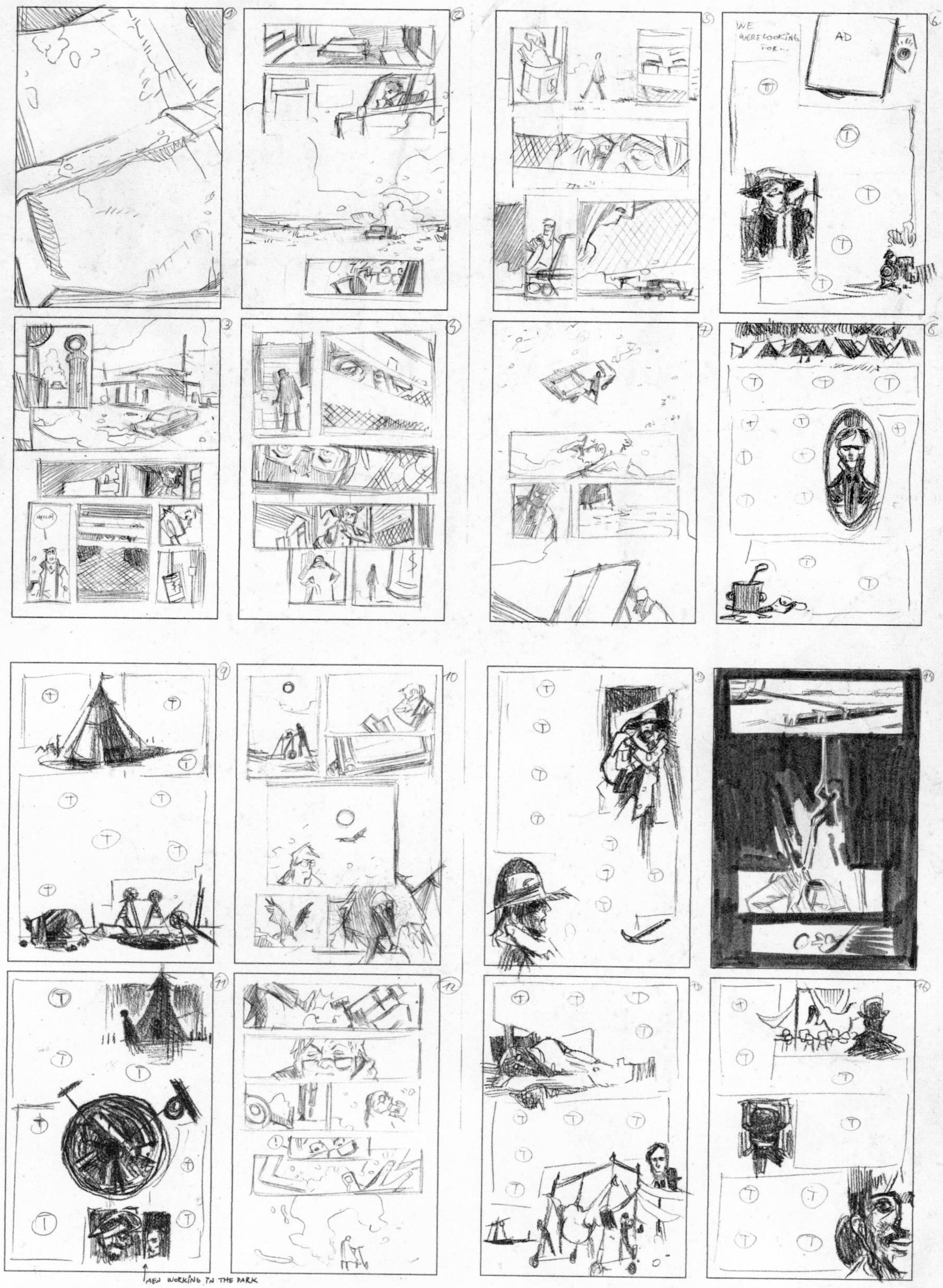

WE WERE LOOKING FOR...
AD
HELLO
MEN WORKING IN THE PARK

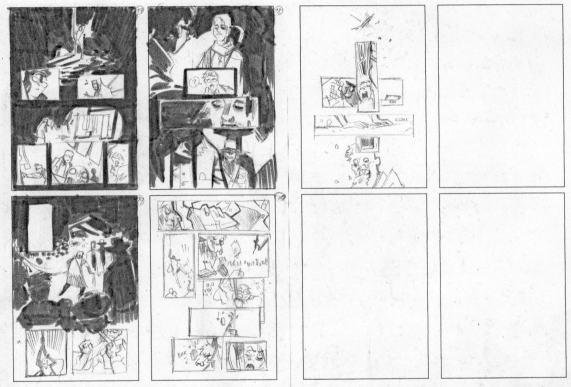

American Vampire #5 layouts by Matías Bergara

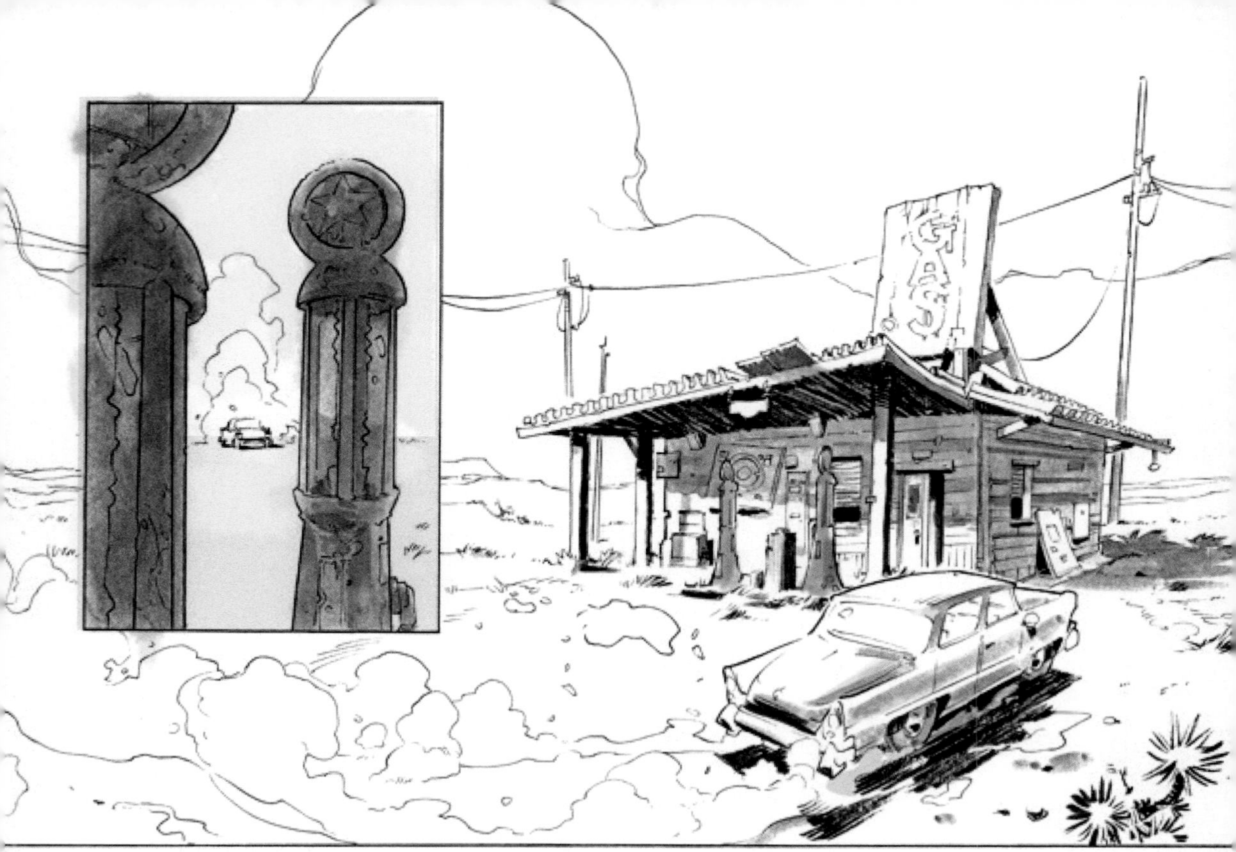
GAS

American Vampire #5 page 3 color study by Matías Bergara

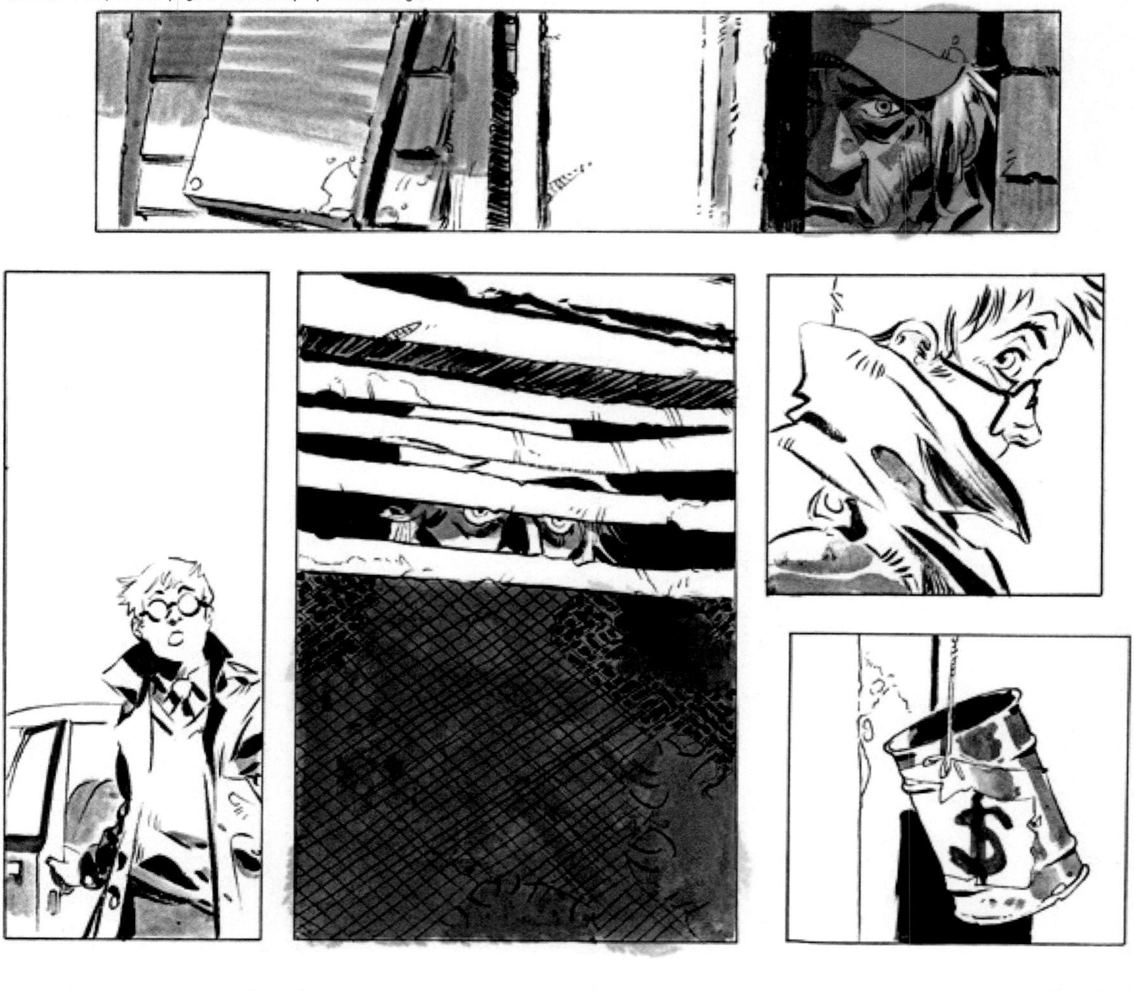

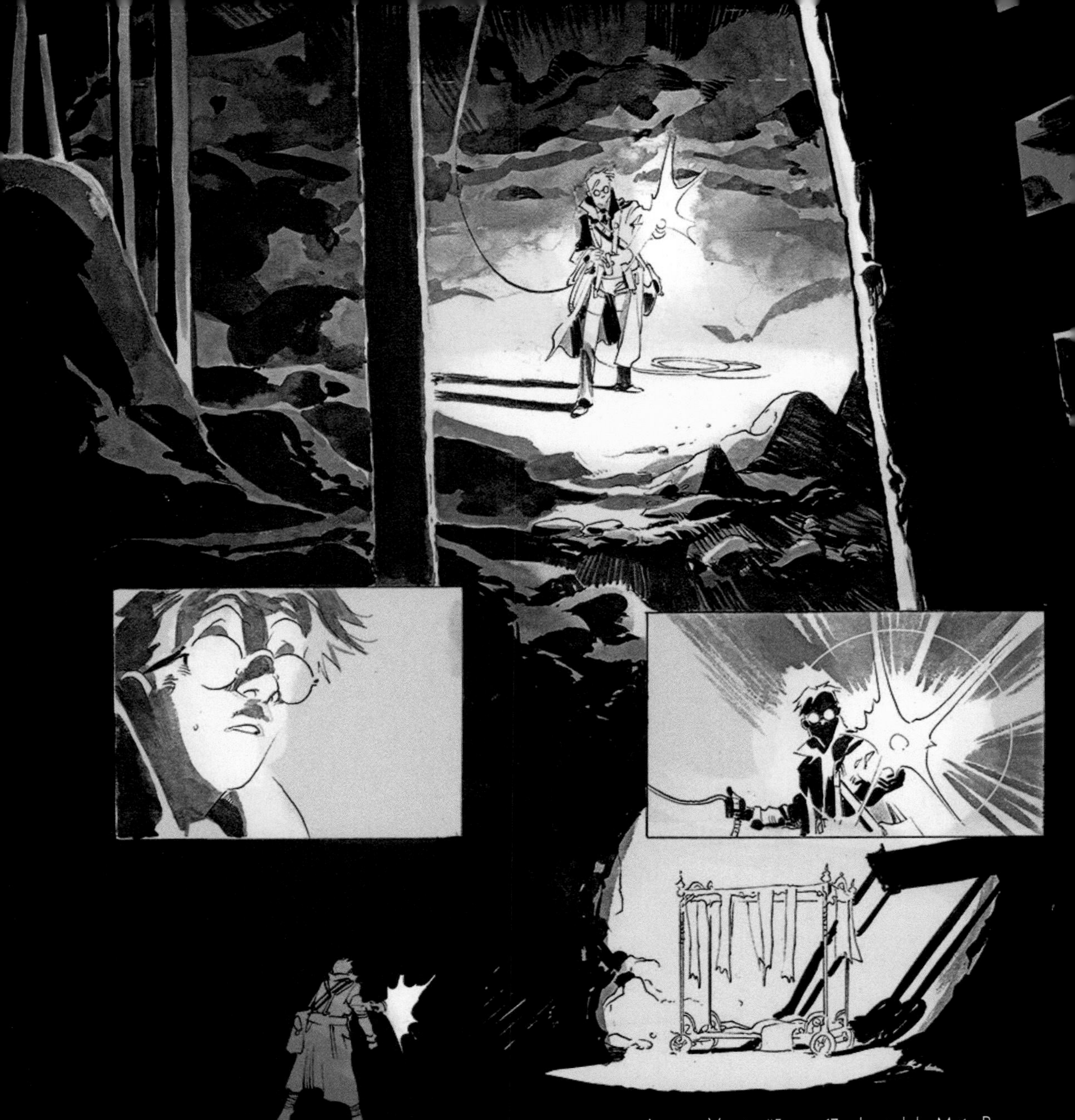

American Vampire #5 page 17 color study by Matías Bergara

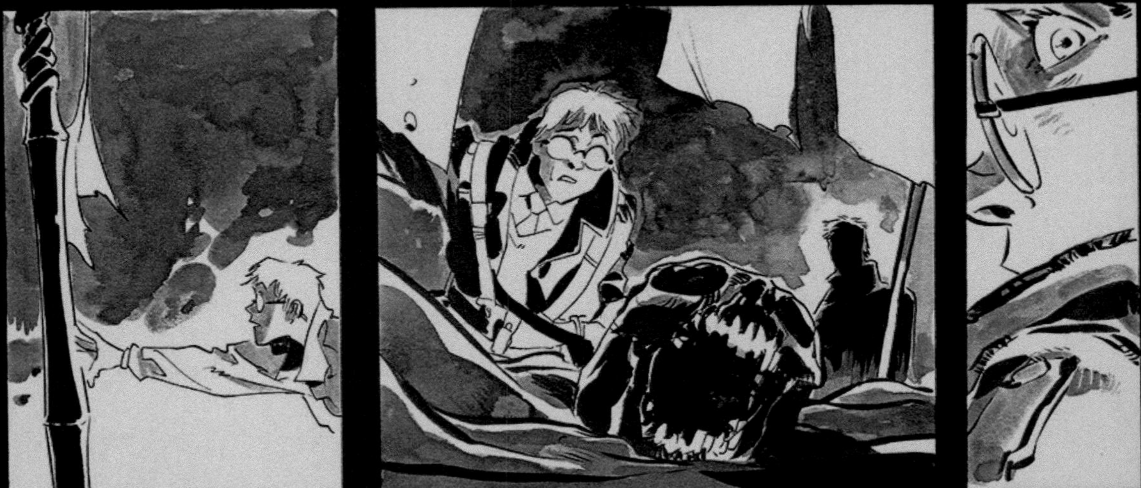

AMERICAN VAMPIRE #2 PAGES BY RAFAEL ALBUQUERQUE

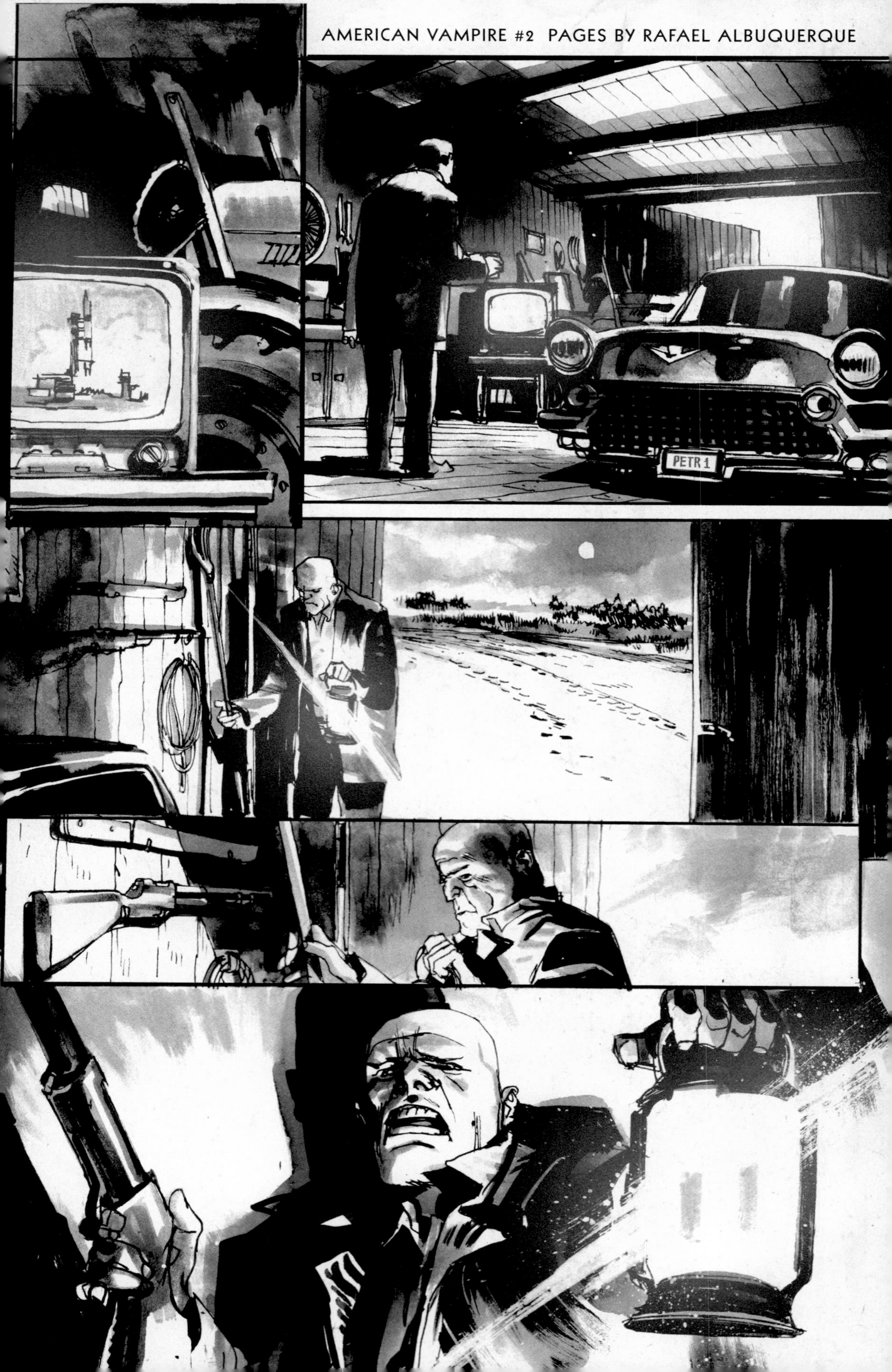
PETR 1

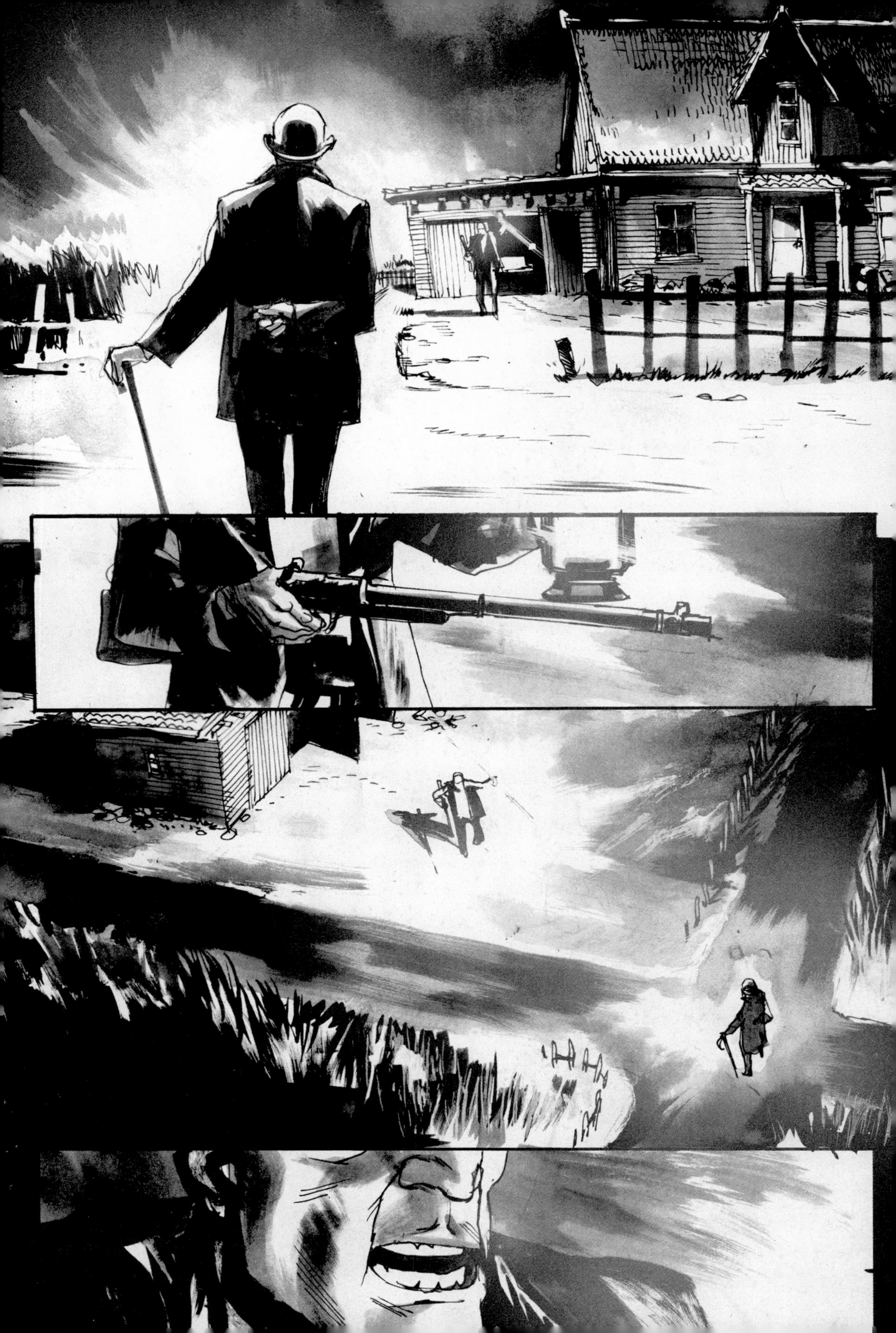

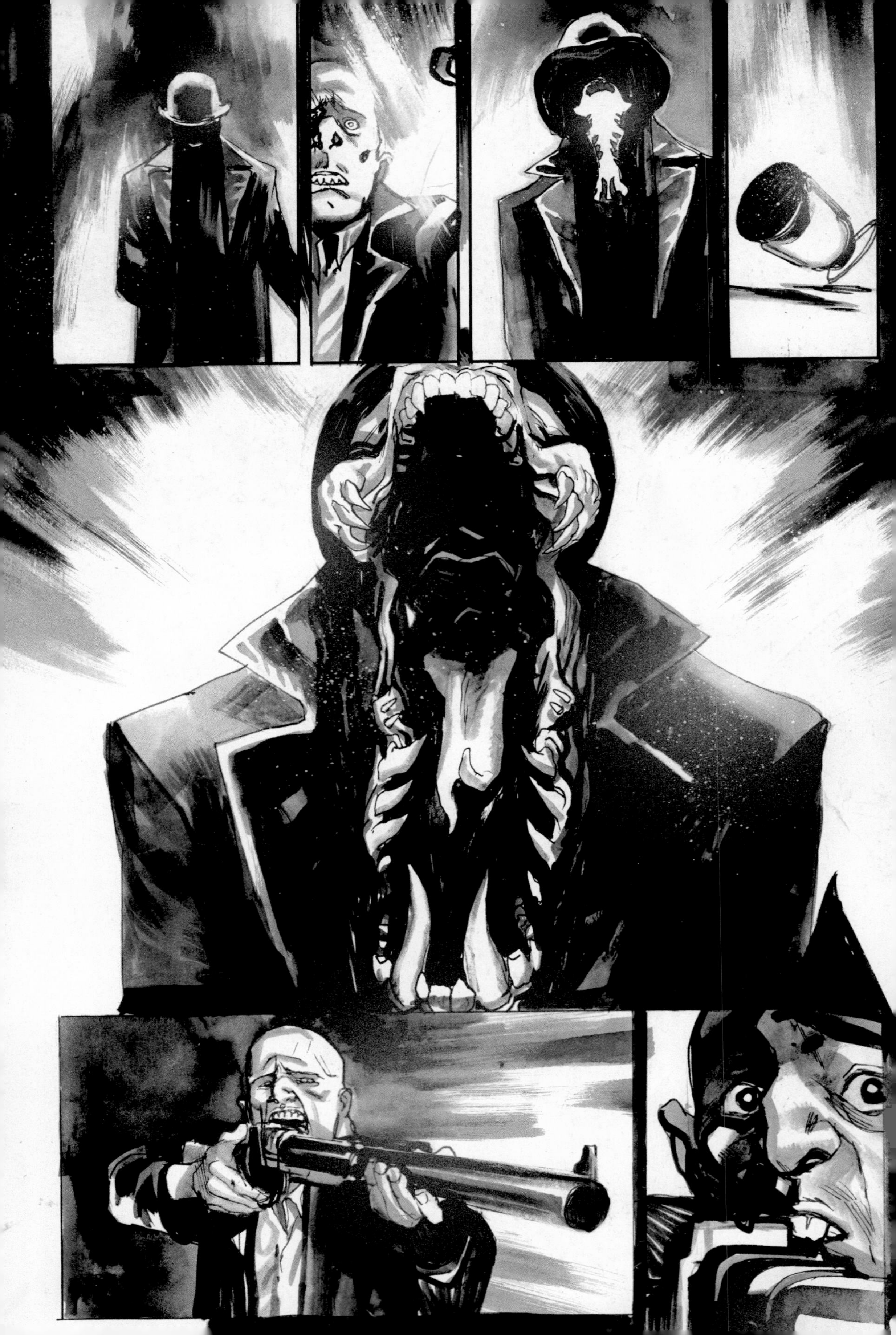

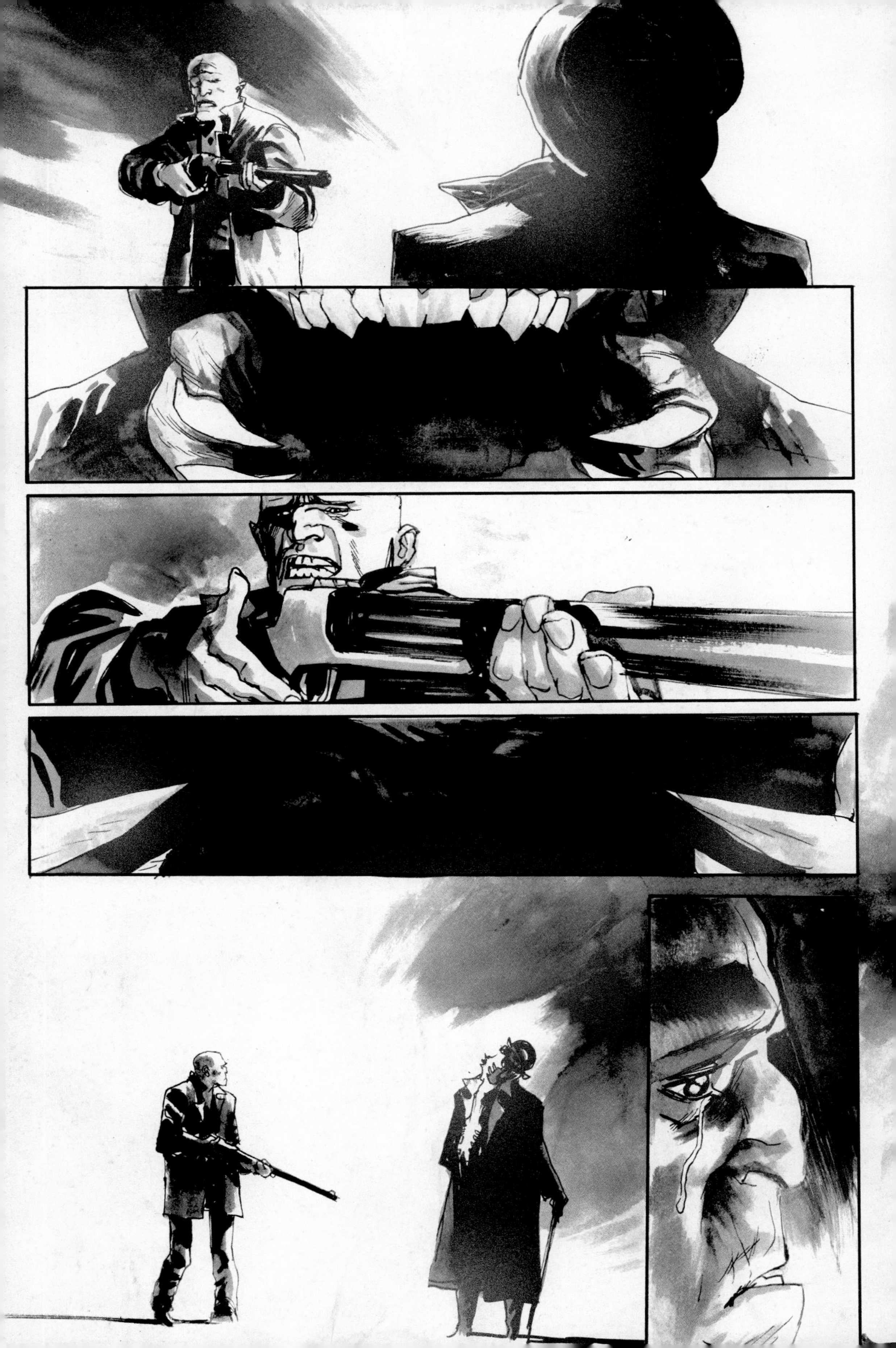

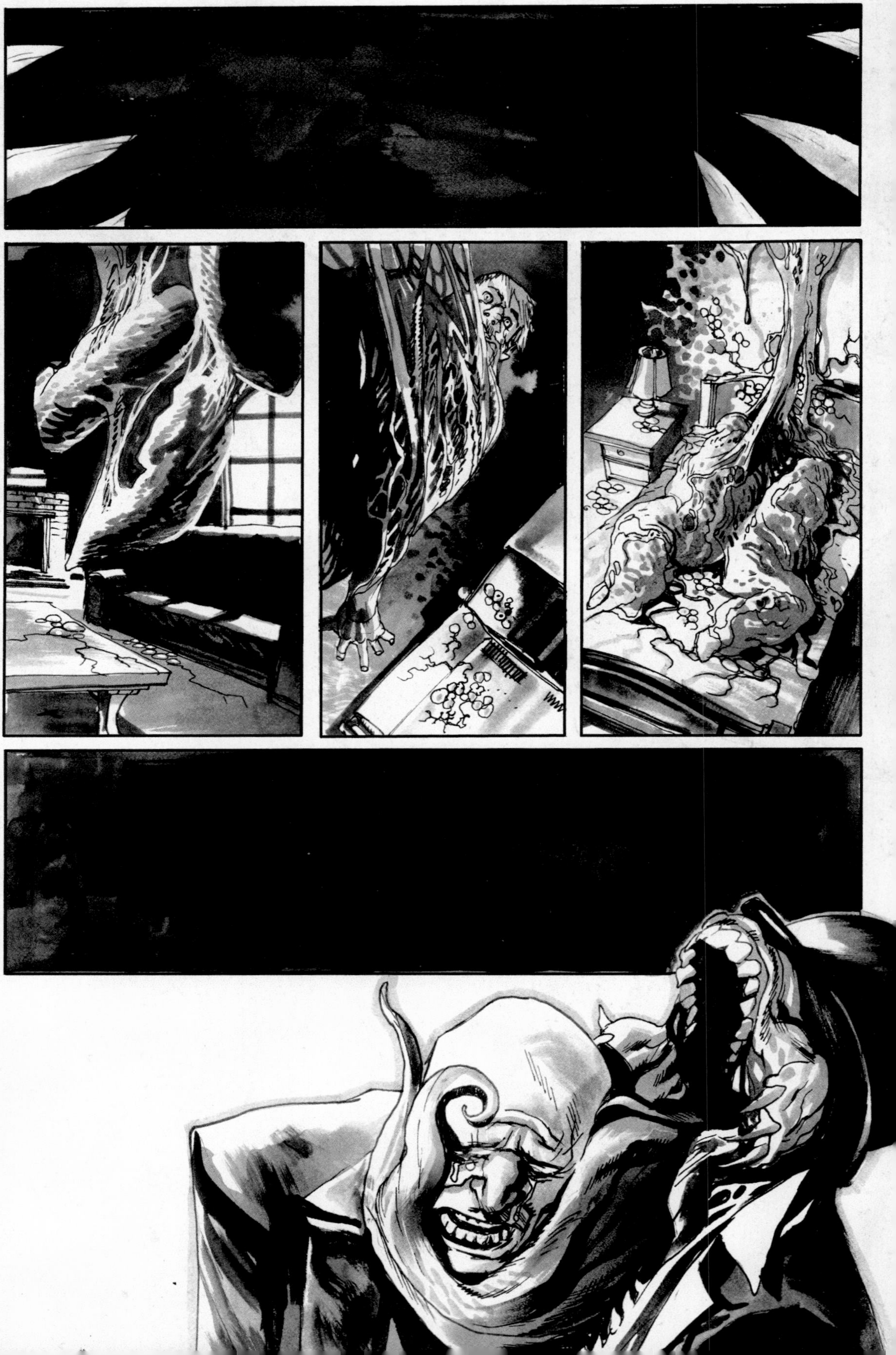

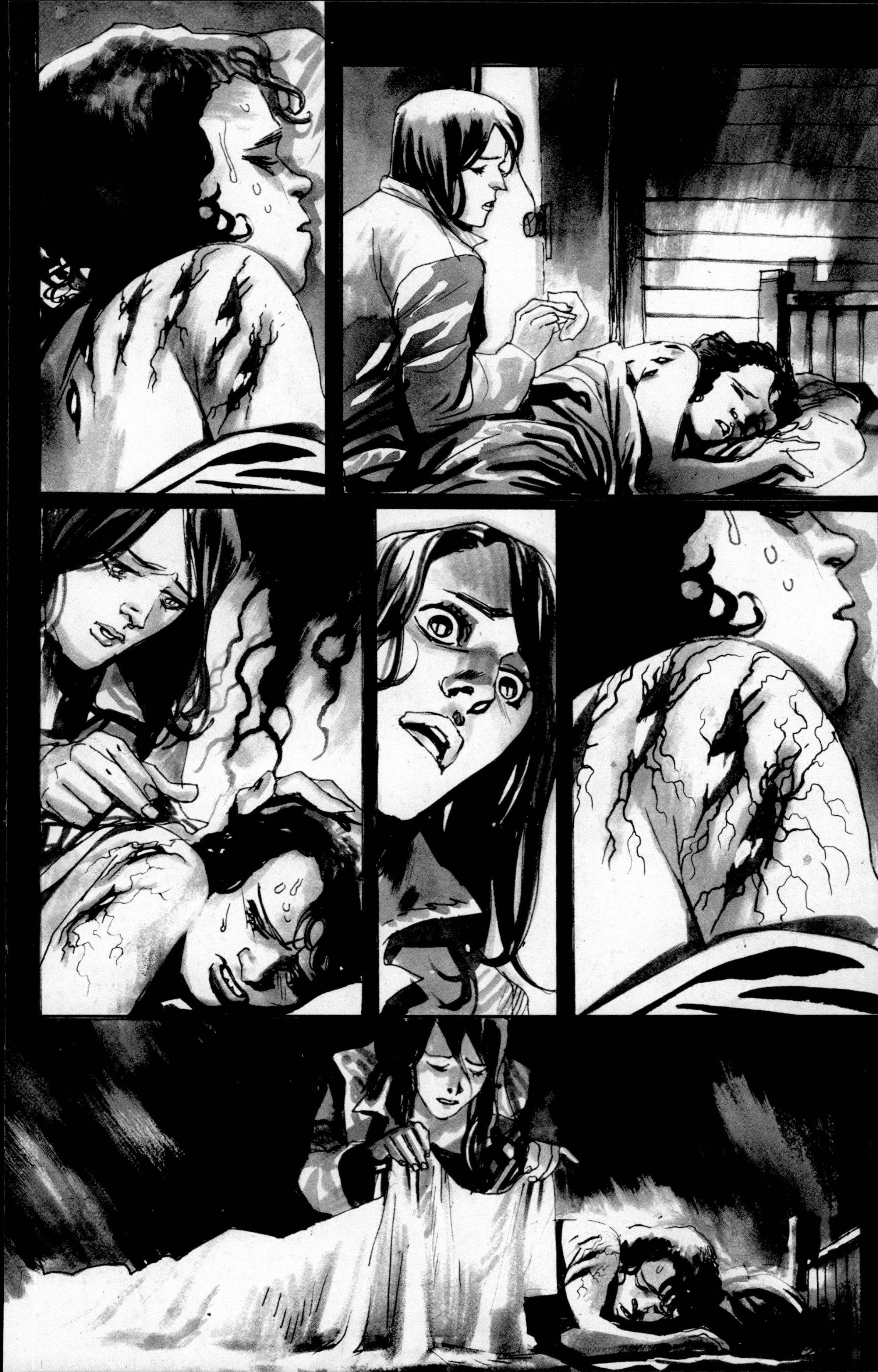

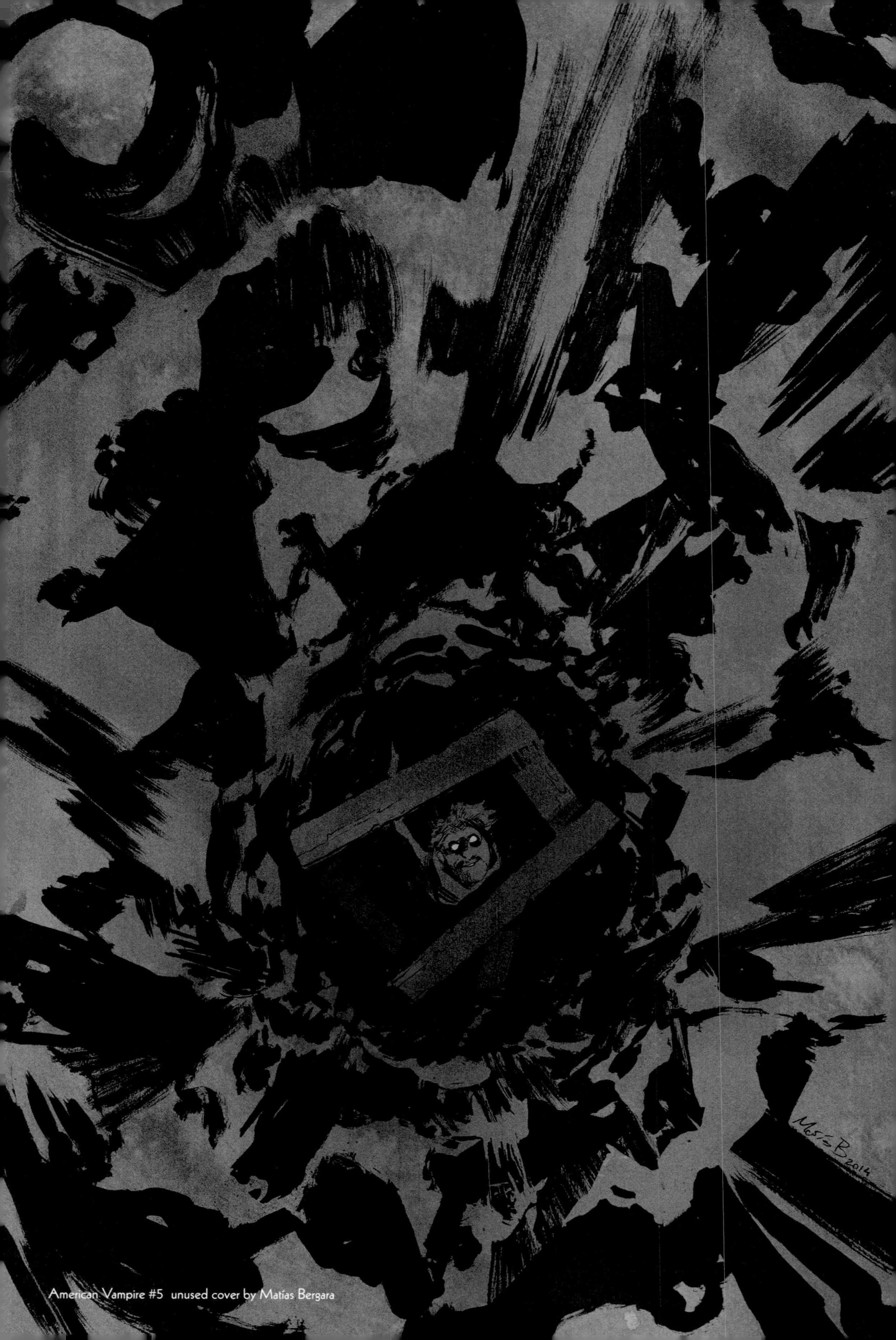

American Vampire #5 unused cover by Matías Bergara

Scott Snyder has written comics for both DC and Marvel, including the best-selling series BATMAN and SWAMP THING, and is the author of the story collection *Voodoo Heart*. He teaches writing at Sarah Lawrence College and Columbia University. He lives on Long Island with his wife, Jeanie, and his sons Jack and Emmett. He is a dedicated and un-ironic fan of Elvis Presley.

Rafael Albuquerque was born in Porto Alegre, Brazil, and has been working in the American comic book industry since 2005. Best known for his work on the *Savage Brothers*, BLUE BEETLE and SUPERMAN/BATMAN, he has also published the creator-owned graphic novels *Crimeland* (2007) and *Mondo Urbano* (2010).

Matías Bergara is an up-and-coming artist from Montevideo, Uruguay. He has previously drawn Zenescope Entertainment's *Grimm Fairy Tales Presents Demons: The Unseen*, and is currently working with BOOM! Studios on *Sons of Anarchy* and *Sleepy Hollow*. AMERICAN VAMPIRE: SECOND CYCLE is his first title for Vertigo.

Dave McCaig was raised by bears in the Canadian tundra and has since pinballed his way across North America to his current digs in New York City. He is probably best known for his work coloring SUPERMAN: BIRTHRIGHT, NORTHLANDERS, and ADAM STRANGE, and as color supervisor on *Batman: The Animated Series*.

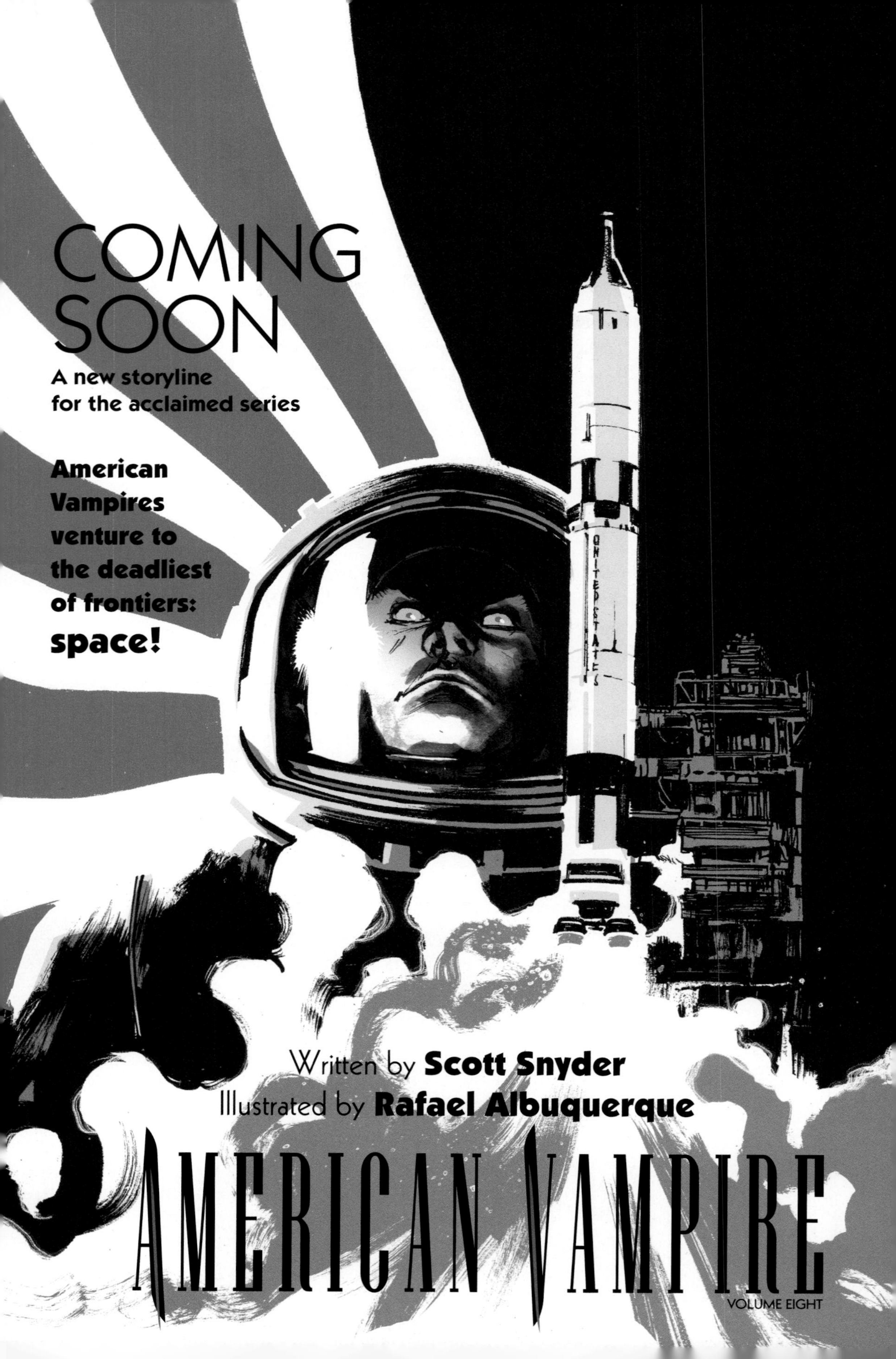
COMING SOON
A new storyline for the acclaimed series
American Vampires venture to the deadliest of frontiers: space!
Written by Scott Snyder
Illustrated by Rafael Albuquerque
AMERICAN VAMPIRE
VOLUME EIGHT

"Looking for a vampire story with some real bite? Then, boys and girls, Scott Snyder has a comic book for you."
—USA WEEKEND

FROM THE *NEW YORK TIMES* #1 BESTSELLING AUTHOR OF *BATMAN VOL. 1: THE COURT OF OWLS*
SCOTT SNYDER
with RAFAEL ALBUQUERQUE and STEPHEN KING

AMERICAN VAMPIRE VOL. 2

with RAFAEL ALBUQUERQUE and MATEUS SANTOLOUCO

AMERICAN VAMPIRE VOL. 3

with RAFAEL ALBUQUERQUE and SEAN MURPHY

AMERICAN VAMPIRE VOL. 4

with RAFAEL ALBUQUERQUE and JORDI BERNET

"At a time when vampire stories engulf pop culture, this one's actually fresh and original."
— ENTERTAINMENT WEEKLY

AMERICAN VAMPIRE
SCOTT SNYDER   RAFAEL ALBUQUERQUE
and
STEPHEN KING

VERTIGO

VERTIGO

"The most intense adult comic in ages."
—SPIN MAGAZINE

"Cool."
—ENTERTAINMENT WEEKLY

"Far and away the best example of the genre I have ever seen."
—THE GUARDIAN

READ THE ENTIRE SERIES!

PREACHER VOL. 3:
PROUD AMERICANS

PREACHER VOL. 6:
WAR IN THE SUN

PREACHER VOL. 1:
GONE TO TEXAS

PREACHER VOL. 2:
UNTIL THE END OF
THE WORLD

PREACHER VOL. 3:
PROUD AMERICANS

PREACHER VOL. 4:
ANCIENT HISTORY

PREACHER VOL. 5:
DIXIE FRIED

PREACHER VOL. 6:
WAR IN THE SUN

PREACHER VOL. 7:
SALVATION

PREACHER VOL. 8:
ALL HELL'S A-COMING

PREACHER VOL. 9:
ALAMO

GARTH ENNIS
with STEVE DILLON

GARTH **ENNIS** STEVE **DILLON**

PREACHER

★★★★ GONE TO TEXAS ★★★★

"More fun than going to the movies."
—Kevin Smith

Introduction by
Joe R. Lansdale

VERTIGO